Writing FCode Programs

 Sun

Editorial/production supervision: *Camille Trentacoste*
Manufacturing manager: *Alexis Heydt*
Acquisitions editor: *Michael Meehan*
Editorial assistant: *Nancy Boylan*

The publisher offers discounts on this book when ordered in bulk quantities. For more information contact:
Corporate Sales Department, PTR Prentice Hall, 113 Sylvan Avenue, Englewood, Cliffs, NJ 07632
Phone: 201-592-2863; FAX: 201-592-2249.

10 9 8 7 6 5 4 3 2 1

ISBN 0-13-107236-6

SunSoft Press
A Prentice Hall Title

Table of Contents

Preface xiii

1. SBus Cards and FCode 1

    FCode PROM Format 1

    Interpreting FCode 2

    Device Identification..2

    Creating and Executing FCode Definitions 2

2. Elements of FCode Programming 5

    Colon Definitions 6

    Stack Operations 7

    Additional Information 7

    Programming Style..8

        Commenting Code 8

        Short Definitions 8

        Stack Comments 8

     A Minimum FCode Program 10

     FCode Classes..11

    Primitive FCodes..12

    System FCodes 12

    Interface FCodes 12

    Local FCodes 13

3. Producing FCode 15

    FCode Source..15

    Tokenizing FCode Source...16

    FCode Binary Format 17

    Testing FCode on the Target Machine 17

    Configuring the Target Machine 18

        Setting Appropriate Configuration Parameters............18

        Modifying The Expansion Bus Probe Sequence 18

Getting to the Forth Monitor 19
Using the Forth Monitor to Download FCode 20
  Using **dload** to Load from Ethernet. 20
  Using **dlbin** to Load From Serial Port A. 21
  Using **boot** to Load From Hard Disk, Floppy Disk, or Ethernet 21
Using the Forth Monitor to Interpret an FCode Program 22
  Interpretation Under OpenBoot 2 22
  Interpretation Under OpenBoot 1 24
Using the Forth Monitor to Browse a Device Node 26
  Device Node Browsing Under OpenBoot 2 27
  Device Node Browsing Under OpenBoot 1 28
Using the Forth Monitor to Test a Device Node Driver 28
  Device Node Methods Under OpenBoot 2. 29
    Using **select-dev** 29
    Using **execute-device-method** 31
  Device Node Methods Under OpenBoot 1 32
Testing FCode in Source Form. 32
Producing an FCode PROM 33
Exercising an Installed FCode PROM 33
  Exercising FCode Under OpenBoot 2 33
  Exercising FCode Under OpenBoot 1 34

4. **Packages** 35
Package Definitions, Package Instances, and Device Nodes. 36
Plug-in Device Drivers. 36
Package Methods 37
  Required Methods. 37
  Recommended Methods. 37
Package Data Definitions. 39
Accessing Other Packages 40
  Instance Arguments and Parameters. 42
  Package Addresses. 44
Debugging Packages. 47
  Package Mappings. 47
  nvramrc 47
  Modifying Package Properties. 48
Standard Support Packages. 48

Sun Disk-Label Support Package 48

TFTP Booting Support Package 49

Deblocker Support Package 50

5. Properties 53

Standard FCode Properties 54

Standard FCode Properties For Cards (General) 54

Device-type Specific Properties For SBus Cards 54

General Properties For Parent Nodes 55

Properties For SBus Parent Nodes 55

Standard Properties 55

Manipulating Properties 70

Property Creation and Modification 70

Property Values 70

Property Encoding 71

Property Retrieval 71

Property Decoding 72

Property-Specific FCodes 72

Block Devices 75

Byte Devices 75

6. Block and Byte Devices 75

Required Methods 76

Required Properties 78

Device Driver Examples 78

Simple Block Device Driver 79

Extended Block Device Driver 79

Complete Block and Byte Device Driver 88

Required Methods 99

Required Properties 99

7. Display Devices 99

Device Driver Examples 100

Simple Display Device Driver 100

Extended Display Device Driver 101

Complete Display Device Driver 105

Required Methods 111

8. **Hierarchical Devices** 111

SBus Addressing 116

SBus Required Properties 116

VMEBus Addressing 116

VMEBus Required Properties 117

Device Driver Examples 117

   Basic Hierarchical Device Driver 118

   Extended Hierarchical Device Driver 120

   Complete Hierarchical Device Driver 128

9. **Network Devices** 145

Required Methods 146

Required Device Properties 147

Optional Device Properties 147

Device Driver Examples 147

   Simple Network Device Example 148

   Sample Driver With Test and Debugging Methods 150

   Bootable Network Device Driver Example 162

Required Methods 189

10. **Serial Devices** 189

Required Properties 190

Device Driver Examples 190

   Simple Serial FCode Program 190

   Extended Serial FCode Program 191

   Complete Serial FCode Program 194

11. **FCode Dictionary** 199

A. **FCode Reference** 337

FCode Primitives 337

FCodes by Function 337

FCodes by Byte Value 361

FCodes by Name 375

Version 2 FCodes 388

B. **OpenBoot Interrupt Testing** 393

For OpenBoot 2 399

C. FCode Memory Allocation 399

   For OpenBoot 1 400

   FCode For OpenBoot 1 Systems 401

D. Changes in OpenBoot 1 FCode Usage 401

   FCode Programming Style 1 402

   FCode Programming Style 2 402

   FCode Programming Style 3 403

   Other OpenBoot 1 Restrictions 403

   Total FCode Program Size 404

   Old-style Memory Mapping And Unmapping 404

   Memory Mapping Size Limits 404

   Large General-purpose Mappings............................... 404

   Memory De-allocation 405

   Total Properties 405

   Interpretation of **my-address** and **my-space** 405

   my-address Volatility 405

   free-virtual and Properties...................................... 405

   Changes in **new-device** and **finish-device** Usage 405

Index 407

Writing FCode Programs

Tables

≡

Table PR-1	Typographic Conventions	xv
Table 2-1	Stack Item Notation	9
Table 3-1	FCode Binary Format	17
Table 3-2	FCode Header Format	17
Table 3-3	File Download/Execute-related Toolkit Commands	20
Table 3-4	Commands for Browsing the Device Tree	26
Table 4-1	Package Access FCodes	41
Table 4-2	Manipulating `phandles` and `ihandles`	41
Table 4-3	Method-Access Words	46
Table 4-4	Sun Disk Label Package Methods	49
Table 4-5	TFTP Package Methods	50
Table 4-6	Deblocker Package Methods	51
Table 5-1	Standard Device Types	58
Table 5-2	Child-Parent Address Relationships	66
Table 5-3	`status` property values	69
Table 5-4	Property-specific FCodes	72
Table 6-1	Required Properties of Block and Byte Devices	78
Table 7-1	Required Display Device Properties	99
Table 8-1	Required SBus Properties	116
Table 8-2	Required VMEbus Properties	117
Table 9-1	Required Network Device Properties	147
Table 9-2	Optional Network Device Properties	147
Table 10-1	Serial Driver Required Properties	190
Table 11-1	Escape Sequences in Text Strings	200
Table 11-2	Tokenizer macros	327
Table A-1	Stack Manipulation	337

Table A-2	Arithmetic Operations	338
Table A-3	Memory Operations	339
Table A-4	Atomic Access	341
Table A-5	Data Exception Test	341
Table A-6	Comparison Operations	341
Table A-7	Text Input	342
Table A-8	ASCII Constants	343
Table A-9	Numeric Input	343
Table A-10	Numeric Primitives	344
Table A-11	Numeric Output	344
Table A-12	General-purpose Output	345
Table A-13	Formatted Output	345
Table A-14	`begin` Loops	345
Table A-15	Conditionals	345
Table A-16	`do` Loops	346
Table A-17	Control Words	346
Table A-18	Strings	346
Table A-19	Defining Words	347
Table A-20	Dictionary Compilation	347
Table A-21	Dictionary Search	348
Table A-22	Conversion Operators	348
Table A-23	Memory Buffers Allocation	349
Table A-24	Miscellaneous Operators	349
Table A-25	Internal Operators, (invalid for program text)	350
Table A-26	Memory Allocation	352
Table A-27	Non-volatile Parameters	352
Table A-28	Properties	352
Table A-29	Commonly-used Properties	353
Table A-30	System Version Information	354
Table A-31	Device Activation Vector Setup	354
Table A-32	Self-test utility Routines	354
Table A-33	Time Utilities	355

Table A-34   Machine-specific Support 355

Table A-35   User-set terminal Emulation Values 355

Table A-36   Terminal Emulator-set Terminal Emulation Values 356

Table A-37   Terminal Emulation Routines* 356

Table A-38   Frame Buffer Parameter Values* 357

Table A-39   Font Operators 357

Table A-40   One-bit Framebuffer Utilities 357

Table A-41   Eight-bit Framebuffer Utilities 358

Table A-42   Package Support 359

Table A-43   Asynchronous Support 360

Table A-44   Miscellaneous Operations 360

Table A-45   Interpretation 361

Table A-46   Error Handling 361

Table A-47   FCodes by Byte Value 361

Table A-48   FCodes by Name 375

Table A-49   Version 2 FCodes 388

Table B-1   Interrrupt-handling words 393

Table B-2   Interrupt register format 396

Writing FCode Programs

Preface

This manual, *Writing FCode Programs*, replaces both *Writing FCode Programs for SBus Cards* and *Writing FCode 2.0 Programs*.

Who Should Use This Book

This manual is written for designers of SBus interface cards and other devices that use the FCode interface language. It assumes that you have some familiarity with SBus card design requirements and Forth programming.

The material covered in this manual is specifically for those developing FCode applications on OpenBoot 2.0 or later SPARCsystems, and those developing SBus cards for either OpenBoot 2.0 only or both OpenBoot 1.0 *and* OpenBoot 2.0 and later systems.

This manual also assumes that you have read and understood the *OpenBoot Command Reference*™ and the SBus specification as published by the IEEE (Reference Number 1496). The SBus Handbook (see below) also contains useful guidelines for SBus hardware developers.

How This Book Is Organized

- **Chapter 1, "SBus Cards and FCode",** introduces the basic relationships between FCode device drivers and the hardware that they control.
- **Chapter 2, "Elements of FCode Programming",** introduces the basic elements of FCode, stack notation, and programming style.
- **Chapter 3, "Producing FCode",** describes the process of producing FCode programs, from source file to testing working programs.
- **Chapter 4, "Packages",** describes the basic units of FCode program function.
- **Chapter 5, "Properties",** describes properties, which define how an FCode device driver program "sees" the hardware that it controls.
- **Chapter 6, "Block and Byte Devices"** through **Chapter 10, "Serial Devices"** describe currently-defined device types, programming requirements, and give some examples of device drivers for the various device types.
- **Chapter 11, "FCode Dictionary",** describes currently-defined FCode words, their functions and use, with brief programming examples.

- **Appendix A, "FCode Reference",** lists all currently-defined FCode words according to functional grouping, name, and byte value.
- **Appendix B, "OpenBoot Interrupt Testing",** describes how to treat interrupts when testing SBus devices, including programming examples.
- **Appendix C, "FCode Memory Allocation",** describes guidelines for memory allocation and deallocation in FCode.
- **Appendix D, "Changes in Version 1 FCode Usage",** describes differences in programming style between OpenBoot 1 and OpenBoot 2 practice, and changes in the usage of FCode words between OpenBoot 1 and OpenBoot 2.

Related Books

This manual does not pretend to cover everything you need to know to write FCode drivers for SBus cards. You'll have to read some other books, too.

For more information about Forth and Forth programming, see:

- *Mastering Forth,* Anita Anderson and Martin Tracy. Brady Communication Company, Inc., 1989.
- *Forth: A Text and Reference*, Mahlon G. Kelly and Nicholas Spies. Prentice Hall.
- *Starting FORTH*, Leo Brody. FORTH, Inc., second edition, 1987.
- *Forth: a New Model*, Jack Woehr. M & T Books, 1992.
- *OpenBoot Command Reference* (see below).

SBus/SCSI Developer's Kit

The SBus/SCSI Developer's Kit, Release III (ISBN 0-13-107202-1) consists of four manuals:

> *SunOS 5.3 Writing Device Drivers* (ISBN 0-13-107228-5) includes a diskette of sample drivers
> *Writing FCode Programs, Version 2.x* (ISBN 0-13-107236-6)
> *OpenBoot™ Command Reference, Version 2.x* (ISBN 0-13-107194-7)
> *SBus Handbook* by Susan A. Mason, Desktop Strategies (ISBN 0-13-107210-2)

This kit is available at all PTR PH Magnet Stores, or directly from Prentice Hall. For single copies, tel: (515) 284-6751, fax: (515) 284-2607 or e-mail *orders@prenhall.com*. For quantity orders (greater than 10 books): tel: (201) 592-2498, fax: (201) 592-2249. International customers: Simon & Schuster International, Customer Service, Attention: Joanne Edwing, 200 Old Tappan Road, Old Tappan, NJ 07675, USA, tel: 201-767-4990, fax: 201-767-5625. Individual manuals are available through local technical bookstores worldwide.

Software Tools

Some programs specifically mentioned in this manual for use in developing FCode programs are included on a diskette packaged with the *SunOS 5.3 Writing Device Drivers* manual published by SunSoft Press/Prentice Hall. This manual is a component of the SBus/SCSI Developer's Kit, Release III (see paragraph above for order information). Instructions for using these programs are included on the diskette.

If you don't have access to a complete SBus/SCSI Developer's Kit, or if your SPARCstation doesn't have a diskette drive, contact the Sun SBus Technical Support Group (sbustech@Sun.com) for the software.

What Typographic Changes and Symbols Mean

The following table describes the typeface changes and symbols used in this book.

Table PR-1 Typographic Conventions

Typeface or Symbol	Meaning	Example
AaBbCc123	The names of commands, files, and directories; on-screen computer output	Edit your `.login` file. Use `ls -a` to list all files. system% You have mail.
AaBbCc123	What you type, contrasted with on-screen computer output	system% **su** Password:
AaBbCc123	Command-line placeholder: replace with a real name or value	To delete a file, type `rm` *filename*.
AaBbCc123	Book titles, new words or terms, or words to be emphasized	Read Chapter 6 in *User's Guide*. These are called *class* options. You *must* be root to do this.
Code samples are included in boxes and may display the following:		
%	UNIX C shell prompt	system%
ok	OpenBoot command prompt	ok
$	UNIX Bourne and Korn shell prompt	system$
#	Superuser prompt, all UNIX shells	system#

This manual follows a number of typographic conventions:

- Text beginning with a capitalized letter indicates a key name or a panel button on a window-based program. For example:

  Press the Control-C key.

  When you see two key names separated by a dash, press and hold the first key down, then press the second key. For example:

  To press Control-C, press and hold Control, then press C.

- In a command line, square brackets indicate an optional entry and italics indicate an argument that you must replace with the appropriate text. For example:

  cd [*directory*]

SBus Cards and FCode

Each SBus card must have a PROM whose contents identify the device and its characteristics.

The SBus card's PROM may also include an optional software driver that lets you use the card as a boot device or a display device during booting. The software driver may also include diagnostic selftest code.

In addition to designing hardware, the process of developing SBus devices may include writing, testing, and installing FCode drivers for the device. These drivers, if present, serve three functions:

- To exercise the device during development, and to verify its functionality.
- To provide the necessary driver to be used by the system boot PROM during power-up.
- To provide device configuration information.

In practice, these functions overlap substantially. The same code needed by the system boot PROM usually serves to significantly test the device as well, although additional code may be desired to fully verify proper behavior of the device. The PROM code is used before and during the boot sequence. After the boot sequence finishes, and while not using the OpenBoot Forth Monitor, most SBus device use is through SunOS drivers.

SBus device PROMs must be written in the FCode programming language, which is similar to Forth-83. FCode is described in more detail in Chapter 2, "Elements of FCode Programming".

FCode PROM Format

An FCode PROM begins at address 0 within the SBus card's physical address space. Its size can range from 30 bytes up to 32K bytes. Typical sizes are 60 bytes (for a simple card that identifies itself but does not need a driver) and 1-4K bytes (for a card with a boot driver). It is good practice to make FCode boot drivers as short as is practical.

An FCode PROM must be organized as follows:

- Header (8 bytes: consisting of magic number, version number, length, checksum).
- Body (FCode program; 0 or more bytes).
- End Token (either End0, a zero byte, or End1, an alternative all 1's byte).

Interpreting FCode

For each SBus slot, the FCode program is interpreted during bootup as follows:

- Location 0 of the SBus PROM is read with an 8-bit or 32-bit access. If there is no response (as when there is no card in that slot), the slot is subsequently ignored.
- If the high-order byte of the value returned from the first access is not the FCode magic numbers 0xfd or 0xf1, the slot is subsequently ignored.
- If the high-order byte is 0xfd or 0xf1, the PROM is assumed to contain a valid FCode program. The FCode is then interpreted by starting at location 0 and reading one byte at a time, executing a procedure associated with each FCode value.
- Interpretation ceases when the FCode 0x00 or 0xff (End0 or End1) is encountered.

Device Identification

An FCode PROM must identify its device. This identification must include, at a minimum, the driver name, used to link the device to its SunOS driver. Identification information may include additional characteristics of the device for the benefit of the operating system and the CPU boot PROM.

In most systems, the CPU's FCode interpreter will store each device's identification information in a **device tree** that has a node for each device. Each **device node** has a **property list** that identifies and describes the device. The property list is created as a result of interpreting the program in the FCode PROM.

Each property must have a name and a value. The name is a string and the value is an array of bytes, which may encode strings, numbers, and various other data types.

See Chapter 5, "Properties" for more information.

Creating and Executing FCode Definitions

Many FCode programs create executable routines, called **colon definitions** (or **methods**) that typically read from and write to device locations to control device functions. These definitions are also stored in the **device tree** node for that device.

Once defined, these routines may typically be executed under any of the following circumstances:

- Interactively at the OpenBoot ok prompt (for selftest or other purposes).
- By the OpenBoot system (for using this boot or display system during system start-up).
- Automatically during FCode interpretation (for power-on initialization or other purposes).

≡ *1*

Elements of FCode
Programming

FCode is based on the Forth-83 dialect of the Forth language, with the following major differences:

- The FCode `tokenizer` program uses normal textfiles, rather than the `BLOCK`s and block editing of Forth-83, and contains its own predefined words for file transfers.

- Forth-83 is designed for 16-bit machines. FCode is designed for 32-bit machines, so FCode handles 16 and 32-bit quantities differently than Forth-83.

FCode has these characteristics:

- The source format is machine and system independent.
- The binary format (FCode) is machine, system, and position independent.
- The binary format is compact.
- The binary format may be interpreted easily and efficiently.
- Programs are easy to develop and debug.
- The source format can easily be translated to binary format.
- The binary format can be untranslated back to a source format.

Forth commands are called **words**, and are roughly analogous to procedures in other languages. Unlike other languages, such as C, which have operators and syntactic characters and procedures, in Forth every word is a procedure.

Forth words consist of one to 31 printable characters, separated by one or more spaces from subsequent words.

Forth uses a left-to-right reverse Polish notation, like some scientific calculators. The basic structure of Forth is: do this, now do that, now do something else, and so on.

New Forth words are defined as sequences of previously existing words. Subsequently, new words may be used to create still more words.

FCode is a byte-coded translation of a Forth program. Translating Forth source code to FCode involves replacing the Forth word names (stored as text strings) with their equivalent FCode numbers. The tokenized FCode takes up less space in PROM than the original ASCII textfile form of the Forth program from which it was derived.

For purposes of this manual, the term FCode indicates both binary-coded FCode and the Forth programs written as ASCII text files for later conversion to binary-coded FCode.

Except where a distinction between the two forms is explicitly stated, the use of FCode in this manual can be assumed to apply equally to both FCode and Forth.

Colon Definitions

Two concepts are critical to understanding FCode (or Forth):

- A **colon definition** creates a new word with the same behavior of a sequence of existing words. A colon definition begins with a colon and ends with a semicolon.

- Most parameter passing is done through a pushdown, last-in, first-out **stack**.

Normally, the action associated with an FCode word is performed when the FCode word is encountered. This is called **interpret state**. However, you can switch from interpret state to **compile state**.

In interpret state, FCode words are executed as they are encountered. Interpret state operates until encountering a ":". The word ":" does the following:

- Allocates a new FCode word and associates it with the name immediately following the colon
- Switches to compile state

During compile state operation, FCodes are saved for later execution, rather than being executed immediately. The sequence thus compiled is installed in the action tables as a new word, and can be later used in the same way as if it were a built-in word.

Compile state continues until a ";" is read, switching operation back to interpret state.

FCode words encountered after the colon are compiled into RAM for later use, until a semicolon is encountered. The word ";"does the following:

- Compiles an end-of-procedure FCode word
- Switches to interpret state

After compilation, the newly-assigned FCode word can be either interpreted or compiled as part of yet another new word.

If you define a new word having the same spelling as an existing word, the new definition supersedes the older one(s), but only for subsequent usages of that word.

Here's an example of a colon definition, defining a new FCode word dac!:

```
: dac! ( data addr reg# -- ) swap dac ! dac + ! ;
```

Stack Operations

Each FCode word is specified by its effect on the stack and any side effects, such as accessing memory. Most FCode words affect only the stack, by removing arguments from the stack, performing some operation on them, and putting the result or results back on the stack.

The stack effects of an FCode word is described by a **stack comment**, included in the colon definition.

In the previous example, the stack comment, beginning with " (" and ending with ") ", shows that `dac!` takes three parameters from the stack, and doesn't replace them with anything when it's done.

You can place stack comments anywhere in a colon definition, and you should include them anywhere that they will enhance clarity.

The rightmost argument is on top of the stack, with any preceding arguments beneath it. In other words, arguments are pushed onto the stack in left to right order, leaving the most recent one (the rightmost one in the diagram) on the top.

Following the stack comment in the preceding example are a series of words that describe the behavior of `dac!`. Executing `dac!` is the same as executing the list of words in its colon definition.

Note that FCode words are separated by spaces, tabs, or newlines; "(data " is *not* the same as "(data ". Any visible character is part of a word, and not a separator.

While case is not significant, by convention FCode is written in lower case.

Additional Information

For more information about Forth programming, needed to use available FCode primitives, refer to the Forth-related books listed in "Related Books," on page xvi.

Programming Style

Some people have described Forth as a write-only language. While it sometimes ends up that way, it *is* possible to write Forth (and FCode) programs that can be read and understood by more than just the original programmer.

Commenting Code

Comment code extravagantly, then consider adding more comments. The comments can help you and others maintain your code, and they don't add to the final size of the resulting FCode PROM.

Typical practice is to use " ( ) " for stack comments and "\" for other descriptive text and comments.

Short Definitions

Keep word definitions short. If your definition exceeds half a page, try to break it up into two or more definitions. If it grows to a page or longer, you *should* break it up, if only to make the code easier to support in the future.

A *good* size for a word definition is one or two lines of code.

Stack Comments

Always include stack comments in word definitions. It can be useful to compare intended function with what the code really does. Here's an example of a word definition with acceptable style.

```
\ xyz-map  establishes a virtual-to-physical mapping for each of the

\ useful addressable regions on the board



: xyz-map  ( -- )



\ Base-address  Offset  Size  create-mapping

\ then save virtual address


   my-address  40.0000 + 4 map-sbus  ( virtaddr )

   is status-register ( )
```

```
    my-address  80.0000 + frame-buf-size  map-sbus ( virtaddr )

    is frame-buffer-adr  ( )


;
```

Stack items are generally written using descriptive names to help clarify correct usage. See the table below for stack item abbreviations used in this manual.

Table 2-1 Stack Item Notation

Notation	Description
|	Alternate stack results, for example: (input -- adr len false | result true).
?	Unknown stack items (changed from ???).
??? or [...]	Unknown stack items.
acf	Code field address.
adr	Memory address (generally a virtual address).
byte b*xx*	8-bit value (smallest byte in a 32-bit word).
char	7-bit value (smallest byte), high bit unspecified.
cnt len size	Count or length.
flag *xxx*?	0 = false; any other value = true (usually -1).
long L*xx*	32-bit value.
n n1 n2 n3	Normal signed values (32-bit).
+n u	Unsigned, positive values (32-bit).
n[64] (n.low n.hi)	Extended-precision (64-bit) numbers (2 stack items).
phys	Physical address (actual hardware address).
pstr	Packed string (`adr len` means unpacked string).
virt	Virtual address (address used by software).
word w*xxx*	16-bit value (smallest two bytes in a 32-bit word).

A Minimum FCode Program

If an SBus card is not needed during the boot process, a minimal FCode program that merely declares the name of the device will often suffice. Here is an example of an acceptable minimum program:

```
fcode-version1

" SUNW,bison"  xdrstring  " name" attribute

my-address h# 20.0000 +

my-space h# 100

" reg" attribute

end0
```

This program creates a "name" property called "SUNW,bison" that will be used by the SunOS driver's identify routine to identify this device, and declares the location and size of on-board registers. The name that you use should always begin with your company name.

Note – To avoid name conflicts between different companies' products, use your company's public stock symbol.

You can also use the following shorthand form. The FCode program generated will be equivalent to the minimum program given above.

```
fcode-version1

" SUNW,bison" name

my-address h# 20.0000 + my-space h# 100 reg

end0
```

You might also want to include additional code to declare additional properties, create selftest routines, or to initialize the device after power-on.

FCode Classes

There are four general classes of FCode source words:

- **Primitives.** These words generally correspond directly to conventional Forth words, and implement functions such as addition, stack manipulation, and control structures.

- **System.** These are extension words implemented in the boot PROMs, and implement functions such as memory allocation and device attribute reporting.

- **Interface.** These are specific to particular types of devices, and implement functions such as draw-character.

- **Local.** These are private words definitions, implemented and used by devices.

Each FCode primitive is represented in the SBus card's PROM as a single byte. Other FCodes are represented in the SBus PROM as two consecutive bytes. The first byte, a value from 1 to 0xf, may be thought of as an escape code.

One-byte FCode numbers range in value from 0x10 to 0xfe. Two-byte FCode numbers begin with a byte in the range 0x01 to 0x0f, and end with a byte in the range 0x00 to 0xff. The single-byte values 0x00 and 0xff signify "end of program" (either value will do; conventionally, 0x00 is used):

Currently-defined FCodes are listed according to both functional groups and in numeric order in Appendix A, "FCode Reference".

Primitive FCodes

There are more than 300 primitive FCode words, most of which exactly parallel Forth-83 words, divided into three groups:

- FCode words that generate a single FCode byte
- tokenizer macros
- tokenizer directives

Primitive FCode words that have an exact parallel with standard Forth-83 words are given the same name as the equivalent Forth-83 word. Chapter 11, "FCode Dictionary", contains further descriptions of primitive FCodes.

There are about another 70 tokenizer macros, most of which also have direct Forth-83 equivalents. These are convenient source code words translated by the tokenizer into short sequences of FCode primitives.

tokenizer **directives** are words that generate no FCodes, but are used to control the interpretation process. Cross-compiler directives include the words

- binary, decimal, hex, and octal
- b#, d#, h#, and o#
- headers and headerless
- \ and (
- .(
- alias

System FCodes

System FCodes are used by all classes of FCode drivers for various system-related functions. System FCodes may be either **service** words or **configuration** words.

- Service words are available to the device's FCode driver when needed for functions such as memory mapping or diagnostic routines.

- Configuration words are included in the driver to document characteristics of the driver itself. These "properties" are passed up to the device's SunOS driver.

Interface FCodes

Interface FCodes are standard routines used by the workstation's CPU to perform the functions of the SBus card's device. Different classes of devices will each use only the appropriate set of interface FCodes.

For example, if the system wants to paint a character on the display screen, it does it by calling the interface FCode routine draw-character. This requires the frame buffer's FCode driver to assign its own definition into the draw-character interface word. It does this as follows

```
: my-draw ( char -- ) \ "local" word to draw a character.

    ...                 \ Definition contents.

;                       \ end of my-draw definition.

: my-install ( -- )   \ local word to install all interfaces.

    ...
```

```
       ['] my-draw is draw-character

       . . .

   ;
```

When `my-install` executes, `draw-character` has the behavior of `my-draw`.

Local FCodes

Local FCodes are assigned, where needed, to words defined within the body of SBus driver code. There are over 2000 FCode byte values allocated for local FCodes. The byte values are meaningful only within the context of a particular driver. Different drivers reuse the same set of byte values.

≡ *2*

Writing FCode Programs

Producing FCode

FCode Source

An FCode source file is essentially a Forth language source code file. The basic Forth words available to the programmer are listed in the FCode Dictionary chapter of this manual. Typically Forth source files are named with a .fth suffix. FCode source files follow the same convention.

FCode programs have the following format:

```
\ Title comment describing the program that follows

fcode-version1

< body of the FCode program >

end0
```

fcode-version1 is a macro which directs the tokenizer to create an FCode header. For a description of the FCode header see "FCode Binary Format" on page 3-17. fcode-version1 produces a header including the version1 FCode. The macro fcode-version2 is similar except it produces a header containing the start1 FCode. This macro may also be used to begin the FCode source. However since OpenBoot version 1 systems only recognize version1, plug-in device FCode that must run in OpenBoot version 1 systems must use fcode-version1.

See Appendix D, "Changes in Version 1 FCode Usage" for more information on differences between version 1 and version 2 FCode usage.

end0 is an FCode that marks the end of an FCode program. It must be at the end of the program or erroneous results may occur. end1 is an alternative but end0 is recommended.

The comment in the first line is not strictly necessary in many cases but it is recommended since some OpenBoot tools require it.

Tokenizing FCode Source

The process of converting FCode source to FCode binary is referred to as *tokenizing*. A tokenizer program coverts FCode source words to their corresponding byte-codes, as indicated in the FCode Dictionary chapter. A tokenizer program together with instructions describing its use is available from the *Sun SBus Support Group*.

An FCode program's source may reside across multiple files. The `fload` tokenizer directive may be used to direct the tokenizer input stream to another file. `fload` acts like an `#include` statement in C. When `fload` is encountered the tokenizer begins processing the file named by the `fload` directive. When the named file is completed, tokenizing continues with the file that issued the `fload`. `fload` directives may be nested.

Typically, the tokenizer produces a file in the following format based on the UNIX[tm] `a.out` format:

- Header - 32 bytes
- FCode header - 8 bytes
- FCode binary - remainder of file

The header has the following format:

- 4 bytes - 0x01030107 (hexadecimal)
- 4 bytes - Size in bytes of the FCode binary
- 4 bytes - 0x0
- 4 bytes - 0x0
- 4 bytes - 0x0
- 4 bytes - Load point of the file
- 4 bytes - 0x0
- 4 bytes - 0x0

You can use this file to load either an FCode PROM or system memory for debugging as described in "Using the Forth Monitor to Download FCode" on page 3-20.

The load point of the file is not used when burning an FCode PROM, but is used by Forth Monitor commands that load FCode files into system memory. The tokenizer available from the SBus Support Group sets the load point to be the recommended 0x4000 address.

By convention, the file output by the tokenizer has the suffix `.fcode`.

FCode Binary Format

The format of FCode binary that is required by the OpenBoot *FCode evaluator* is as follows:

Table 3-1   FCode Binary Format

Element	Structure
FCode header	eight bytes
Body	0 or more bytes
End byte-code	1 byte either the `end0` or `end1` byte-code

The format of the FCode header is:

Table 3-2   FCode Header Format

Byte(s)	Content
0	One of the FCodes: `version1`,`start1`,`start2`,`start3`,`start4`
1	reserved
2 and 3	16-bit checksum of the FCode body
4 through 7	count of bytes in the FCode binary image including the header

Testing FCode on the Target Machine

Once you have created the FCode binary you may test it using the OpenBoot Forth Monitor. The Forth Monitor provides facilities to allow you to load your program into system memory and direct the FCode evaluator to interpret it from there. This allows you to avoid having to burn a PROM and attach it to your plug-in board with each FCode revision during the debug process. See the *OpenBoot Command Reference* for complete documentation on the use of the Forth Monitor.

The FCode testing process generally involves the following steps:

1. Configuring the target machine. This includes installing the hardware associated with the FCode program into the target machine and powering-up the machine to the OpenBoot Forth Monitor.

2. Loading the FCode program into memory from a serial line, a network, a hard disk, or a floppy disk.

3. Interpreting the FCode program to create a *device node(s)* on the OpenBoot *device tree.*

4. Browsing the device node(s) to verify proper FCode interpretation.

5. Exercising the FCode program's device driver *methods* complied into the device node, if any.

If the FCode program does not include any methods which involve using the actual hardware then the program may be tested without installing the hardware.

Configuring the Target Machine

Setting Appropriate Configuration Parameters

Before powering-down the target machine to install the target hardware, a few NVRAM parameters should be set to appropriate values. You can set them from the Forth Monitor as follows:

```
ok setenv auto-boot? false

ok setenv fcode-debug? true
```

Setting `auto-boot?` to `false` tells OpenBoot not to boot the OS upon a machine reset but rather to enter the Forth Monitor at the ok prompt.

Setting `fcode-debug?` to `true` tells the OpenBoot FCode evaluator to save the names of words created by interpreting FCode words which were tokenized with `headers` on. This is in addition to words defined with `external` on - whose names are always saved. `fcode-debug?` defaults to `false` to conserve RAM space in normal machine operation. With the names saved, the debugging methods described in later sections will be easier since it will be easier to read decompiled FCode.

Modifying The Expansion Bus Probe Sequence

The start-up sequence in the machine's OpenBoot implementation will be programmed to examine all expansion buses at well-known locations for the presence of plug-in devices and their onboard FCode PROM program. It then invokes the FCode evaluator to interpret the program. This process is called *probing* the device.

When using the Forth Monitor to load and interpret an FCode program in system memory, it is better to configure OpenBoot to not automatically try to probe the device. The probing will be done manually (as explained later) from the Forth Monitor after the FCode program is loaded into memory.

Configuring an OpenBoot implementation not to probe a given slot on a given expansion bus may be done in various ways which are implementation dependent. That is, they will be different for different systems and different expansion buses.

Many machines have an NVRAM parameter called `sbus-probe-list` which defines which SBus card slots will be probed during start up and the order in which they will be probed.

For example, on the SPARCstation2, `sbus-probe-list` has a default value of 0123. Setting `sbus-probe-list` to 013 directs OpenBoot during start-up to probe first SBus slots 0 (built-in devices), then slot 1, and finally slot 3. This leaves SBus slot 2 unprobed, free for use by the device under development.

Methods to prevent probing a given slot for other types of expansion buses may involve using the `nvramrc`. An `nvramrc` script could be used to patch an implementation specific OpenBoot word which defines the bus's probe sequence or to modify a property of the expansion buses device node which describes the sequence.

After the FCode program is debugged and programmed in PROM on the device and you want to do a full system test (including automatic probing of the new device), restore the expansion bus probing configuration to the default.

Getting to the Forth Monitor

After completing the configuration described above, power-down the machine and install the device. Then power-up the system and it should stop at the `ok` prompt ready for Forth Monitor commands.

Note – On the SPARCstation1 and SPARCstation1+, SBus slot 3 may be used *only* for SBus slave devices, such as framebuffers. Unlike slots 1 and 2, it may *not* be used for SBus master devices, such as disk drive or network interfaces.

3

Using the Forth Monitor to Download FCode

Complete directions for using the Forth Monitor to download files to system memory are provided in the *OpenBoot Command Reference*. This chapter contains a synopsis for FCode program files. FCode words used to help download and execute FCode source files are shown below.

Table 3-3   File Download/Execute-related Toolkit Commands

FCode	Stack Notation	Function
begin-package	(arg-adr arg-len reg-adr reg-len path-adr path-len --)	Initialize device tree for executing FCode.
select-dev	(path-adr path-len --)	Open specified device node and make it the current node.
set-args	(arg-adr arg-len reg-adr reg-len --)	Sets values returned by `my-args`, `my-space` and `my-address` for the current node.
end-package	(--)	Complete device tree entry and return to Forth Monitor environment.
unselect-dev	(--)	Closes current node and return to Forth Monitor environment.
new-slot-node (*1.x only*)	(--)	Prepare device tree for new entry.
execute-device-method	(... path-adr path-len cmd-adr cmd-len -- ... ok?)	Execute named command within the specified device tree node.
probe-slot (1.x only)	(slot# --)	Setup and execute FCode in the given SBus slot.

Using `dload` to Load from Ethernet

`dload` loads files over Ethernet at a specified address, as shown below.

```
ok  4000  dload filename
```

In the above example, *filename* must be relative to the server's root. Use **4000** (hex) as the address for `dload` input.

FCode programs loaded with `dload` must be in the format described in "Tokenizing FCode Source".   The tokenizer provided by the *SBus Support Group* can output these files.

`dload` uses the trivial file transfer protocol (TFTP), so the server may need to have its permissions adjusted for this to work.

Using `dlbin` to Load From Serial Port A

`dlbin` may be used to load files over serial line A. Connect the target system's serial port A to a machine that is able to transfer a file on request. The following example assumes a `tip` window setup on a Sun system which will provide the FCode file. (See the *OpenBoot Command Reference* for information on setting `tip` connections.)

1. At the `ok` prompt, type:

```
ok dlbin
```

2. In the `tip` window of the other system, send the file:

```
~C (local command) cat filename
(Away two seconds)
```

The `ok` prompt will reappear on the screen of the target system.

FCode programs loaded with `dlbin` must be in the format described in "Tokenizing FCode Source". `dlbin` loads the files at the entry point indicated in the file header. It is recommended that this address be 0x4000.

Using `boot` to Load From Hard Disk, Floppy Disk, or Ethernet

You can also load an FCode program with `boot`, the command normally used to boot the operating system. Use the following format:

```
ok boot [device-specifier]  [filename]  -h
```

device-specifier is either a full device path name or a device alias. See the *OpenBoot Command Reference* for information on device path names and aliases.

For a hard disk or floppy partition, *filename* is relative to the resident file system. See the *OpenBoot Command Reference* for information on creating a bootable floppy disk. For a network, *filename* is relative to the system's root partition on its root server. In both cases, the leading / must be omitted from the file path.

The -h flag specifies that the program should be loaded, but not executed. This flag must be included since otherwise boot will attempt to automatically execute the file assuming it is executable binary.

boot uses intermediate booters to accomplish its task. When loading from a hard disk or floppy disk, the OpenBoot firmware first loads the disk's boot block, which in turn loads a second-level booter. When loading over a network, the firmware uses TFTP to load the second-level booter. In both cases, *filename* and -h are passed to these intermediate booters.

The output file produced by a tokenizer may need to be converted to the format required by the secondary boot program. For example, Solaris 2.*x* intermediate booters require ELF format. fakeboot, a program available from the Sun SBus Support Group, may be useful in this process.

The location in memory where the FCode program is loaded depends on the secondary boot program and the fakeboot program.

Using the Forth Monitor to Interpret an FCode Program

FCode program interpretation involves creating a *device node* on the *device tree*.

There are some basic differences between the device tree of version 2 and of version 1. Improvements were made in version 2 that involve the form of physical addresses associated with device nodes and the ability to include device driver methods in device nodes. Thus use of the FCode evaluator to interpret an FCode Program differs for OpenBoot version 2 and OpenBoot version 1 systems.

Interpretation Under OpenBoot 2

For version 2, device nodes are also known as *packages*. Creating a device node from downloaded FCode involves the following steps:

1. Setting up the environment with begin-package.

For example, a begin-package call for creating a device node for an SBus card installed in slot #3 of a SPARCstation2 looks like:

```
ok 0 0 " 3,0" " /sbus" begin-package
```

In the example, the string, /sbus, indicates that the device node which will be created by the FCode program is to be a *child node* of the /sbus node in the device tree.

In general, any device node which supports child nodes - called *parent* nodes - may be used as this argument to begin-package. The device node defined by the FCode program will be made a child of that node. The full device pathname from the root node must be given. Another example of an SBus parent node is on a SPARCstation10 where its device pathname is /iommu/sbus.

In the example, the string, "3,0" indicates the SBus slot number, 3, and byte-offset, 0, within the slot's address space where the device node is to be based.

In general, this string is a pair of values separated by a comma which identify the physical address associated with the expansion slot. The form of this physical address depends on the physical address space defined by the parent node. For children of an SBus node, the form is slot-number,byte-offset. Other parent nodes will define different address spaces.

The physical address pair value is retrieved within the FCode program with both the my-address and my-space FCodes.

In the example, the initial 0 0 represents a null argument string passed to the FCode program.

This argument string is retrieved within the FCode program with the my-args FCode. Generally, FCode programs do not take arguments at interpretation time so this will usually be the null string. (For the SPARCstation2, when the FCode PROM on an SBus card is automatically interpreted during system power-on, this is set to a null string).

begin-package is defined as:

```
: begin-package  select-dev new-device set-args ;
```

select-dev (adr len --) - Opens the input device node (the parent node) and makes it the *current instance.*

new-device (--) - Initializes a new device node as a child of the currently active node and makes it the current instance.

set-args (arg-adr arg-len reg-adr reg-len --) - Sets the values returned by my-args, my-space, and my-address for the current instance.

2. Interpreting the loaded FCode with byte-load

byte-load is the Forth Monitor command that invokes the FCode evaluator to compile the FCode program into the current instance.

For FCode programs downloaded with dload or dlbin use:

```
ok 4000 1 byte-load
```

4000 is the load address recommended to be used as input to dload and as the entry point in the file loaded by dlbin. The argument, 1, is the byte spacing between FCode byte-codes which byte-load is to expect. For FCode loaded into memory this is always 1.

For FCode programs downloaded with boot, the address at which the FCode is loaded depends on the second level booter and the program that is used to convert the FCode file to a format accepted by the booter, such as fakeboot. For example, if the file is loaded with the FCode binary starting at 4030 use:

```
ok 4030 1 byte-load
```

3. Closing the environment with end-package.

end-package finishes up the creation of the device tree node.

```
ok end-package
```

It is defined as:

```
: end-package finish-device unselect-dev ;
```

finish-device (--) Completes the device tree node initialized by new-device and changes the current instance to be the parent node.

unselect-dev (--) Closes the parent device tree node and returns to the normal Forth Monitor environment. That is, there is no longer a current instance or active package.

Interpretation Under OpenBoot 1

OpenBoot Version 1 was only implemented in early SPARCstations which only contain the SBus expansion bus. Thus the following discussion assumes an FCode program for an SBus plug-in device on early SPARCstations.

1. Setting up the environment

In version 1, the user sets only the value of `my-address`. Unlike version 2, `my-address` is defined as the offset - from the base of the SBus in the systems root address space - of the SBus slot in which the device is installed.

Set `my-address` as in the following example for SBus slot 1:

```
ok 200.0000 is my-address
```

Hexadecimal slot offsets for the SPARCstation1/1+, SPARCstation IPC and SPARCstation 1E are:

- 0x200.0000 - Slot 1
- 0x400.0000 - Slot 2
- 0x600.0000 - Slot 3

In version 1 the user prepares the device tree for a new entry by issuing the `new-slot-node` command. This command assumes that the new device will be the child of the SBus nexus node in the slot indicated by `my-address`.

```
ok new-slot-node
```

`new-slot-node` is not in OpenBoot versions 1.0 or 1.1, but you can download it with the `reheader.fth` file available from the *Sun SBus Support Group*, or enter the following patch directly:

```
\ For OpenBoot version 1.0

: new-slot-node ( -- )

  ffe9b192 execute

  my-address ffe93da0 execute

  slot# ffe9bd6e execute

;

\ For OpenBoot version 1.1
```

```
: new-slot-node ( -- )

  ffe9b152 execute

  my-address ffe9499c execute

  slot# ffe9bd56 execute

;
```

2. Interpreting the downloaded FCode with `byte-load`

For version 1, use `byte-load` to interpret the FCode program as described for version 2.

Using the Forth Monitor to Browse a Device Node

The capability to view device nodes as well as what is contained in device nodes is different in OpenBoot versions 1 and 2. In version 2, the Forth Monitor has built-in many more commands to navigate the device tree.

Table 3-4 lists available OpenBoot commands supporting device node browsing:

Table 3-4   Commands for Browsing the Device Tree

Command	Description
.attributes	Display the names and values of the current node's properties.
cd *device-path*	Select the indicated device node, making it the current node.
cd *node-name*	Search for a node with the given name in the subtree below the current node, and select the first such node found.
cd ..	Select the device node that is the parent of the current node.
cd /	Select the root machine node.
device-end	De-select the current device node, leaving no node selected.
find-device	(*path-adr path-len* --) Select device node, like `cd`.
get-attribute	(name-adr name-len -- true | value-adr value-len false) Returns property value.
ls	Display the names of the current node's children.

Table 3-4   Commands for Browsing the Device Tree

Command	Description
pwd	Display the device path name that names the current node.
show-devs [*device-path*]	Display all the devices known to the system directly beneath a given level in the device hierarchy. show-devs used by itself shows the entire device tree.
words	Display the names of the current node's methods.

Device Node Browsing Under OpenBoot 2

Once a device node has been created, you may use the Forth Monitor to browse the node. See the *OpenBoot Command Reference* for a more complete discussion on this. Below is a brief synopsis of the available commands.

- show-devs displays all known devices in the device tree.

- cd sets the active package to a named node so its contents may be viewed. For example, to make the ACME company's SBus device named "ACME,widget" the active package on a SPARCstation2:

```
ok cd /sbus/ACME,widget
```

- find-device is essentially identical to cd differing only in the way the input pathname is passed.

```
ok " /sbus/ACME,widget" find-device
```

- .attributes displays the names and values of all the properties created for the active package.
- get-attribute returns the value of the specified property from the active package.
- ls displays the names of all child nodes, if any, of the active package.

- words shows the names of the device node methods, if any, created by the FCode program. It shows all words which were defined with external and, if fcode-debug? was true when the FCode was interpreted, the words defined with headers.

- see *wordname* decompiles *wordname*.

- device-end undoes the effects of the cd or find-device command putting the system back into the normal Forth Monitor environment.

- pwd displays the device pathname of the active package.

Device Node Browsing Under OpenBoot 1

For version 1, only device node properties are included in device nodes and there are no commands built in the Forth Monitor to view them. Here is some Forth code which may be loaded into a version 1 system to view device nodes and their properties. It defines the command, .dev, with the following usage:

Code Example 3-1   Device Node Properties Example

```
\ Forth program to display device node properties
3 /1* constant /prop
: printable?  ( char -- flag )  bl  h# 7e  between  ;
: .cstring  ( adr -- )  begin  dup c@ dup  while  emit 1+  repeat  2drop  ;
: xtype  ( adr len -- )
   bounds  ?do  i c@  dup printable?  if  emit  else  drop  then  loop
;
: xdump  ( adr len -- )  bounds  ?do  i unaligned-@ .h  /1 +loop ;
: to-column  ( column# -- )  #out @ -  1 max  spaces  ;
: .props  ( prop-adr -- )
   begin  dup 1@  while
      dup 1@ .cstring
      dup 1a1+ 1@  over 2 1a+ 1@ swap
      d# 16 to-column 2dup xtype
      d# 32 to-column xdump cr
      /prop +
   repeat drop
;
: .dev  ( adr -- [ next-adr' ] [ child-adr ] )
   ." Node at: " dup .h cr
   dup 2 1a+ 1@ ?dup  if  .props  then
   dup  >r  1@ ?dup  if  ." Next: "  dup .h  then
   r> 1a1+  1@ ?dup  if  ." Child: " dup .h  then cr
;
ok root-info .dev
(displays root node)
ok .dev
(displays next node)
ok .dev
```

Using the Forth Monitor to Test a Device Node Driver

The Forth Monitor provides the capability to test the device node driver methods of an FCode program by allowing the user to execute individual methods from the Forth Monitor prompt.

OpenBoot version 2 has much more robust support for device node methods than version 1. In version 2, there are basically two ways to invoke device node methods. They are described below. For version 1 considerations see the third part of this section.

Device Node Methods Under OpenBoot 2

Using `select-dev`

`select-dev` initializes an execution environment for the methods of the input device node methods. It allows the user to subsequently execute the methods directly by name.

For example, on a SPARCstation2 execute this command as follows:

```
ok " /sbus/ACME,widget" select-dev
```

`select-dev` performs the following:

- It effectively calls `"cd /sbus/ACME,widget"` to make the named device the active package. This makes all the device methods "visible" to the Forth Monitor.

- Establishes a chained set of package instances for each node in the path. In particular, this makes an instance of all data items of the device node available to its methods.

- Opens all device nodes in the path by calling the `open` method of each. `select-dev` assumes `open` (and `close`) methods in each node in the path and so the device node under test must have one.

Once these steps are performed the current device node methods may be executed by simply typing their name at the prompt. For example:

```
ok clear-widget-register

ok fetch-widget-register .

0

ok
```

As is generally true of the Forth language, if execution of the method exposes an error in the code, the error may be isolated by executing the component words of the method step-by-step. Use see to decompile the method. And then type the component words individually until the error is evident. For example:

```
ok see clear-widget-register

: clear-widget-register

    enable-register-write

    0 widget-register r1!

    disable-register-write

;

ok enable-register-write

ok 0 widget-register r1!

ok disable-register-write
```

This process may be performed recursively by decompiling the component words and then individually executing their component words. This is much easier if most of the words were defined with the headers directive. Use showstack to enable automatic printing of the Forth stack after the execution of each step to ensure correct stack behavior.

Device nodes may also be modified "on-the-fly" by any of the following:

- Entering new methods definitions. These methods are compiled into the device node like the methods in the FCode program that created the node.

- Redefining a method to include some function neglected in the first definition. (Only subsequent uses of the method are affected.) For example:

```
ok : open open initialize-widget-register-2 ;
```

- Use patch to edit word definitions. See the *OpenBoot Command Reference* for information on how to use this command.

Of course these modifications only stay in effect until the machine is reset and once they are working you'll probably want to include the modifications to the FCode program source.

`unselect-dev` reverses the effects of `select-dev` by calling the `close` method of each device in the path of the current active node, destroying the package instance of each node, and returning to the normal Forth Monitor environment. Execute `unselect-dev` as follows:

```
ok unselect-dev
```

Using `execute-device-method`

`execute-device-method` is used to execute a method directly from the normal Forth Monitor environment. That is, it is not necessary to manually make the device node the current instance before executing the method. For example:

```
ok " /sbus/ACME,widget" " test-it" execute-device-method
```

`execute-device-method` returns `true` if it successfully executes the method; `false`, if not.

`execute-device-method` performs the following steps before invoking the method:

- Temporarily sets the named device node to be the active package.

- Temporarily establishes a chained set of package instances for each node in the path. In particular, this makes an instance of all data items of the device node available to its methods.

- Temporarily opens all device nodes in the name device path *except* the last device node in the pathname.

Note that the last item in the above list is a significant departure from how `select-dev` works. Since the device `open` method is not executed, any method invoked in this manner must be able to stand alone - not requiring any preestablished state which normally is created by `open`.

In summary, `execute-device-method` is provided to allow execution of device node methods which have been designed to provide their own state initialization and therefore to execute without previous execution of the `open` method. A typical example is a `selftest` method.

3

Device Node Methods Under OpenBoot 1

With the exception of framebuffer device drivers, it not recommended to make use of device node methods in version 1. Since booting from plug-in boards is not supported in version 1 the only beneficial methods would be for device diagnostics.

Some reasons to avoid device methods in version 1 are:

1. There are several FCode words not supported in version 1. Therefore methods designed to run on version 2 and version 1 must use the old, less functional, set of FCodes.

2. Plug-in board device methods are not compiled into the associated device node. They are compiled into the main Forth vocabulary. This makes it impossible to provide a standard way for users to invoke diagnostic methods across different devices. The methods must be named specially and users must be informed of that name in order to pick them out of the many OpenBoot Forth words.

3. There is limited dictionary space in many version 1 systems.

Testing FCode in Source Form

The Forth Monitor provides the capability to skip the tokenizer and download FCode program source directly. This practice is not recommended since there is not much advantage to this except to save a small amount of time tokenizing the program. And, in fact, there are some down sides:

• It may cause problems in the long run since generally the Forth Monitor recognizes a larger number of words that does the FCode evaluator. So the FCode program developer who tests with FCode source may develop and test a program only to find that some of the words he used are not FCode words and will not be accepted by the tokenizer and the FCode evaluator. This will require the developer to rewrite code.

• To load source you should comment out `fcode-version1` and `end0`.

• Since the download commands accept only one file any `fload`ed files must be put in-line.

To load an ASCII Forth source file over serial line A you use the command, `dl`. In addition to loading the file over the serial line it compiles the Forth source while it is loading without requiring a extra command. Therefore the developer must execute `begin-package` before downloading. See the *OpenBoot Command Reference* for details on the use of `dl`.

To load a program over a network with `dload` or from a disk with `boot` follow the instructions in the *OpenBoot Command Reference.* These commands do not evaluate the Forth source so downloading may be done before `begin-package`. `dload` requires that the source file begin with the two characters,
"\ " (backslash space).

For OpenBoot version 1, using source code directly may cause problems since some FCode words do not have name headers and will thus be unrecognized. A file named `reheader.fth`, available from the *Sun SBus Support Group*, may be downloaded and executed to provide the missing words.

Producing an FCode PROM

The output of the tokenizer program is used to make an actual FCode PROM. If your PROM burning tools do not accept the format, you may need to develop a format conversion utility.

Exercising an Installed FCode PROM

You may either let OpenBoot automatically evaluate the FCode program from the PROM or you may remove the device from the OpenBoot probing as discussed earlier in "Configuring the Target Machine".

The same process discussed for testing FCode programs which are loaded to system memory may be used to test FCode programs already loaded into PROM on the device.

Exercising FCode Under OpenBoot 2

If you take the device out of the probing sequence, a device node may be built manually as in the following example for a SPARCstation2 with the device installed in SBus slot 1:

```
ok 10000 constant rom-size

ok " /sbus" select-dev

ok " 1,0"  decode-unit          ( offset space )

ok rom-size  map-in             ( fcode-vadr )

ok new-device                   ( fcode-vadr )
```

```
ok " " " 1,0" set-args          ( fcode-vadr )

ok dup 1 byte-load              ( fcode-vadr )

ok finish-device               ( fcode-vadr )

ok rom-size    map-out

ok unselect-dev
```

This is essentially the same sequence as outlined for evaluating FCode loaded into system memory except that the user must map in and map out the FCode PROM by using the decode-unit and use the map-in and map-out methods of the parent device node. For more information about these methods, see Chapter 8, "Hierarchical Devices".

You may browse the device node and exercise the device methods in the same way as described earlier. You may also define new methods and patch existing ones. Of course these modifications will only remain until a system reset.

Exercising FCode Under OpenBoot 1

If you take the device out of the probing sequence, a device node may be built manually as in the following example with the device installed in SBus slot 2:

```
ok 2 probe-slot
```

In this case, probe-slot is equivalent to:

```
ok 400.0000 is my-address

ok new-slot-node

ok my-address 10000 map-sbus    ( fcode-vadr)

ok dup 1 byte-load              ( fcode-vadr )

ok 10000 free-virtual
```

Packages

4 ≡

A *package* is a group of functions, or methods, that implements a specific interface. A package implements a library of functions that may then be called, as needed, by FCode programs.

For many devices, this is not particularly useful, but it will be useful for FCode programs that:

- implement bootable devices
- call functions or properties from other packages, or
- implement functions intended to be called from other packages

A **plug-in package** is a package that is not permanently resident in the main OpenBoot PROM. Plug-in packages are written in FCode. Since FCode is represented with a machine-independent binary format, it lets the same plug-in packages be used on machines with different CPU instruction sets.

A package's references to OpenBoot PROM system functions are resolved and the functions defined by the package are made available to other parts of the OpenBoot during the linking process. This is performed at run-time, when OpenBoot interprets (probes) the package. Thus, plug-in packages do not need to be pre-linked with a particular OpenBoot implementation.

OpenBoot only needs to know the beginning address of the package in order to probe it. Once probed, the package becomes a working part of OpenBoot, until the system is reset or turned off. A package exports its interface to OpenBoot, and to other packages, as a vocabulary of Forth words.

Many packages implement a specific interface; a standard set of functions. Different packages may implement the same interface. For example, there may be two display device driver packages, each implementing the standard display device interface, but for two different display devices.

There may also be multiple instances of a single package. For example, a plug-in disk driver may have as many instances as there are disks of that type.

Package Definitions, Package Instances, and Device Nodes

A package consists of

- **methods** (software procedures)
- **properties** (externally-visible information describing the package), and
- **data** (information used internally by the package).

Package data consists of uninitialized data, corresponding to Forth buffers, and initialized data, corresponding to Forth variables, values and deferred words. The initial values of the initialized data are stored within the package.

Each package is associated with exactly one device node, so you can use the terms *package* and *device node* interchangeably.

The *active package* is the package whose methods are currently visible.

An *instance* is a set of values for a package's data. Before a package's methods may be executed, an *instance* must be created. You create an instance from a package by allocating memory for the package's data and setting the contents of that memory to the initial values stored in the package. Multiple instances may be created from the same package, and may exist simultaneously.

The *current* instance is whatever instance is in use at a given time. When a package method accesses a data item, it refers to the copy of that data item that is associated with the current instance.

Plug-in Device Drivers

Plug-in device drivers are plug-in packages implementing simple device drivers. The interfaces to these drivers are designed to provide a primitive I/O capability.

Plug-in drivers are used for such functions as booting the operating system from that device, or displaying text on the device before the operating system has activated its own drivers. Plug-in drivers are made available to other parts of the OpenBoot PROM during the probing phase of the OpenBoot PROM start-up sequence.

Plug-in drivers must be programmed to handle portability problems, such as hardware alignment restrictions and byte ordering of external devices. With care, you can write a driver so that it is portable to a variety of systems in which the device could conceivably operate.

Plug-in drivers are intended to be stored in ROM located on the device itself, so that the act of installing the device automatically makes its plug-in driver available to the OpenBoot PROM.

For devices with no provision for such a plug-in driver ROM, the plug-in driver could be located elsewhere, perhaps in ROM located on a different device or in an otherwise unused portion of the main OpenBoot PROM.

Package Methods

Required Methods

A package that is intended for use by OpenBoot (bootable, for example) must always implement the two following methods:

open
(-- ok?)

Prepare the package for subsequent use. open typically allocates resources, maps, initializes devices, and performs a brief sanity check (no check at all may be acceptable). true is returned if successful, false if not. When open is called, the parent instance chain has already been opened, so this method may call its parent's methods.

close
(--)

Restore the package to its "not in use" state. close typically turns off devices, unmaps, and deallocates resources. close is executed before its parent is closed, so the parent's methods are available to close. It is an error to close a package which is not open.

Recommended Methods

The following methods are highly recommended. If possible, they should be present even if they are only stubs.

reset
--)

Put the package into a "quiet" state. reset is primarily for packages that do not automatically assume a quiet state after a hardware reset, such as devices that turn on with interrupt requests asserted.

selftest
(-- error#)

Test the package. `selftest` is invoked by the OpenBoot `test` word. It returns 0 if no error found or a package-specific error number if a failure is noticed.

`test` does not open the package before executing `selftest`, so `selftest` is responsible for establishing any state necessary to perform its function prior to starting the tests, and for releasing any resources allocated after completing the tests. There should be no user interaction with `selftest`, as the word may be called from a program with no user present.

If the device was already open when `selftest` is called, a new instance will still be created and destroyed. A well-written `selftest` should handle this possibility correctly, if appropriate.

If the device is already open, but it is not possible to perform a complete selftest without destroying the state of the device, the integrity of the open device should take precedence, and the selftest process should test only those aspects of the device that can be tested without destroying device state. The inability to fully test the device should not be reported as an error result; an error result should occur only if selftest actually finds a device fault.

The "device already open" case happens most commonly for display devices, which are often used as the console output device, and thus remain open for long periods of time. When testing a display device that is already open, it is not necessary to preserve text that may already be on the screen, but the device state should be preserved to the extent that further text output can occur and be visible after selftest exits. Any error messages that are displayed by the selftest method will be sent to the console output device, so when testing an already-open display device, such error messages should be avoided during times when selftest has the device in a state where it is unable to display text.

`selftest` is *not* executed within an open/close pair. When `selftest` executes, a new instance is created (and destroyed). It will have its own set of variables, values, and so forth. These quantities are not normally shared with an instance opened with the normal `open` routine for the package.

Note – `selftest` should be written to do its own mapping and unmapping.

Package Data Definitions

The usual Forth words can be used to create and use package data areas:

```
variable bar

5 value grinch

defer stub

create ival  x , y , z ,

7 buffer: foo

ival foo 7 move
```

The data areas defined above are shared among all open instances of the package. If a value is changed, for instance, the new value will persist until it is changed again, independent of the creation and destruction of package instances.

All open instances of a package can access and change the value, which changes it for all other instances.

Usually a package does not share values among open instances. Consequently, you will usually want to use the following constructions to define package data areas local to a given package instance:

```
instance variable bar

5 instance value grinch

instance defer stub

7 instance buffer: foo
```

You should use the `instance` approach whenever possible. Using `instance` defines data areas that are re-initialized every time a package instance is created (usually by opening the package), so each instance gets its own copy of the data area. For example, changes to *bar* in one instance will not affect the contents of *bar* in another instance. (Note that `create` operates across all the instances, and cannot be made instance-specific.)

The total amount of data space consumed by that package is remembered as part of the package definition when `finish-device` executes to finish the package definition. Also, the contents of all the `variables`, `values`, and `defer`s at the time `finish-device` executes are also stored as part of the package definition.

An instance of the package is created when that package is later opened. Data space is allocated for that instance (the amount of which was remembered in the package definition). The portion of that data space corresponding to the initialized `variables`, `values`, and `defer`s is initialized from the values stored in the package definition. Data space associated with `buffer:`'s is not initialized.

You can add new methods and new properties to a package definition at any time, even after `finish-device` has been executed for that package. To do so, select the package and proceed to create definitions or properties.

However, it is *not* possible to add new data items to a package definition after `finish-device` has been executed for that package. `finish-device` sets the size of the data space for that package, and from then on it is fixed.

Accessing Other Packages

A particular package can often use the support of other, previously defined packages. There are two types of packages whose methods can be used directly:

- the parent of the package being defined
- standard support packages in the `/packages` node of the device tree

Phandles and Ihandles

A package definition is identified by its `phandle`. `find-package` returns the `phandle` of a package definition in the `/packages` node. The `phandle` is then used to open that support package. For example:

```
" deblocker" find-package
```

returns either `false` (not found), or `phandle true`.

Opening a support package with `open-package` returns an `ihandle`. This `ihandle` is used primarily to call the methods of the support package, and to close the support package when it is no longer needed.

An instance argument string must be supplied when opening any package (it may be null). The instance argument string can then be accessed from within the opened package with the my-args FCode (see below for details). For example (assume that phandle has already been found):

```
" 5,3,0" phandle open-package (ihandle)
```

If the package cannot be opened, an ihandle of 0 is returned.

The following FCodes are used to find and open packages (within the /packages node):

Table 4-1   Package Access FCodes

Name	Stack Comment	Description
find-package	(name-adr name-len -- false | phandle true)	Find the package specified by the string *name-adr* name-len within /packages. Returns the *phandle* of the package, if found.
open-package	(arg-adr arg-len phandle -- ihandle | 0)	Open an instance of the package *phandle*, return the ihandle of the opened package, or 0 if unsuccessful. The package is opened with an instance argument string specified by *arg-adr arg-len*.
$open-package	(arg-adr arg-len name-adr name-len -- ihandle | 0)	Shortcut word to find and open a package within the /packages node in one operation.

An example of using $open-package follows:

```
" 5,3,0" " deblocker"

$open-package ( ihandle | 0 )
```

Table 4-2   Manipulating phandles and ihandles

Name	Stack Comment	Description
my-self	(-- ihandle)	Return the instance handle of the currently-executing package instance.
my-parent	(-- ihandle)	Return the instance handle of the parent of the currently-executing package instance.
ihandle>phandle	(ihandle -- phandle)	Convert an instance handle to a package handle.
close-package	(ihandle --)	Close an instance of a package.

Don't confuse phandle with ihandle. Here's how to use them:

1. Find the phandle of a package.

2. Use this phandle to open an instance of the package; this will give an ihandle.

3. Use the ihandle to access the methods of the package.

4. When done accessing the methods of the package, use the ihandle to close the instance of the package with `close-package`.

Use `ihandle>phandle` to open another instance of the current package or its parent. `my-self` and `my-parent` return ihandles, which can be converted into phandles with `ihandle>phandle`.

To open another instance of the current package, use:

```
my-self ihandle>phandle open-package
```

To open another instance of the parent package, use:

```
my-parent ihandle>phandle open-package
```

Instance Arguments and Parameters

An instance argument (*my-args*) is a string that is passed to a package when it is opened. The string may contain parameters of any sort, based on the needs of the package, or can simply be a null-string if no parameters are needed. A null string is generated either with `"  "` or `0 0`.

The instance argument passed may be accessed from inside the package with the `my-args` FCode.

Note – A package is not required to inspect the passed arguments.

If the argument string contains several parameters separated by a common character, you can pick off the pieces from within the package with `left-parse-string`. You can use any character as the separator; a comma is commonly used for this.

Note – Avoid using blanks or the / character, since these will confuse the parsing of any pathname.

A new value for my-args is passed every time a package is opened. This can happen under a number of circumstances:

1. The my-args string will be null when FCode on an SBus card is interpreted automatically by the OpenBoot system at power-on.

2. The my-args string is determined by a parameter to the begin-package tool used to set up the device tree when FCode is downloaded and interpreted interactively.

3. The my-args string can be set with set-args before a particular slot is probed, if SBus probing is being controlled from nvramrc.

The above three instances happen only once, when the package FCode is interpreted for the first time. If you want to preserve the initial value for my-args, the FCode program should copy it into a local buffer to preserve the information.

Whenever a package is reopened, a new value for my-args is supplied at that time. The method for supplying this new value depends on the method used to open the package, as described below.

4. The instance argument (my-args) is supplied as a string parameter to the commands open-package or $open-package.

5. Monitor commands, such as select-dev, test, and execute-device-method, supply the entire pathname to the device being opened. This approach lets an instance argument be supplied as part of the pathname itself. For example, to open the SBus device "SUNW,bwtwo" with the argument string "5,3,0", enter:

```
ok " /sbus/SUNW,bwtwo:5,3,0" select-dev

ok
```

A more complicated (and fictitious) example is the following:

```
ok " /sbus/SUNW,fremly:test/grumpin@7,32:print/SUNW,fht:1034,5"

ok select-dev

ok
```

Here the string "test" is passed to the SUNW,fremly package as it is opened, the string "print" is passed to the grumpin package as it is opened, and the string "1034,5" is passed to the SUNW,fht package as it is opened.

Package Addresses

Another piece of information available to a package is its address relative to its parent package. Again, there are two main ways to pass this address to the package:

- Part of the pathname of the package
- A string parameter given to the probe words

As an example of the first method, suppose the following package is being opened:

```
ok "/sbus/esp/sd@3,0:b" select-dev
```

Then the address of the /sd package relative to the /esp package is 3,0. Note that this address must match the initial value of the "reg" property (if present) of the /sd package.

The package can find its relative address with my-unit, which returns the address as a pair of numbers. The first number (*high*) is the number before the comma in the example above, and the second number (*low*) is the number after the comma. Note that these are numbers, not strings.

As an example of the second method, suppose a test version of an FCode package is being interpreted:

```
ok 0 0  " 3,0"  " /sbus" begin-package

ok
```

Here the my-args parameters for the new FCode are null, the initial address is 3,0 and it will be placed under the /sbus node.

The initial address can be obtained through my-address and my-space. Typically, you use my-space and my-address (plus an offset) to create the package's "reg" property, and also to map in needed regions of the device.

Executing Methods

A method is identified by its execution token, which is returned by find-method for other packages. The token is actually the Forth acf for the word. For words in the package being defined, the Forth word ['] returns an execution token.

The execution token is used to execute a method in another package, and also to schedule a method for automatic, repeated execution by the system clock interrupt. See the alarm FCode.

Accessing the methods of a package can be done in one of the following ways (there are other ways as well, but these cover the common cases), with the last approach generally the best:

```
$open-package $call-method

find-package open-package $call-method

find-package open-package find-method call-package
```

Because finding is inherently a slow process, if a method is to be used repeatedly, the last technique is recommended. The idea is to save the ihandle and phandle of the package in question, together with the execution token of the method needed, so that the overhead of finding them gets paid only one time, instead of every time the method is executed.

For example, the following method is simple, but if slow called repeatedly:

```
: add-offset  ( x.byte# -- x.byte#' )

  my-args " disk-label" $open-package (ihandle)

  " offset" rot  (name-adr name-len ihandle)

  $call-method

;
```

A more complex, but if called repeatedly, much faster construct:

```
0 value label-ihandle                \ place to save the other package's
ihandle

0 value offset-method                \ place to save found method's acf

: init  ( -- )

    my-args "  disk-label" $open-package ( ihandle ) is label-ihandle
```

```
    " offset"  label-ihandle ihandle>phandle ( name-adr name-len phandle
) find-method if

        ( acf ) is offset-method

    else  ." Error: can't find method"

    then

;

: add-offset  ( d.byte# -- d.byte#' )

    offset-method label-ihandle call-package

;
```

Because device access time often dominates I/O operations, the benefit of this extra code probably won't be noticed. It is only justified if the particular method will be called often.

A shortcut word to call a method in the parent package is `$call-parent`. This is equivalent to using `my-parent $call-method`.

Table 4-3   Method-Access Words

Name	Stack Comment	Description
find-method	(adr len phandle -- false | acf true)	Find the method named *adr len* within the package *phandle*. Returns *false* if not found.
call-package	([...] acf ihandle -- [...])	Execute the method *acf* within the instance *ihandle*.
$call-method	([...] adr len ihandle -- [...])	Shortcut word to find and execute the method adr *len* within the package instance *ihandle*.
$call-parent	([...] adr len -- [...])	Execute the method *adr len* within the parent's package instance. Exactly equivalent to calling `my-parent  $call-method`.

Debugging Packages

Package Mappings

Mappings set up by a package persist across instances (unless explicitly unmapped). Passing the mapped addresses between instances is not usually worth the convolutions involved. It is usually better for each new instance to do its own mappings, being sure to unmap resources as they are no longer needed.

If you save virtual addresses into a `value`, be sure to use the `instance` declarations (see "Package Data Definitions" on page 4-39).

nvramrc

Machines that support packages will generally also support the `nvramrc` facility. `nvramrc` is a special area in the `NVRAM` that can contain Monitor commands to be executed by OpenBoot as the machine powers on. These commands can be used to specify behavior during start up or to define changes for later execution.

For example: assume a card in SBus slot#2 (named `XYZ,me`) needs custom attributes set by the user. `nvramrc` contents would include:

```
probe-all

cd /sbus/XYZ,me

" type5" xdrstring " xyzmode" attribute

device-end

install-console

banner
```

After editing `nvramrc`, turn on the nvram parameter `use-nvramrc?` and reset the machine to activate the contents of `nvramrc`. See *OpenBoot Command Reference* for more about editing `nvramrc` contents.

Modifying Package Properties

To modify the properties of a package, first probe the package to get it into memory. Normally, probing is done automatically after the `nvramrc` commands are executed.

See Chapter 5, "Properties", for more information about properties.

Standard Support Packages

The `/packages` node of the device tree is special. It is a hierarchical node, but instead of describing a physical bus, `/packages` serves as a parent node for some software package nodes. The children of `/packages` are general-purpose software packages not attached to any particular hardware device. The "physical address space" defined by `/packages` is a trivial one: all addresses are the same — 0,0. Its children are distinguished by name alone.

The children of `/packages` are used by other packages to implement commonly used functions. They may be opened with the FCodes `open-package` or `$open-package`, and closed with `close-package`. There are three support packages that are included as standard children of `/packages`.

Sun Disk-Label Support Package

Disk (block) devices are random-access, block-oriented storage devices with fixed-length blocks. Disks may be subdivided into several logical "partitions", as defined by a *disk label*—a special disk block, usually the first one, containing information about the disk. The disk driver is responsible for appropriately interpreting a disk label. The driver may use the standard support package `/disk-label` if it does not implement a specialized label.

`/disk-label` interprets a standard Sun disk label, reading any "partitioning" information contained in it. It includes a first stage disk boot protocol for the standard label. `load` is the most important method defined by this package.

This package uses the `read` and `seek` methods of its parent (in practice, the package which opens this one to use the support routines). `/disk-label` defines the following methods:

Table 4-4   Sun Disk Label Package Methods

Name	Stack diagram	Description
open	(-- flag)	Reads and verifies the disk label accessed by the `read` and `seek` methods of its parent instance. Selects a disk partition based upon the text string returned by `my-args`. For the standard Sun disk label format, the argument is interpreted as follows: <table><tr><td>Argument</td><td>Partition</td></tr><tr><td><none></td><td>0</td></tr><tr><td>a or A</td><td>0</td></tr><tr><td>b or B</td><td>1</td></tr><tr><td>...</td><td>...</td></tr><tr><td>g or G</td><td>7</td></tr></table> Returns -1 if the operation succeeds. As a special case, if the argument is the string "`nolabel`", `open` returns -1 (success) without attempting to read or verify the label.
close	(--)	Frees all resources that were allocated by `open`.
load	(adr -- size)	Reads a stand-alone program from the "standard" disk boot block location for the partition specified when the package was opened. Places the program at memory address `adr`, returning its length `size`. For the standard Sun disk format, the stand-alone program is 7.5K bytes beginning 512 bytes from the start of the partition.
offset	(x.rel-- x.abs)	Returns the 64-bit absolute byte offset `x.abs` corresponding to the 64-bit partition-relative byte offset `x.rel`. In other words, adds the byte location of the beginning of the selected partition to the number on the stack.

TFTP Booting Support Package

The `/obp-tftp` package implements the Internet Trivial File Transfer Protocol (TFTP) for use in network booting. It is typically used by a `network` device driver for its first stage network boot protocol. Again, `load` is the most important method defined by this package.

This package uses the `read` and `write` methods of its parent, and defines the following methods:

Table 4-5   TFTP Package Methods

Name	Stack diagram	Description
open	(-- flag)	Prepares the package for subsequent use, returning -1 if the operation succeeds and 0 otherwise.
close	(--)	Frees all resources that were allocated by `open`.
load	(adr -- size)	Reads the default stand-alone program from the default `TFTP` server, placing the program at memory address *adr* and returning its length *size*. For the standard Sun `TFTP` booting protocol, `RARP` (Reverse Address Resolution Protocol) is used to acquire the `IP` address corresponding to the system's `MAC` address (equivalent to its Ethernet address). From the `IP` address, the default file name is constructed, of the form *<Hex-IP-Address>.<architecture>* (for example, `C0092E49.SUN4C`). Then `obp-tftp` tries to `TFTP` read that file, first trying the server that responded to the `RARP` request, and if that fails, then broadcasting the `TFTP` read request.

Deblocker Support Package

The `/deblocker` package makes it easy to implement byte-oriented device methods, using the block-oriented or record-oriented methods defined by devices such as disks or tapes. It provides a layer of buffering between the high-level byte-oriented interface and the low-level block-oriented interface. `/deblocker` uses the `max-transfer`, `block-size`, `read-blocks` and `write-blocks` methods of its parent, and defines the following methods:

Table 4-6   Deblocker Package Methods

Name	Stack diagram	Description
open	(-- flag)	Prepares the package for subsequent use, allocating the buffers used by the deblocking process based upon the values returned by the parent instance's `max-transfer` and `block-size` methods. Returns -1 if the operation succeeds, 0 otherwise.
close	(--)	Frees all resources that were allocated by `open`.
read	(adr len -- actual)	Reads at most *len* bytes from the device into the memory buffer beginning at `adr`. Returns `actual`, the number of bytes actually read, or 0 if the read operation failed. Uses the parent's `read-blocks` method as necessary to satisfy the request, buffering any unused bytes for the next request.
write	(adr len -- actual)	Writes at most `len` bytes from the device into the memory buffer beginning at `adr`. Returns `actual`, the number of bytes actually read, or 0 if the write operation failed. Uses the parent's `write-blocks` method as necessary to satisfy the request, buffering any unused bytes for the next request.
seek	(x.position -- flag)	Sets the device position at which the next `read` or `write` will take place. The position is specified by the 64-bit number `x.position`. Returns 0 if the operation succeeds or -1 if it fails.

Properties   5 ▤

Properties are created by FCode PROMs. The CPU's boot PROM understands certain property names that tell it things such as the type of the device (disk, tape, network, display, and so on). The CPU boot PROM may use this information to determine how to use the device (if at all) during the boot process.

SunOS understands other property names that give information used for configuring the operating system automatically. These properties include the driver name, the addresses and sizes of the device's registers, and interrupt levels and interrupt vectors used by the device.

Other properties may be used by individual SunOS device drivers. The names of such properties and the interpretation of their values is subject to agreement between the writers of the FCode PROM and the SunOS driver, but may otherwise be arbitrarily chosen. For example, a display device might declare width, height, and depth properties to allow a single SunOS driver to automatically configure itself for one of several similar but different devices.

A package's properties identify the characteristics of the package and its associated physical device, if any. You can create a property either with the `attribute` FCode, or with the `name`, `reg`, `intr`, `model`, and `device-type` FCodes, described below.

For example, a framebuffer package might export its register addresses, interrupt levels, and framebuffer size. Every package has an associated property list, which is arbitrarily extensible. Use the Forth Monitor command `.attributes` to display the names and values of the current node's properties.

Each property has a **property name** and a **property value**.

- The *property name* identifies the particular property. This name is composed of a string of printable characters. Uppercase characters should not be used in the name string since some systems may convert them to lower case.
- The *property value* specifies the contents, or value, of a particular property. The value is an array of bytes that may be used to encode integer numbers, text strings, or other forms of information.

Many derived data types can be encoded into the primitive "array of bytes" data type, for example:

- *integer.* Encoded as 4 bytes, big endian
- *text string.* Encoded as a null-terminated sequence of bytes
- *physical address range.* Encoded as 3 integers: *space*, *offset*, *size*
- *structure.* The concatenation of other types, with no padding or internal alignment
- *array.* The concatenation of *n* examples of some type

If an FCode program tries to create the same property (with the same name) more than once for a given package, the new property supercedes the old one.

You can add new properties during the lifetime of a product. For backward compatibility, an FCode or device driver program that needs the value of a particular property should consider the possibility that the property does not exist, in which case the program should supply its own default value.

Standard FCode Properties

A number of FCode properties have been defined and used by some or all current implementations of OpenBoot. These are listed below.

A package should never create any property using any of the following names, unless the defined meanings and structures are used. Doing otherwise can result in system errors occurring.

Standard FCode Properties For Cards (General)

- address
- device_type
- interrupts
- intr
- model
- name
- params
- parity-generated
- reg
- slave-burst-sizes
- status

Device-type Specific Properties For SBus Cards

- `address-bits`, (network)
- `character-set`, (display)

- `down-burst-sizes`, (sbus)
- `local-mac-address`, (network)
- `mac-address`, (network)
- `max-frame-size`, (network)

General Properties For Parent Nodes

- clock-frequency
- ranges
- scsi-initiator-id

Properties For SBus Parent Nodes

- burst-sizes
- bus-parity-generated
- one-pending-retry
- slave-only
- slot-address-bits
- up-burst-sizes

Standard Properties

"address"

This is an optional property that declares currently-mapped device virtual addresses. It is generally used to declare large regions of existing mappings, in order to enable the SunOS device driver to reuse those mappings to conserve system resources.

The contents of the property are an arbitrary number of virtual addresses. The correspondence between declared addresses and the set of mappable regions of a particular device is device-dependent.

```
-1 value my-buffers

-1 value my-dma-adr

: map-me ( -- )

  my-address 10.0000 +  my-space 1.0000  " map-in" $call-parent  ( virt1 )
```

```
    is my-buffers

    2000 " dma-alloc" $call-parent   ( virt2 )   is my-dma-adr

    my-buffers xdrint   my-dma-adr xdrint   xdr+   " address" attribute

;

: unmap-me   ( -- )

    my-dma-adr 2000 " dma-free" $call-parent

    my-buffers 1.0000 " map-out" $call-parent

    " address" delete-attribute

;
```

See also: `free-virtual`, `attribute`

"address-bits"

This optional property, when declared in "`network`" devices, indicates the number of address bits needed to address this device on its network. Used as:

```
    d# 48  xdrint   " address-bits"   attribute
```

See also: `attribute` and Chapter 9, "Network Devices".

"burst-sizes"

This required property is located in every SBus controller node in the system. Its value is a bit mask of burst transfer sizes supported by this SBus implementation. If bit n is 1, then transfer size 2^n bytes is supported. For instance, 9 means that 8-byte and 1-byte transfers are supported.

Support for the extended (64-bit) SBus protocol is also indicated by this property, using the next-higher 16 bits of the value.

Thus, an SBus controller which supports transfer sizes of 1,2,4,8,16,32,64 bytes would have a "burst-sizes" value of 0x007f. An SBus controller which also supports extended (64-bit) transfers of 8,16,32,64,128 bytes would have a "burst-sizes" value of 0x00f8007f.

Notice that particular destination devices may be more restrictive in the allowed transfer sizes. This property only describes the transfer sizes allowed by the SBus controller itself.

It is acceptable for an SBus controller to omit this property, as long as some parent node is assured of having the correct value. A plug-in device should use get-inherited-attribute to query this property.

Some early systems only support 16-byte bursts (as well as 1,2,4 byte transfers), but do not declare the "burst-sizes" property at all. Thus, a missing "burst-sizes" should be assumed to be equivalent to a "burst-sizes" value of 0x0017. Used as:

```
h# 7f xdrint " burst-sizes" attribute
```

See also: slave-burst-sizes, attribute, Chapter 8, "Hierarchical Devices".

"bus-parity-generated"

This optional property, when present on an SBus controller node, indicates that this SBus is generating parity on SBus transactions. A null value is used.

See also Chapter 8, "Hierarchical Devices".

"character-set"

This optional property, when declared in "display" or "serial" devices, indicates the recognized character set for this device. The contents are a text string.

A typical value is "ISO8859-1". 8859-1 is the number of the ISO specification for that particular character set, which essentially covers the full range of western European languages. To get a list of possible values, consult the X registry. There is an address for it in the X11R5 documentation.

Used as:

```
" ISO8859-1" xdrstring " character-set" attribute
```

See also: attribute, Chapter 7, "Display Devices" and Chapter 10, "Serial Devices".

"clock-frequency"

This property may be queried (using `get-inherited-attribute`) by a plug-in device, to determine the clock frequency for this bus (if appropriate). The value is returned in Hertz (cycles per second).

Any bus nexus node implementing a bus with a basic clock frequency (such as SBus) must either publish this property, or ensure that the correct value will be returned if a child queries for this value using `get-inherited-attribute`. For example:

```
d# 2.000.000 xdrint

" clock-frequency" attribute
```

See also: Chapter 8, "Hierarchical Devices".

"device_type"

This optional property declares the type of this plug-in device. The type need not be declared, unless this device is intended to be usable for booting. If this property is declared, using one of the following key values listed next, then the FCode program *must* follow the required conventions for that particular type of device, by implementing a specified set of properties and procedures (methods). Used as:

```
" display" xdrstring   " device_type"   attribute
```

Defined key values for this property are:

Table 5-1   Standard Device Types

Device Type	Device Characteristics
display	Framebuffer or other similar display device, usable for message display during booting. See Chapter 7, "Display Devices" for the requirements of this type of device.
network	Packet-oriented network device, such as Ethernet, usable as a boot file source. See Chapter 9, "Network Devices" for the requirements of this type of device.
block	Random-access, block-oriented device, such as a disk drive, usable as a boot file source. See Chapter 6, "Block and Byte Devices" for the requirements of this type of device.

Table 5-1   Standard Device Types

Device Type	Device Characteristics
byte	Random-access, byte-oriented device, such as a tape drive, usable as a boot file source. See Chapter 6, "Block and Byte Devices" for the requirements of this type of device.
serial	Byte-oriented device, such as a serial port, usable for console input and/or console output. See Chapter 10, "Serial Devices" for the requirements of this type of device.
sbus	SBus controller node, which lets you attach plug-in SBus devices. Some SBus controller nodes set their "device_type" to "hierarchical" and set their "name" to "*sbus*". See Chapter 8, "Hierarchical Devices" for the requirements of this type of device.

See also: device-type, attribute

"down-burst-sizes"

This optional property, when declared in an SBus slave acting as a bus bridge (such as an "sbus" device), denotes transfer sizes allowed to the subordinate bus. The value is encoded similarly to "burst-sizes".

See also Chapter 8, "Hierarchical Devices".

"interrupts"

This optional property declares the interrupt level(s) for this plug-in device. The contents are one or more integers. Note that the bus-level interrupt (not the CPU-level interrupt) is specified.

For SBus devices, SBus interrupt levels 1-7 are allowed. The correct choice for your interrupt level will depend on your latency requirements. Typical usage is: video - SBus level 5, Ethernet - SBus level 4, SCSI and DMA - SBus level 3. SBus levels 6 and 7 should only be used with great care, otherwise significant system performance degradation may occur.

Because of previous usage of the "intr" property instead of the "interrupts" property in earlier systems, we recommend that both "intr" and "interrupts" be declared in FCode for SBus cards. However, cards which only declare "intr" should continue to work, as current systems automatically generate the "interrupts" property for you as required.

To declare a single interrupt (level 5), used as:

```
5 xdrint   " interrupts"   attribute

5  0 intr
```

To declare two interrupts (levels 3 and 5), used as:

```
5 xdrint   3 xdrint   xdr+   " interrupts"   attribute

3 sbus-intr>cpu   xdrint              \ Interrupt#1

0                 xdrint   xdr+       \ Null vector#1

5 sbus-intr>cpu   xdrint   xdr+       \ Interrupt#2

0                 xdrint   xdr+       \ Null vector#2

" intr"   attribute
```

See also: "intr", intr, attribute

"intr"

This property was used in early systems, but has now been superceded by the "interrupts" property.

Creation of this property automatically creates an "interrupts" property in most systems, except in the case where an "interrupts" property has already been created by the FCode for this device.

See also: "interrupts", intr, attribute

"local-mac-address"

This optional property, when declared in "network" devices, indicates the built-in Media Access Control address for this device (if any). The system may or may not use this address in order to access this device.

Used as:

```
"  "(08,04,fe,23,46,9e)"   xdrbytes   " local-mac-address"  attribute
```

See also: `mac-address`, "`mac-address`", `attribute`, and Chapter 9, "Network Devices".

"mac-address"

This property must be declared in "`network`" devices, to indicate the Media Access Control (MAC) address that this device is currently using. This value may or may not be the same as the "`local-mac-address`" property, if any.

Here's how it all fits together.

1. If a plug-in device has an assigned MAC address from the factory, this address is published as the value for "`local-mac-address`".

2. The system (based on various factors such as presence or absence of "`local-mac-address`" and/or the value of the NVRAM parameter "`local-mac-address?`") decides which address it prefers the plug-in device to use. The value returned by the `mac-address` FCode is set to this address.

3. The plug-in device then reports the address which it is actually using, by publishing the "`mac-address`" property.

Following are code examples for three typical situations.

For a well-behaved plug-in "`network`" device (which has a factory-unique MAC address but can use another system-supplied MAC address if desired by the system), the FCode would appear as:

```
"  "(08,04,fe,23,46,9e)"   xdrbytes   " local-mac-address"  attribute

mac-address                 xdrbytes   " mac-address"         attribute

(plus code to "assign" the correct mac-address value into registers)
```

For a plug-in "network" device that has a factory-unique MAC address and is unable to alter its behavior to a different address, the FCode would appear as:

```
" "(08,04,fe,23,46,9e)"  xdrbytes  " local-mac-address"  attribute

" "(08,04,fe,23,46,9e)"  xdrbytes  " mac-address"        attribute
```

For a plug-in "network" device which does not have any built-in MAC address, the FCode would appear as:

```
mac-address              xdrbytes  " mac-address"        attribute

(plus code to "assign" the correct mac-address value into
registers)
```

See also: mac-address, "local-mac-address", attribute and Chapter 9, "Network Devices".

"max-frame-size"

This optional property, when declared in "network" devices, indicates the maximum allowable size of a packet (in bytes). Used as:

```
4000 xdrint  " max-frame-size"  attribute
```

See also: attribute and Chapter 9, "Network Devices".

"model"

This optional property identifies the model name/number for a plug-in card, for manufacturing and field-service purposes.

The "model" property is useful to identify the specific piece of hardware (the plug-in card), as opposed to the "name" property (since several different but functionally-equivalent cards would have the same "name" property, thus calling the same device driver). Although the "model" property is good to have in general, it generally does not have any other specific purpose.

Used as:

> " SUNW,501-1415" xdrstring " model" attribute

See also: model, attribute

"name"

This property is used to match a particular SunOS device driver with the appropriate plug-in device. All device nodes *must* publish this property.

The contents are an arbitrary string. Any combination of printable characters is allowed, except for "@", ":" or "/". Embedded spaces are not allowed. The convention is to use a string of the form SUNW,xxxxxx.

(In place of SUNW, use your company's over-the-counter stock symbol. If you're not a publicly-traded company, pick a name that isn't being used.) This technique greatly reduces the chance that the value for your name property will accidentally collide with a name chosen by someone else.

Used as:

> " SUNW,bison-printer" xdrstring " name" attribute

The name command may also be used to create this property.

See also: name, attribute, device-name.

"one-pending-retry"

This optional property, if present in the SBus controller node, indicates a system restriction on the use of SBus retry cycles. A null value is used.

If this property is present, the SBus controller restricts retries from a particular slot to use the same address until the retry cycle is completed, as opposed to being able to interleave retries with different addresses.

Any SBus master capable of interleaving pending retries with accesses to other addresses, must check for the absence of this property in the parent before enabling that feature.
Used as:

> 0 0 " one-pending-retry" attribute

See also: Chapter 8, "Hierarchical Devices".

"params"

This optional property contains the information to be passed when the `my-params` FCode is executed. This feature is obsolescent and should not be used.

See also: `my-params`, `attribute`.

"parity-generated"

This optional property, if present, indicates that this SBus device is currently generating correct parity on the SBus. This means that whenever this device presents data (or a virtual address) on the SBus data lines, the Parity signal is also driven to correct (odd) parity. The value of the property is null.

This does not deal with the methods for enabling or disabling parity *checking*. Presence of this property merely provides the necessary information to determine that parity is being generated, so that any decision as to whether or not to check parity can be made with adequate information.

If the device has the capability to turn parity-generation on and off, this property should be created and deleted accordingly. Used as:

```
0 0 " parity-generated" attribute
```

See also: `attribute`.

"ranges"

The `ranges` property is a list of child-to-parent physical address correspondences required for most hierarchical devices.

`ranges` is a property for bus devices, particularly those buses whose children can be accessed with CPU load and store operations (as opposed to buses like SCSI, whose children are accessed with a command protocol).

The `ranges` property value describes the correspondence between the part of the physical address space of the bus node's parent available for use by the bus node (the parent address space), and the physical address space defined by the bus node for its children (the child address space).

The `ranges` property value is a sequence of

```
child-phys parent-phys size
```

specifications.

- *child-phys* is a starting address in the child physical address space defined by the bus node
- *parent-phys* is a starting address in the physical address space of the parent of the bus node
- *size* is the length in bytes of the address range.

The specification means that there is a one-to-one correspondence between the child addresses and the parent addresses within that range. The parent addresses given are always relative to the parent's address space.

Each starting address is represented using the physical address representation as two 32-bit numbers (one for `space` and one for `offset`). *size* is encoded as an unsigned integer.

The total size of each such specification is five 32-bit numbers (two for each of the two addresses, plus one for the size). Successive specifications are encoded sequentially. A space with length 2**(number of bits in a machine word) is represented with a size of 0.

The specifications should be sorted in ascending order of the child address. The address ranges thus described need not be contiguous in either the child space or the parent space. Also, the entire child space must be described in terms of parent addresses, but not all of the parent address space available to the bus device need be used for child addresses (the bus device might reserve some addresses for its own purposes, for instance).

For example, suppose that a 4-slot 25-bit SBus is attached to a machine whose physical address space consists of a 32-bit "memory" space (space=0) and a 32-bit "io" space (space=1). The SBus slots appear in "io" space at address 0xf800.0000, 0xfa00.0000, 0xfc00.0000, and 0xfe00.0000. In terms of the SBus's parent address space, the SBus device has available for its purposes the offsets from 0xf800.0000 through 0xffff.ffff in space 1 of its parent.

The SBus device defines for its children the spaces 0, 1, 2, and 3, all starting at offset 0 and running for 0x200.0000 bytes. In this case the SBus device uses all the address space given to it by its parent for the SBus children, and reserves none of the addresses for itself. The ranges property for the SBus device would contain the encoded form of the following sequence of numbers:

Table 5-2 Child-Parent Address Relationships

Child Address		Parent Address		Size
Space, Offset		Space,	Offset	
0,	0	1,	f800.0000	200.0000
1,	0	1,	fa0.00000	200.0000
2,	0	1,	fc00.0000	200.0000
3,	0	1,	fe00.0000	200.0000

Here the high components of the child address represent the SBus slot numbers, and the high component of the parent address represents "io space."

If ranges exists but its value is of 0 length, the bus's child address space is identical to its parent address space.

If the ranges property for a particular bus device node is nonexistent, code using that device should use an appropriate default interpretation. Some examples include the following:

- SBus node: Missing ranges means that the version of OpenBoot was created before the ranges property came into existence. Code should supply the correct ranges based on the machine type, from the finite set of machines that existed before ranges came into existence.
- Machine node: The machine node has no parent. Therefore the correspondence between its child and parent address spaces is meaningless, and there is no need for ranges.
- SCSI host adapter node: The child address space is not directly addressable, thus ranges would be meaningless.

The distinction between reg and ranges is as follows:

- reg is supposed to represent the actual device registers in the parent address space. For a bus adapter, this would be such as configuration/mode/initialization registers.
- ranges represents the correspondence between a bus adapter's child and parent address spaces.

Most packages do not need to be concerned with `ranges`. These properties are mainly to communicate with stand-alone programs. One exception could be a bus extender or adaptor.

See also: Chapter 8, "Hierarchical Devices".

"reg"

This property declares the location and size of onboard registers for its device. The FCode program for every plug-in SBus device *must* declare this property.

The contents are one or more (`phys`, `size`) pairs. Each pair specifies an addressable region of the device. An FCode PROM at location 0 of the device is generally *not* declared, except in the case where there are no other regions to declare.

For example, to declare two register fields at 10.0000-10.00ff and 20.0000-20.037f, use the following:

```
my-address 10.0000 +   my-space   xdrphys              \ Offset#1

100 xdrint                                   xdr+      \ Merge size#1

my-address 20.0000 +   my-space   xdrphys   xdr+       \ Merge offset#2

380 xdrint                                   xdr+      \ Merge size#2

" reg" attribute
```

In some cases, the `reg` command may also be used to create this property.

See also: `reg`, `attribute`.

"scsi-initiator-id"

This optional property is located in one of the parent nodes of the system. It may be queried (using `get-inherited-attribute`) by a plug-in device.   Its value is an integer, 0-15, indicating the address of the main SCSI host adapter of this system (if any). The value also indicates the suggested address for the host adapter for any plug-in SCSI controller.

The SCSI controller node for a plug-in SCSI controller may also publish this property, to indicate the current address of this host adapter. Used as:

```
7 xdrint  " scsi-initiator-id"  attribute
```

See also: `attribute`.

"slave-burst-sizes"

This optional property uses a bitmask to indicate the set of SBus transfer sizes which this device will accept. It contains a set of integer values. The number of entries is the same as the number of (`phys`, `size`) entries in the "`reg`" property, and each entry in "`slave-burst-sizes`" describes the transfer sizes accepted by the corresponding "`reg`" entry. The encoding of each "`slave-burst-sizes`" entry is the same as the encoding for the "`burst-sizes`" property.

This property may be defined for any device which is capable of acting as an SBus slave. The value is a "hint" to the operating system, or to other devices which may desire to access this SBus device. Used as:

```
h# 3f xdrint  h# 17 xdrint  xdr+  " slave-burst-sizes" attribute
```

See also: `burst-sizes`, `reg`, `attribute`

"slave-only"

This optional property, if present in the SBus controller node or other parent nodes, uses a bitmask to indicate that certain SBus slots support slave-only access. If bit n is 1, then slot#$2^{\wedge\wedge}n$ is slave-only. For example, a value of 8 indicates that slot#3 is slave-only.

A plug-in device should use `get-inherited-attribute` to query this property.

If this property is not found (for example, if the system contains a version 1 boot PROM that was released before this property was defined), then slot#3 is slave-only.

This affects SPARCstation1 and SPARCstation 1+ only (SPARCstation IPC only has two slots). Used as:

```
8 xdrint " slave-only" attribute
```

See also: `attribute` and Chapter 8, "Hierarchical Devices".

"slot-address-bits"

This required property in the SBus controller node specifies the number of address lines available to each SBus card. Typical values are either 25 or 28. It is acceptable for an SBus controller to omit this property, as long as some parent node is assured of having the correct value. A plug-in device should use `get-inherited-attribute` to query this property.

If this property is not found (for example, if the system contains a version 1 boot PROM that was released before this property was defined), then a value of 25 should be assumed. Used as:

```
d# 25 xdrint " slot-address-bits" attribute
```

See also: `attribute`.

"status"

This optional property indicates that this device has failed an internal selftest and is thus unavailable for use.

Absence of this property means that this device is believed to be operational.

If this property is present, the value is a string indicating the status of the device, as follows:

Table 5-3 `status` *property values*

Status Value	Meaning
"okay"	The device is believed to be operational.
"disabled"	The device represented by this node is not operational, but it might become operational in the future (e.g. an external switch is turned off, or something isn't plugged in).
"fail"	The device represented by this node is not operational because a fault has been detected, and it is unlikely that the device will become operational without repair. No additional failure details are available.
"fail-xxx"	The device represented by this node is not operational because a fault has been detected, and it is unlikely that the device will become operational without repair. "xxx" is additional human-readable information about the particular fault condition that was detected.

Used as:

```
" disabled" xdrstring  " status" attribute
```

See also: attribute.

"up-burst-sizes"

This optional property, when present on an SBus controller node, indicates the set of allowed transfer sizes up though the node to its parent bus. The value is encoded similarly to that of "burst-sizes".

See also: Chapter 8, "Hierarchical Devices".

Manipulating Properties

Property Creation and Modification

By far the most common activity done with a property is to create or modify one. The FCode attribute is the general property publishing word. It will create a new property or change the value of an existing property for the current package.

There are some special property publishing FCodes, designed for use in common situations:

- reg is used to create a "reg" property that describes where the package's physical resources are located.
- intr creates "intr" and "interrupts" properties to describe what interrupts and vectors are used by the physical hardware of the package.
- model can be used to create the "model" property to differentiate among similar packages.
- name is an FCode macro for creating the "name" property.
- device-name can also be used to create the "name" property.
- Use delete-attribute to completely remove a property.

Property Values

Various kinds of information may be stored in a property value byte array by using an *external data representation* (xdr) encoding/decoding method. The encoding format is machine-independent; the representation of the property values is independent of the byte organization and word alignment characteristics of particular processor.

Note – This encoding is not related to xdr-type encodings described in architecture documents for various other computer systems.

The data type of any particular property must be implicitly known by any software that wishes to use it. In other words, property value data types are not self-identifying. Furthermore, the presence or absence of a property with a particular name can encode a true/false flag; such a property may have a zero-length property value.

Property Encoding

The second most common activity in connection with properties is to encode the value for a property in the external data representation, usually in preparation for publishing the property using attribute. There are four FCodes used to encode a basic piece of data, and one FCode for amalgamating the basic pieces for a property that has multiple values.

xdrint encodes a number. xdrstring encodes a string. xdrphys encodes a physical address (hiding all the relative addressing information). And finally, xdrbytes encodes a sequence of bytes.

xdr+ is used to amalgamate two basic pieces of data.

Property Retrieval

Somewhat less common is for a package to retrieve the value of a property. There are three property value retrieving words, get-my-attribute, get-inherited-attribute, and get-package-attribute.

- Use get-inherited-attribute if the property in question is one that exists somewhere in the chain of parent instances between the package being defined and the root node of the machine.
- Use get-my-attribute if the property desired already exists for the package being defined.
- Use get-package-attribute if the property exists in some other support package. In this last case, you must find the support package first to get its phandle.

For an example, suppose a particular SBus FCode package wants to use DVMA to transfer some data between a device and memory.

It could use get-inherited-attribute to find the value of a property named slave-only. slave-only will be a property of one of the parent nodes of the package being defined, if it exists.

The value of the property is a bitmask of the SBus slots that do *not* support DVMA. Then the package would look at `my-unit` or `my-space` to get its slot number. The two pieces of information will tell the package whether or not it can use DVMA.

Property Decoding

Once a package has searched for and found the value of a property of interest, it must decode the value to forms it can understand. Usually the value is the representation of an integer; use `xdrtoint` to generate the actual number as a binary number on the stack. Occasionally the value of interest is the representation of a string, in which case use `xdrtostring`. Both of these FCodes act as parsers — they will also return the unused portion of the value for further decoding.

Other kinds of values can be decoded by `left-parse-string` or package-specific decoders. Note that the package must know how to decode the value of a property it wishes to use.

Property-Specific FCodes

Following is a summary of attribute-specific FCodes. Those introduced with OpenBoot 2.0 are noted by **V2**. See the individual dictionary entries in Chapter 11, "FCode Dictionary" for more information.

Table 5-4   Property-specific FCodes

Name	Stack Comment	Description
Property Creation		
attribute	(xdr-adr xdr-len name-adr name-len --)	Create an property named *name-adr name-len*, with the value `xdr-adr xdr-len`.
device-type	(adr len --)	Shorthand word to create the "`device_type`" property, with the value *adr len*.
intr	(intr-level vector --)	Shorthand word to create the "`intr`" and "`interrupts`" properties.
model	(adr len --)	Shorthand word to create the "`model`" property, with the value *adr len*.
name	(adr len --)	Shorthand macro to create the "`name`" property, with the value *adr len*.
reg	(phys space size --)	Shorthand word to create the "`reg`" property.

Table 5-4   Property-specific FCodes (Continued)

Name	Stack Comment	Description
device-name	(adr len --)	Shorthand word to create the "name" property, with the value *adr len*. Similar to name, but uses only one FCode instead of creating a macro. **V2**.
delete-attribute	(name-adr name-len --)	Delete the desired property. **V2**.

xdr Encoding

Name	Stack Comment	Description
xdrint	(n -- xdr-adr xdr-len)	Converts an integer to xdr-format.
xdrphys	(phys space -- xdr-adr xdr-len)	Converts a physical unit pair to xdr-format.
xdrstring	(adr len -- xdr-adr xdr-len)	Converts a text string to xdr-format.
xdr+	(xdr-adr1 xdr-len1 xdr-adr2 xdr-len2 -- xdr-adr xdr-len1+2)	Merge two xdr-format structures. They must have been created sequentially.
xdrbytes	(adr len -- xdr-adr xdr-len)	Converts a byte array to xdr-format. Similar to xdrstring, except no trailing null is appended. **V2**.

xdr Decoding

Name	Stack Comment	Description
xdrtoint	(xdr-adr xdr-len -- xdr-adr2 xdr-len2 n)	Converts an xdr-format string to an integer. **V2**.
xdrtostring	(xdr-adr xdr-len -- xdr-adr2 xdr-len2 adr len)	Converts an xdr-format string to a normal string. **V2**.

Attribute Retrieval

Name	Stack Comment	Description
get-my-attribute	(adr len -- true | xdr-adr xdr-len false)	Returns the xdr-format contents for the property *adr len* within the current instance, or true if not found. **V2**.
get-package-attribute	(adr len phandle -- true | xdr-adr xdr-len false)	Returns the xdr-format contents for the property *adr len* within the package *phandle*, or true if not found. **V2**.
get-inherited-attribute	(adr len -- true | xdr-adr xdr-len false)	Returns the xdr-format contents for the property *adr len*, or true if not found. The current package instance is searched first. If not found, the parent is searched next, then the parent's parent, and so on. **V2**.

≡ 5

Writing FCode Programs

Block and Byte Devices 6 ≡

Block Devices

Block devices are nonvolatile mass storage devices whose information can be accessed in any order. Examples of block devices include hard disks, floppy disks, and CD-ROMs. OpenBoot firmware typically uses block devices for booting.

This device type generally applies to disk devices, but as far as OpenBoot is concerned, it simply means that the device "looks like a disk" at the OpenBoot software interface level.

The block device FCode must declare the `block` device-type, and must implement the methods `open` and `close`, as well as the methods described below in "Required Methods" on page 6-76".

Although packages of the `block` device type present a byte-oriented interface to the rest of the system, the associated hardware devices are usually block-oriented i.e. the device reads and writes data in "blocks" (groups of, for example, 512 or 2048 bytes). The standard `/deblocker` support package assists in the presentation of a byte-oriented interface "on top of" an underlying block-oriented interface, implementing a layer of buffering that "hides" the underlying "block" length.

Block devices are often subdivided into several logical "partitions", as defined by a disk label - a special block, usually the first one, containing information about the device. The driver is responsible for appropriately interpreting a disk label. The driver may use the standard disk label support package if it does not implement a specialized label. The `/disk-label` support package interprets a system-dependent label format. Since the disk booting protocol usually depends upon the label format; the standard disk label support package also implements a `load` method for the corresponding boot protocol.

Byte Devices

Byte devices are sequential-access mass storage devices, for example tape devices. OpenBoot firmware typically uses byte devices for booting.

The byte device FCode program must declare the `byte` device type, and must implement the `open` and `close` methods in addition to those described in "Required Methods".

Although packages of the `byte` device type present a byte-oriented interface to the rest of the system, the associated hardware devices are usually record-oriented; the device reads and writes data in records containing more than one byte. The records may be fixed length or variable length. The standard `/deblocker` support package assists in presenting a byte-oriented interface on top of an underlying record-oriented interface, implementing a layer of buffering that hides the underlying record structure.

Required Methods

block-size

```
( -- bytes )
```

All data transfers to or from the device are in records of n bytes each. The most common value for n is 512.

This method is only required if the `/deblocker` support package is used.

load

```
( adr -- len )
```

`load` works a bit differently for block and byte devices:

With block devices, it loads a stand-alone program from the device into memory at `adr`. `len` is the size in bytes of the program loaded. If the device can contain several such programs, the instance arguments returned by `my-args` can be used to select the specific program desired. `open` is executed before `load` is invoked.

With byte devices, `load` reads a stand-alone program from the tape file specified by the value of the argument string given by `my-args`. That value is the string representation of a decimal integer. If the argument string is null, tape file 0 is used. `load` places the program in memory at `adr`, returning the size `len` of the read-in program in bytes.

max-transfer

```
( -- bytes )
```

The size in bytes of the largest single transfer that the device can perform. `max-transfer` is expected to be a multiple of `block-size`.

This method is only required if the `/deblocker` support package is used.

read

```
( adr len -- actual )
```

Read at most `len` bytes from the device into memory at `adr`. `actual` is the number of bytes actually read. If the number of bytes read is 0 or negative, the read failed. Note that `len` need not be a multiple of the device's normal block size.

read-blocks
```
( adr block# #blocks -- #read )
```

Read #blocks records of length block-size bytes each from the device, starting at device block block#, into memory at address adr. #read is the number of blocks actually read.

This method is only required if the /deblocker support package is used.

seek
```
( poslow poshigh -- error? )          for block
( offset file# -- error? )            for byte
```

seek works a bit differently depending on whether it's being used with a block or byte device.

For block devices, seek sets the device position for the next read or write. The position is the byte offset from the beginning of the device specified by the 64-bit number which is the concatenation of poshigh and poslow. error? is -1 if the seek fails, and 0 if it succeeds.

For byte devices, it seeks to the byte offset within file file#. If offset and file# are both 0, rewind the tape. error? is -1 if seek fails, and 0 if seek succeeds.

write
```
( adr len -- actual )
```

Write len bytes from memory at adr to the device. actual is the number of bytes actually written. If actual is less than len, the write did not succeed. If actual is -1, some other error occurred. len need not be a multiple of the device's normal block size.

write-blocks
```
( adr block# #blocks -- #written )
```

Write #blocks records of length block-size bytes each to the device, starting at block block#, from memory at adr. #written is the number of blocks actually written.

This method is only required if the /deblocker support package is used.

Required Properties

Table 6-1   *Required Properties of Block and Byte Devices*

Property Name	Sample Value
name	"SUNW,googly"
reg	my-address h# 12.0000 + my-space h# 20
device_type	" block" or " byte"

Device Driver Examples

The structure of the device tree for the sample card supported by the sample device drivers in this chapter is as follows:

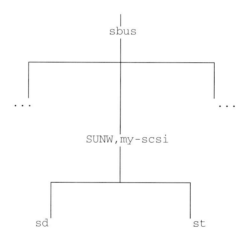

Figure 6-1   Sample Device Tree

Simple Block Device Driver

Code Example 6-1   Simple Block Device Driver

```
\ This is at a stage where each leaf node can be used only as a
\ non-bootable device.
\ It only creates nodes and publishes necessary properties
\ to identify the device.
fcode-version1
hex
   " SUNW,my-scsi"   xdrstring " name" attribute

   3 xdrint " interrupts" attribute
   3 0 intr

   h# 20.0000    constant scsi-offset
   h# 40         constant /scsi
   my-address scsi-offset + my-space /scsi   reg
   d# 25.000.000 xdrint  " clock-frequency" attribute

   new-device  \ missing "reg" indicates a SCSI "wild-card" node
      " sd"      xdrstring " name" attribute
   finish-device

   new-device  \ missing "reg" indicates a SCSI "wild-card" node
      " st"      xdrstring " name" attribute
   finish-device
end0
```

Extended Block Device Driver

Code Example 6-2   Sample Driver for "my-scsi" device

```
\ sample driver for "my-scsi" device.
\ It is still a non-bootable device.
\ The purpose is to show how an intermediate stage of driver can
\ be used to debug board during development.
\ In addtion to publishing the properties, this sample driver
\ shows methods to access, test and control "SUNW,my-scsi" device.
\ Following main methods are provided for "SUNW,my-scsi" device.
\   open   ( -- success? )
\   close  ( -- )
\   reset  ( -- )
\   selftest  ( -- fail? )
fcode-version2
   hex
```

Code Example 6-2   Sample Driver for "my-scsi" device

```
\ sample driver for "my-scsi" device.
  headers

  h# 20.0000     constant scsi-offset
  h# 40          constant /scsi
  d# 25.000.000 constant clock-frequency
  my-address constant my-sbus-address
  my-space    constant my-sbus-space

  : identify-me ( -- )
     " SUNW,my-scsi"   xdrstring " name" attribute
     " scsi"                     device-type
     \ sbus interrupt level generated by card
     3 xdrint " interrupts" attribute
     3 0 intr

     my-sbus-address scsi-offset + my-sbus-space /scsi   reg
     clock-frequency  xdrint  " clock-frequency" attribute
  ;
  identify-me




  \ Tokenizer 2.1 or later has the word 'instance'
  : instance ( -- ) version h# 20001 >=  if  instance   then  ;

  h# 10.0000 constant dma-offset
  h# 10       constant /dma
  -1 instance value dma-chip

  \ methods to access/control dma registers
  : dmaaddress  ( -- addr )  dma-chip 4 +  ;
  : dmacount  ( -- addr )  dma-chip 8 +  ;
  : dmaaddr@  ( -- n )  dmaaddress rl@  ;
  : dmaaddr!  ( n -- )  dmaaddress rl!  ;
  : dmacount@  ( -- n )  dmacount rl@  ;
  : dmacount!  ( n -- )  dmacount rl!  ;
  : dma-chip@  ( -- n )  dma-chip rl@  ;
  : dma-chip!  ( n -- )  dma-chip rl!  ;
  : dma-btest  ( mask -- flag )  dma-chip@  and  ;
  : dma-bset  ( mask -- )  dma-chip@  or  dma-chip!  ;
  : dma-breset  ( mask -- )  not dma-btest  dma-chip!  ;

  external
```

Code Example 6-2   Sample Driver for "my-scsi" device

```
\ sample driver for "my-scsi" device.

  \ methods to allocate, map, unmap, free dma buffers
  : decode-unit  ( adr len -- low high )  decode-2int  ;
  : dma-alloc  ( n -- vaddr )  " dma-alloc" $call-parent  ;
  : dma-free  ( vaddr n -- )    " dma-free" $call-parent  ;
 : dma-map-in ( vaddr n cache? -- devaddr )  " dma-map-in" $call-parent  ;
 : dma-map-out  ( vaddr devaddr n -- )       " dma-map-out" $call-parent  ;
  \ Dma-sync could be dummy routine if parent device doesn't support.
  : dma-sync  ( virt-addr dev-addr size -- )
     " dma-sync" my-parent ['] $call-method catch  if
        2drop 2drop 2drop
     then
  ;
  : map-in ( adr space size -- virt ) " map-in" $call-parent  ;
  : map-out ( virt size -- ) " map-out" $call-parent  ;

  headers
  : dma-open ( -- )
     my-sbus-address dma-offset +  my-sbus-space  /dma
     map-in  is dma-chip
  ;
  : dma-close ( -- )
     dma-chip /dma map-out
     -1 is dma-chip
  ;


  -1 instance value scsi-init-id
  -1 instance value scsi-chip
  h# 20 constant /mbuf
  -1 instance value mbuf
  -1 instance value mbuf-dma
  d# 6 constant /sense
  -1 instance value sense-command
  -1 instance value sense-cmd-dma
  d# 8 constant #sense-bytes
  -1 instance value sense-buf
  -1 instance value sense-buf-dma
  -1 instance value mbuf0
  d# 12 constant /cmdbuf
  -1 instance value cmdbuf
  -1 instance value cmdbuf-dma
  -1 instance value scsi-statbuf
```

Code Example 6-2   Sample Driver for "my-scsi" device

```
\ sample driver for "my-scsi" device.

   \ mapping and allocation routines for scsi
   : map-scsi-chip  ( -- )
     my-sbus-address scsi-offset +  my-sbus-space /scsi map-in
     is scsi-chip
   ;
   : unmap-scsi-chip
     scsi-chip /scsi map-out
     -1 is scsi-chip
   ;

   \ After any changes to sense-command by cpu or any changes
   \ to sense-cmd-dma by device, synchronize changes by issuing
   \ " sense-command sense-cmd-dma /sense dma-sync "
   \ Similarly after any changes to sense-buf, sense-buf-dma,
   \ mbuf, mbuf-dma, cmdbuf or cmdbuf-dma,  synchronize changes
   \ by appropriately issuing dma-sync

   \ map scsi chip and allocate buffers for "sense" command and status
   : map-scsi  ( -- )
     map-scsi-chip
     /sense dma-alloc is sense-command
     sense-command /sense false
     dma-map-in is sense-cmd-dma
     #sense-bytes dma-alloc is sense-buf
     sense-buf #sense-bytes false
     dma-map-in is sense-buf-dma
     2 alloc-mem is scsi-statbuf
   ;

   \ free buffers for "sense" command and status and unmap scsi chip
   : unmap-scsi  ( -- )
     scsi-statbuf 2 free-mem
     sense-buf sense-buf-dma #sense-bytes dma-sync  \ redundant
     sense-buf sense-buf-dma #sense-bytes dma-map-out
     sense-buf #sense-bytes dma-free
     sense-command sense-cmd-dma /sense dma-sync     \ redundant
     sense-command sense-cmd-dma /sense dma-map-out
     sense-command /sense dma-free
     -1 is sense-command
     -1 is sense-cmd-dma
     -1 is sense-buf
     -1 is scsi-statbuf
     -1 is sense-buf-dma
```

Code Example 6-2   Sample Driver for "my-scsi" device

```
\ sample driver for "my-scsi" device.
    unmap-scsi-chip
  ;

  \ constants related to scsi commands
  h#  0 constant nop
  h#  1 constant flush-fifo
  h#  2 constant reset-chip
  h#  3 constant reset-scsi
  h# 80 constant dma-nop

  \ words to get scsi register addresses.
  \ Each chip register is one byte, aligned on a 4-byte boundary.
  : scsi+  ( offset -- addr )  scsi-chip + ;
  : transfer-count-lo     ( -- addr )  h#  0 scsi+  ;
  : transfer-count-hi     ( -- addr )  h#  4 scsi+  ;
  : fifo                  ( -- addr )  h#  8 scsi+  ;
  : command               ( -- addr )  h#  c scsi+  ;
  : configuration         ( -- addr )  h# 20 scsi+  ;
  : scsi-test-reg         ( -- addr )  h# 28 scsi+  ;

  \ Read only registers:
  : scsi-status           ( -- addr )  h# 10 scsi+  ;
  : interrupt-status      ( -- addr )  h# 14 scsi+  ;
  : sequence-step         ( -- addr )  h# 18 scsi+  ;
  : fifo-flags            ( -- addr )  h# 1c scsi+  ;

  \ Write only registers:
  : select/reconnect-bus-id  ( -- addr )  h# 10 scsi+  ;
  : select/reconnect-timeout ( -- addr )  h# 14 scsi+  ;
  : sync-period              ( -- addr )  h# 18 scsi+  ;
  : sync-offset              ( -- addr )  h# 1c scsi+  ;
  : clock-conversion-factor  ( -- addr )  h# 24 scsi+  ;

  \ words to read from/store to scsi registers.
  : cnt@      ( -- w )
    transfer-count-lo rb@
    transfer-count-hi rb@
    bwjoin
  ;
  : fifo@     ( -- c )  fifo rb@  ;
  : cmd@      ( -- c )  command rb@  ;
  : stat@     ( -- c )  scsi-status rb@  ;
  : istat@    ( -- c )  interrupt-status rb@  ;
  : fifo-cnt  ( -- c )  fifo-flags rb@  h# 1f and ;
```

Code Example 6-2   Sample Driver for "my-scsi" device

```
\ sample driver for "my-scsi" device.
  : data@    ( -- c )  begin  fifo-cnt  until  fifo@  ;
  : seq@     ( -- c )  sequence-step rb@  h# 7 and ;

  : fifo! ( c -- )  fifo rb!  ;
  : cmd!     ( c -- )  command rb!  ;
  : cnt!     ( w -- )
    wbsplit
    transfer-count-hi rb! transfer-count-lo rb!
  ;
  : targ!    ( c -- )  select/reconnect-bus-id rb!  ;
  : data!    ( c -- )  begin  fifo-cnt d# 16 <>  until  fifo!  ;


  \ scsi chip noop  and initialization
  : scsi-nop   ( -- )  nop cmd!  ;
  : init-scsi  ( -- )  reset-chip cmd!  scsi-nop  ;

  : wait-istat-clear  ( -- error? )
    d# 1000
    begin
      1 ms 1-  ( count )
      dup 0=   ( count expired? )
      istat@   ( count expired? istat )
      0= or    ( count clear? )
    until      ( count )
    0=  if
      istat@ 0<>  if
        cr ." Can't clear ESP interrupts: "
        ." Check SCSI Term. Power Fuse." cr
        true  exit
      then
    then
    false
  ;

  : clk-conv-factor ( -- n )
    clock-frequency d# 5.000.000 / 7 and
  ;

  \ initialize scsi chip, tune time amount,
  \ set async operation mode, and set scsi bus id
  : reset-my-scsi ( -- error? )
    init-scsi
    h# 93 select/reconnect-timeout rb!
```

Code Example 6-2   Sample Driver for "my-scsi" device

```
\ sample driver for "my-scsi" device.
    0 sync-offset rb!
    clk-conv-factor clock-conversion-factor rb!
    h# 4 scsi-init-id 7 and or  configuration rb!
    wait-istat-clear
;

: reset-bus ( -- error? )
   reset-scsi cmd!  wait-istat-clear
;

: init-n-test  ( -- ok? ) reset-my-scsi 0=  ;

: get-buffers ( -- )
   h# 8000 dma-alloc is mbuf0
   /cmdbuf dma-alloc is cmdbuf
   cmdbuf /cmdbuf false dma-map-in
   is cmdbuf-dma
;

: give-buffers ( -- )
   mbuf0 h# 8000 dma-free  -1 is mbuf0
   cmdbuf cmdbuf-dma /cmdbuf dma-sync          \ redundant
   cmdbuf cmdbuf-dma /cmdbuf dma-map-out
   cmdbuf /cmdbuf dma-free
   -1 is cmdbuf -1 is cmdbuf-dma
;

: scsi-selftest ( -- fail? )  reset-my-scsi  ;

\ dma-alloc and dma-map-in mbuf-dma
: mbuf-alloc ( -- )
   /mbuf dma-alloc is mbuf
   mbuf /mbuf false dma-map-in is mbuf-dma
;

\ dma-map-out and dma-free mbuf-dma
: mbuf-free ( -- )
   mbuf mbuf-dma /mbuf dma-sync                \ redundant
   mbuf mbuf-dma /mbuf dma-map-out
   mbuf /mbuf dma-free
   -1 is mbuf
   -1 is mbuf-dma
;
```

Code Example 6-2   Sample Driver for "my-scsi" device

```
\ sample driver for "my-scsi" device.
  external
  \ If any routine was actually using buffers allocated by dma-alloc,
  \ and dma mapped by dma-map-in, it would have dma-sync those buffers
  \ after any changes to them.
  : open  ( -- success? )
     dma-open
     " scsi-initiator-id" get-inherited-attribute 0=  if
        xdrtoint  is scsi-init-id
        2drop
        map-scsi
        init-n-test                 ( ok? )
        dup if                      ( true )
           get-buffers              ( true )
        else
           unmap-scsi dma-close     ( false )
        then                        ( success? )
     else
        ." Missing initiator id" cr  false
        dma-close
     then                              ( success? )
  ;

  : close  ( -- )
     give-buffers unmap-scsi dma-close
  ;

  : reset  ( -- )
     dma-open map-scsi
     h# 80 dma-breset
     reset-my-scsi drop reset-bus drop
     unmap-scsi dma-close
  ;

  \ if scsi-selftest was actually using buffers allocated by mbuf-alloc,
  \ it would have to do dma-sync after any changes to mbuf or mbuf-dma.
  : selftest  ( -- fail? )
     map-scsi
     mbuf-alloc
     scsi-selftest
     mbuf-free
     unmap-scsi
  ;

  new-device  \ missing "reg" indicates a SCSI "wild-card" node
```

Code Example 6-2   Sample Driver for "my-scsi" device

```
\ sample driver for "my-scsi" device.
    " sd"      xdrstring " name" attribute
  finish-device

  new-device  \ missing "reg" indicates a SCSI "wild-card" node
    " st"      xdrstring " name" attribute
  finish-device
end0
```

Complete Block and Byte Device Driver

Code Example 6-3   Sample driver for bootable devices

```
\ sample fcode driver for bootable devices.
\ It supports "block" and "byte" type bootable devices,
\ by using standard "deblocker" and "disk-label" packages.

fcode-version2
   hex
   headers

   : copyright  ( -- )
      ." Copyright 1990 Sun Microsystems, Inc.  All Rights Reserved" cr
   ;
   h# 20.0000    constant scsi-offset
   h# 40         constant /scsi
   d# 25.000.000 constant clock-frequency
   my-address constant my-sbus-address
   my-space    constant my-sbus-space

   : identify-me ( -- )
      " SUNW,my-scsi"   xdrstring " name" attribute
      " scsi"                     device-type
      3 xdrint " interrupts" attribute
      3 0 intr
      my-sbus-address scsi-offset + my-sbus-space /scsi   reg
      clock-frequency  xdrint  " clock-frequency" attribute
   ;
   identify-me

   \ Tokenizer 2.1 or later has the word 'instance'
   : instance ( -- ) version h# 20001 >=  if  instance  then  ;




   h# 10.0000 constant dma-offset
   h# 10       constant /dma
   -1 instance value dma-chip

   external
   : decode-unit  ( adr len -- low high )  decode-2int  ;
   : dma-alloc  ( n -- vaddr )  " dma-alloc" $call-parent  ;
   : dma-free  ( vaddr n -- )    " dma-free" $call-parent  ;
  : dma-map-in ( vaddr n cache? -- devaddr )  " dma-map-in" $call-parent ;
  : dma-map-out  ( vaddr devaddr n -- )       " dma-map-out" $call-parent ;
```

Code Example 6-3   Sample driver for bootable devices

```
\ sample fcode driver for bootable devices.
  \ Dma-sync could be dummy routine if parent device doesn't support.
  : dma-sync  ( virt-addr dev-addr size -- )
    " dma-sync" my-parent ['] $call-method catch  if
       2drop 2drop 2drop
    then
  ;

  : map-in ( adr space size -- virt ) " map-in" $call-parent  ;
  : map-out ( virt size -- ) " map-out" $call-parent  ;

  headers
  \ variables/values for sending commands, mapping etc.
  -1 instance value scsi-init-id
  -1 instance value scsi-chip
  -1 instance value mbuf
  -1 instance value mbuf-dma
  h# 20 constant /mbuf
  ...

  \ mapping and allocation routines for scsi
  : map-scsi-chip  ( -- )
    my-address scsi-offset +  my-space /scsi map-in
    is scsi-chip
  ;

  : unmap-scsi-chip
    scsi-chip /scsi map-out
    -1 is scsi-chip
  ;

  : map-scsi  ( -- )
    map-scsi-chip
    \ allocate buffers etc. for "sense" command and status
    ...
  ;

  : unmap-scsi  ( -- )
    \ free buffers etc. for "sense" command and status
    ...
    unmap-scsi-chip
  ;

  \ words related to scsi commands and register access.
  ...
```

Code Example 6-3   Sample driver for bootable devices

```
\ sample fcode driver for bootable devices.


   : reset-my-scsi ( -- error? )   ... ;
   : reset-bus ( -- error? )   ... ;

   : init-n-test  ( -- ok? ) ...  ;
   : get-buffers ( -- )  ... ;
   : give-buffers ( -- )  ... ;
   : scsi-selftest ( -- fail? )  ... ;

   d# 512 constant ublock
   0 instance value /block
   0 instance value /tapeblock
   instance variable fixed-len?
   ...

   external
   : set-timeout  ( n -- ) ... ;
   : send-diagnostic ( -- error? )
       \ run diagnostics and return any error.
       ...
   ;

   : device-present?  ( lun target -- present? ) ...  ;
   : mode-sense  ( -- true | block-size false ) ...  ;
   : read-capacity  ( -- true | block-size false ) ...  ;

   \ Spin up a SCSI disk, coping with a possible wedged SCSI bus
   : timed-spin  ( target lun -- ) ...  ;

   : disk-r/w-blocks ( adr block# #blocks direction? -- #xfered )
     ...                 ( #xfered )
   ;

   \ Execute "mode-sense" command.  If failed, execute read-capacity
command.
   \ If this also failed, return d# 512 as the block size.
   : disk-block-size  ( -- n )
      mode-sense if  read-capacity  if d# 512  then  then
      dup is /block
   ;

   : tape-block-size ( -- n ) ... ;
   : fixed-or-variable  ( -- max-block fixed? )  ... ;
```

Code Example 6-3   Sample driver for bootable devices

```
\ sample fcode driver for bootable devices.
  : tape-r/w-some  ( adr block# #blks read? -- actual# error? ) ...  ;

  headers
  : dma-open ( -- )
    my-address dma-offset +  my-space  /dma
    map-in  is dma-chip
  ;
  : dma-close ( -- )
    dma-chip /dma map-out
    -1 is dma-chip
  ;

  \ After any changes to mbuf by cpu or any changes
  \ to mbuf-dma by device, synchronize changes by issuing
  \ " mbuf mbuf-dma /mbuf dma-sync "
  : mbuf-alloc ( -- )
    /mbuf dma-alloc is mbuf
    mbuf /mbuf false dma-map-in is mbuf-dma
  ;

  \ dma-map-out and dma-free mbuf-dma
  : mbuf-free ( -- )
    mbuf mbuf-dma /mbuf dma-sync                 \ redundant
    mbuf mbuf-dma /mbuf dma-map-out
    mbuf /mbuf dma-free
    -1 is mbuf
    -1 is mbuf-dma
  ;

  external
  \ external methods for scsi bus ( "SUNW,my-scsi" node)
  : open  ( -- success? )
    dma-open
    " scsi-initiator-id" get-inherited-attribute 0=  if
      xdrtoint  is scsi-init-id
      2drop
      map-scsi
      init-n-test                   ( ok? )
      dup if                        ( true )
        get-buffers                 ( true )
      else
        unmap-scsi dma-close        ( false )
      then                          ( success? )
    else
```

Code Example 6-3   Sample driver for bootable devices

```
\ sample fcode driver for bootable devices.
        ." Missing initiator id" cr  false
      dma-close
    then                                 ( success? )
  ;

  : close  ( -- )  give-buffers unmap-scsi dma-close  ;

  : reset  ( -- )
    dma-open map-scsi
    ...
    reset-my-scsi drop reset-bus drop
    unmap-scsi dma-close
  ;

  : selftest  ( -- fail? )
    map-scsi
    mbuf-alloc
    scsi-selftest
    mbuf-free
    unmap-scsi
  ;

  headers

\ start of child block device

  new-device  \ missing "reg" indicates SCSI "wild-card" node

    " sd"     xdrstring " name" attribute
    " block"        device-type

    0 instance value offset-low
    0 instance value offset-high
    0 instance value label-package

    \ The "disk-label" package interprets the disk label,
    \ interpreting any partition information contained in
    \ the disk label. The "load" method of "block" device
    \ uses load method provided by "disk-label"
    : init-label-package  ( -- okay? )
      0 is offset-high  0 is offset-low
      my-args  " disk-label"  $open-package is label-package
      label-package  if
        0 0  " offset" label-package $call-method
```

Code Example 6-3   Sample driver for bootable devices

```
\ sample fcode driver for bootable devices.
         is offset-high is offset-low
         true
      else
         ." Can't open disk label package"  cr  false
      then
   ;


   0 instance value deblocker
   : init-deblocker  ( -- okay? )
      " "  " deblocker" $open-package  is deblocker
      deblocker  if
         true
      else
         ." Can't open deblocker package"  cr  false
      then
   ;

   : device-present? ( lun target -- present? )
      " device-present?" $call-parent
   ;

   \ Following methods are needed for "block" device:
   \ open, close, selftest, reset, read, write, load, seek,
   \ block-size, max-transfer, read-blocks, write-blocks.
   \ Carefully notice the relationship between methods for
   \ "block" device and methods pre-defined for
   \ "disk-label" and "deblocker"

   external
   \ external methods for "block" device ( "sd" node)

   : spin-up  ( -- )  my-unit  " timed-spin" $call-parent  ;

   : open  ( -- ok? )
      my-unit device-present?  0= if  false exit  then
      spin-up      \ Start the disk if necessary

      init-deblocker  0= if  false exit  then
      init-label-package  0= if
         deblocker close-package false exit
      then
      true
   ;
```

Code Example 6-3   Sample driver for bootable devices

```
\ sample fcode driver for bootable devices.
     : close  ( -- )
        label-package close-package  0 is label-package
        deblocker close-package  0 is deblocker
     ;

     : selftest ( -- fail? )
        my-unit device-present?  if
           " send-diagnostic" $call-parent  ( fail? )
        else
           true                              ( error )
        then
     ;
     : reset  ( -- )  ...   ;


     \ The "deblocker" package assists in the implementation
     \ of byte-oriented read and write methods for disks and
     \ tapes. The deblocker provides a layer of buffering to
     \ implement a high level byte-oriented interface
     \ "on top of" a low-level block-oriented interface.

     \ The "seek", "read" and "write" methods of this block
     \ device use corresponding methods provided by "deblocker"

     \ In order to be able to use "deblocker" package this
     \ device has to define following four methods, which the
     \ deblocker uses as its low-level interface to the device:
     \ 1) block-size, 2) max-transfer, 3) read-blocks and
     \ 4) write-blocks

     : block-size ( -- n )   " disk-block-size" $call-parent  ;
     : max-transfer ( -- n ) block-size h# 40 * ;

     : read-blocks  ( adr block# #blocks -- #read )
        true " disk-r/w-blocks" $call-parent
     ;
     : write-blocks  ( adr block# #blocks -- #written )
        false " disk-r/w-blocks" $call-parent
     ;

     : dma-alloc ( #bytes -- vadr ) " dma-alloc" $call-parent  ;
     : dma-free  ( vadr #bytes -- ) " dma-free" $call-parent  ;
     : seek  ( offset.low offset.high -- okay? )
        offset-low offset-high  x+  " seek"   deblocker $call-method
```

Code Example 6-3   Sample driver for bootable devices

```
\ sample fcode driver for bootable devices.
    ;
    : read  ( adr len -- actual-len )  " read"  deblocker $call-method  ;
    : write ( adr len -- actual-len )  " write" deblocker $call-method  ;
    : load  ( adr -- size )            " load"  label-package $call-method  ;

  finish-device  \ finishing "block" device "sd"

  headers

\ start of child byte device

  new-device  \ missing "reg" indicates "wild-card" node
    " st"      xdrstring " name" attribute
    " byte"         device-type

    false instance value write-eof-mark?
    instance variable file-mark?
    true instance value scsi-tape-first-install

    : scsi-tape-rewind    ( -- [[xstatbuf] f-hw] error? ) ... ;

    : write-eof  ( -- [[xstatbuf] f-hw] error? ) ...  ;

    0 instance value deblocker
    : init-deblocker ( -- okay? )
       " "  " deblocker" $open-package  is deblocker
       deblocker  if
          true
       else
          ." Can't open deblocker package"  cr  false
       then
    ;

    : flush-deblocker  ( -- )
       deblocker close-package  init-deblocker drop
    ;
    : fixed-or-variable ( -- max-block fixed? )
      " fixed-or-variable" $call-parent
    ;

    : device-present? ( lun target -- present? )
      " device-present?" $call-parent
    ;
```

Code Example 6-3   Sample driver for bootable devices

```
\ sample fcode driver for bootable devices.
     \ Following methods are needed for "byte" device:
     \ open, close, selftest, reset, read, write, load, seek,
     \ block-size, max-transfer, read-blocks, write-blocks.
     \ Carefully notice the relationship between methods for
     \ "byte" device and methods pre-defined for
     \ standard deblocker package.

    external
    \ external methods for "byte" device ( "st" node)

    \ The "deblocker" package assists in the implementation
    \ of byte-oriented read and write methods for disks and
    \ tapes. The deblocker provides a layer of buffering to
    \ implement a high level byte-oriented interface
    \ "on top of" a low-level block-oriented interface.

    \ The "read" and "write" methods of this "byte"
    \ device use corresponding methods provided by "deblocker"

    \ In order to be able to use "deblocker" package this
    \ device has to define following four methods, which the
    \ deblocker uses as its low-level interface to the device:
    \ 1) block-size, 2) max-transfer, 3) read-blocks and
    \ 4) write-blocks
    : block-size  ( -- n )    " tape-block-size" $call-parent  ;

    : max-transfer  ( -- n )
       fixed-or-variable  ( max-block fixed? )
       if
          \ Use the largest multiple of /tapeblock that is <= h# fe00
          h# fe00  over  / *
       then
    ;

    : read-blocks  ( adr block# #blocks -- #read )
       file-mark? @  0=  if
          true " tape-r/w-some" $call-parent  file-mark? !   ( #read )
       else
          3drop 0
       then
    ;

    : write-blocks  ( adr block# #blocks -- #written )
       false " tape-r/w-some" $call-parent file-mark? !
```

Code Example 6-3   Sample driver for bootable devices

```
\ sample fcode driver for bootable devices.
    ;



    : dma-alloc ( #bytes -- vadr ) " dma-alloc" $call-parent  ;
    : dma-free  ( vadr #bytes -- ) " dma-free" $call-parent   ;
    : open  ( -- okay? )  \ open for tape
      my-unit  device-present?  0=  if  false exit  then
      scsi-tape-first-install  if
          scsi-tape-rewind  if
             ." Can't rewind tape" cr
             0= if  drop  then
             false exit
          then
          false is scsi-tape-first-install
      then
      \ Set fixed-len? and /tapeblock
      fixed-or-variable 2drop
      init-deblocker  0=  if  false exit  then
      true
    ;
    : close  ( -- )
      deblocker close-package  0 is deblocker
      write-eof-mark?  if
          write-eof  if
             ." Can't write EOF Marker."
             0=  if  drop  then
          then
      then
    ;
    : reset  ( -- )  ...  ;
    : selftest ( -- fail? )
      my-unit device-present?  if
         " send-diagnostic" $call-parent  ( fail? )
      else
         true                             ( error )
      then
    ;


    : read ( adr len -- actual-len )  " read"  deblocker $call-method  ;
    : write ( adr len -- actual-len )
       true is write-eof-mark?
       " write" deblocker $call-method
```

Code Example 6-3   Sample driver for bootable devices

```
\ sample fcode driver for bootable devices.
     ;

    : load  ( adr -- size )
       \ use my-args to get tape file-no
       ...  ( adr file# )

       \ position at requested file
       ...
       dup  begin                    ( start-adr next-adr )
          dup max-transfer read      ( start-adr next-adr #read )
         dup 0>                  ( start-adr next-adr #read got-some? )
       while                         ( start-adr next-adr #read )
          +                          ( start-adr next-adr' )
       repeat                        ( start-adr end-adr 0 )
       drop swap -                   ( size )
     ;

    : seek  ( byte# file# -- error? )
       \ position at requested file
       ...                                  ( byte# )

       flush-deblocker                      ( byte# )
       begin  dup 0>  while                 ( #remaining )
          " mbuf0" $call-parent
          over ublock min  read             ( #remaining #read )
          dup  0=  if                       ( #remaining 0 )
             2drop  true
             exit                           ( error )
          then                              ( #remaining #read )
          -                                 ( #remaining' )
       repeat                               ( 0 )
       drop false                           ( no-error )
     ;

  finish-device  \ finishing "byte" device "st"
end0
\ finishing "SUNW,my-scsi"
```

Display Devices 7

This device type applies to framebuffers and other devices that appear to be memory to the processor with associated hardware to convert the memory image to a visual display. Display devices can be used as console output devices.

Required Methods

The display device FCode must declare the `display` device-type, and must implement the methods `open` and `close`.

System `defer` words are loaded by appropriate routines. `is-install`, `is-remove` and `is-selftest` are used to create the `open`, `close` and `selftest` routines.

For display devices, created methods interact with OpenBoot commands in a way that is different from that of other device types. Other device types provide methods that are found by dictionary searches looking for specific names.

Some FCodes are specifically designed for display devices. See Table A-35 through Table A-41 in Appendix A, "FCode Reference".

Required Properties

Table 7-1   *Required Display Device Properties*

Property Name	Typical Value
name	SUNW,cgsix *{any name chosen by the manufacturer}*
device_type	display *{required for display devices}*
reg	list of registers *{depends on the device}*

Device Driver Examples

Simple Display Device Driver

This is a sample FCode program for a display device that does not need to be usable as a console display device during system power-up.

Code Example 7-1   Basic display device driver example

```
\ Basic display device driver



\ cg6 (Lego) frame buffer driver
\ This version doesn't use the graphics accelerator because of
\ conflicts with the window system's use of same.

hex
fcode-version1
   " SUNW,cgsix" name
   " SUNW,501-xxxx" model

   h# 20.0000 constant dac-offset   h#      10 constant /dac
   h# 30.0000 constant fhc-offset   h#      10 constant /fhc
   h# 30.1800 constant thc-offset   h#      20 constant /thc
   h# 70.0000 constant fbc-offset   h#      10 constant /fbc
   h# 70.1000 constant tec-offset   h#      10 constant /tec
   h# 80.0000 constant fb-offset    h# 10.0000 constant /frame

   : >reg-spec ( offset size -- xdrreg )
     >r my-address + my-space xdrphys r> xdrint xdr+
   ;
   dac-offset /dac >reg-spec
   fhc-offset /fhc >reg-spec     xdr+
   thc-offset /thc >reg-spec     xdr+
   fbc-offset /fbc >reg-spec     xdr+
   tec-offset /tec >reg-spec     xdr+
   fb-offset  /frame >reg-spec   xdr+
   " reg" attribute

   5  0   intr

   5  xdrint " interrupts" attribute

end0
```

Extended Display Device Driver

This sample FCode program has added code to initialize and test the device, but still is
not usable as a console display device during system power-up.

Code Example 7-2   Extended display device driver example

```
                     \ Extended Display device driver


\ cg6 (Lego) frame buffer driver
\ This version doesn't use the graphics accelerator because of
\ conflicts with the window system's use of same.

hex
fcode-version1
   " SUNW,cgsix" name
   " SUNW,501-xxxx" model

   h# 20.0000 constant dac-offset   h#       10 constant /dac
   h# 30.0000 constant fhc-offset   h#       10 constant /fhc
   h# 30.1800 constant thc-offset   h#       20 constant /thc
   h# 70.0000 constant fbc-offset   h#       10 constant /fbc
   h# 70.1000 constant tec-offset   h#       10 constant /tec
   h# 80.0000 constant fb-offset    h# 10.0000 constant /frame

   : >reg-spec ( offset size -- xdrreg )
      >r my-address + my-space xdrphys r> xdrint xdr+
   ;
   dac-offset /dac >reg-spec
   fhc-offset /fhc >reg-spec      xdr+
   thc-offset /thc >reg-spec      xdr+
   fbc-offset /fbc >reg-spec      xdr+
   tec-offset /tec >reg-spec      xdr+
   fb-offset  /frame >reg-spec    xdr+
   " reg" attribute

   5   xdrint " interrupts" attribute

   5   0   intr

   -1 value dac-adr
   -1 value fhc-adr
```

Code Example 7-2   Extended display device driver example

```
                    \ Extended Display device driver
   -1 value thc-adr
   -1 value fbc-adr
   -1 value tec-adr
   -1 value fb-adr


   : copyright  ( -- adr len )   " Copyright (c) 1989 by Sun Microsystems,
Inc. "  ;


   : do-map-in  ( offset size -- )   swap my-address +  swap  map-sbus  ;
   : do-map-out ( vadr size --  )   free-virtual  ;


   : dac-map    ( -- )   dac-offset  /dac  do-map-in     is dac-adr  ;
   : dac-unmap  ( -- )   dac-adr     /dac  do-map-out -1 is dac-adr  ;

   : fhc-map    ( -- )   fhc-offset /fhc  do-map-in     is fhc-adr  ;
   : fhc-unmap  ( -- )   fhc-adr    /fhc  do-map-out  -1 is fhc-adr  ;

   : thc-map    ( -- )   thc-offset /thc  do-map-in     is thc-adr  ;
   : thc-unmap  ( -- )   thc-adr    /thc  do-map-out  -1 is thc-adr  ;

   : fbc-map    ( -- )   fbc-offset /fbc  do-map-in     is fbc-adr  ;
   : fbc-unmap  ( -- )   fbc-adr    /fbc  do-map-out -1 is fbc-adr  ;

   : tec-map    ( -- )   tec-offset /tec  do-map-in     is tec-adr  ;
   : tec-unmap  ( -- )   tec-adr    /tec  do-map-out -1 is tec-adr  ;

   : fb-map     ( -- )   fb-offset  /frame  do-map-in     is fb-adr  ;
   : fb-unmap   ( -- )   fb-adr     /frame  do-map-out -1 is fb-adr  ;

   : map-regs   ( -- )  dac-map   fhc-map   thc-map   fbc-map    tec-map  ;
   : unmap-regs ( -- )  tec-unmap  fbc-unmap  thc-unmap  fhc-unmap  dac-
unmap  ;

   \ Brooktree DAC interface section

   \ The Brooktree DAC has an internal address register which helps to
   \ select the internal register which is to be accessed.
   \ First, the address is written to register 0, then the data is written
   \ to one of the other registers.
   \ Ibis has 3 separate DAC chips which appear as the three least-
significant
   \ bytes of a longword.  All three chips may be simultaneously updated
```

Code Example 7-2   Extended display device driver example

```
                    \ Extended Display device driver
    \ with a single longword write.

    : dac!  ( data reg# -- ) >r dup 2dup bljoin r> dac-adr + l!  ;
    : dac-ctl! ( data int.adr reg# -- )  swap 0 dac!  dac!  ;

    \ color! sets an overlay color register.
    \ In order to be able to use either the Brooktree 457 or 458 dacs, we
    \ set the address once, then store the color 3 times.  The chip
internally
    \ cycles each time the color register is written, selecting in turn the
    \ red color, the green color, and the blue color.
    \ The chip is used in "RGB mode".

    : color!  ( r g b c# -- )
       0 dac!        ( r g b )
       swap rot      ( b g r )
       4 dac!        ( b g )
       4 dac!        ( b )
       4 dac!        (  )
    ;

    : lego-init-dac  ( -- )

       40 06  8 dac-ctl!  \ Control reg: enable off, overlay off, RGB on
       0  05  8 dac-ctl!  \ Blinking off
       ff 04  8 dac-ctl!  \ Read mask set to all ones
       ff ff ff 0   color!  \ White in overlay background color register
       0  0  0  ff  color!  \ Black in overlay foreground color register
       64 41 b4  1  color!  \ SUN-blue for logo
    ;

    \ End of Brooktree DAC code

    \ Lego Selftest section

    : fbc!  ( value offset -- )  fbc-adr + l!  ;
    : fbc@  ( offset -- value )  fbc-adr + l@  ;
    : tec!  ( value offset -- )  tec-adr + l!  ;

    : lego-selftest ( -- failed? )  false  ;

    \ Hardware configuration register section

    : fhc!  ( value offset -- )  fhc-adr + l!  ;
```

Code Example 7-2   Extended display device driver example

```
                  \ Extended Display device driver
  : thc!   ( value offset -- )   thc-adr + l! ;

  : set-res-params   ( hcvd hcvs hchd hchsdvb hchs fhc-conf -- )
     0 fhc!  0 thc!  4 thc!  8 thc!  c thc!  10 thc!
  ;

  \ Resolution params:        hcvd     hcvs     hchd hchsdvb  hchs fhc-conf

  : r1024x768   ( -- params )  2c032c  32c0005  110051  490000   510007
3bb  ;
  : r1152x900   ( -- params )  2403a8    10005  15005d  570000    10009  bbb  ;
  : r1024x1024  ( -- params )  200426    10005  180054  520000    10009
3bb  ;
  : r1152x870   ( -- params )  2c0392    20005  120054  540000    10009  bbb  ;
  : r1600x1280  ( -- params )  340534   534009  130045  3d0000   450007
1bbb  ;

  0 value lego-rez-width
  0 value lego-rez-height

  0 value sense-code

  : set-resolution  ( sense-code -- )
     case
        0 of  d# 1152  d#  900  endof
       12 of  d# 1024  d# 1024  endof
       13 of  d# 1600  d# 1280  endof
       drop   d# 1152  d#  900  0
     endcase
     is lego-rez-height  is lego-rez-width
  ;

  8f value thc-misc
  : lego-video-on  ( -- )  thc-misc  400 or  18  thc!  ;
  : lego-video-off ( -- )  thc-misc          18  thc!  ;

  : lego-init-hc  ( -- )
     sense-code  case
        0 of  r1152x900   endof
       12 of  r1024x1024  endof
       13 of  r1600x1280  endof
       drop    r1152x900   0
     endcase                   ( resolution-params )
     set-res-params
```

Code Example 7-2   Extended display device driver example

```
                  \ Extended Display device driver

    016b 14  thc!          \ THC_HCREFRESH
    148f 18  thc!          \ THC_HCMISC
    \   48f 18  thc!        \ THC_HCMISC
    lego-video-off         \ Turn video on at install time
  ;

  \ End of hardware configuration register section

end0
```

Complete Display Device Driver

This sample FCode program is for a device that would be usable as a system console device.

Code Example 7-3   Complete display device driver example

```
              \ Complete Display device driver


\ cg6 (Lego) frame buffer driver
\ This version doesn't use the graphics accelerator because of
\ conflicts with the window system's use of same.

hex
fcode-version1
   " SUNW,cgsix" name
   " SUNW,501-xxxx" model
   " display"  device-type

   h# 20.0000 constant dac-offset   h#      10 constant /dac
   h# 30.0000 constant fhc-offset   h#      10 constant /fhc
   h# 30.1800 constant thc-offset   h#      20 constant /thc
   h# 70.0000 constant fbc-offset   h#      10 constant /fbc
   h# 70.1000 constant tec-offset   h#      10 constant /tec
   h# 80.0000 constant fb-offset    h# 10.0000 constant /frame

   : >reg-spec ( offset size -- xdrreg )
      >r my-address + my-space xdrphys r> xdrint xdr+
   ;
```

Code Example 7-3   Complete display device driver example

```
          \ Complete Display device driver
dac-offset /dac >reg-spec
fhc-offset /fhc >reg-spec      xdr+
thc-offset /thc >reg-spec      xdr+
fbc-offset /fbc >reg-spec      xdr+
tec-offset /tec >reg-spec      xdr+
fb-offset  /frame >reg-spec    xdr+
" reg" attribute

5  xdrint " interrupts" attribute

5  0   intr

-1 value dac-adr
-1 value fhc-adr
-1 value thc-adr
-1 value fbc-adr
-1 value tec-adr
-1 value fb-adr


: copyright  ( -- adr len )   " Copyright (c) 1989 by Sun Microsystems,
Inc. "  ;


: do-map-in  ( offset size -- )  swap my-address +  swap  map-sbus  ;
: do-map-out ( vadr size --   )  free-virtual  ;


: dac-map     ( -- )  dac-offset  /dac  do-map-in     is dac-adr  ;
: dac-unmap   ( -- )  dac-adr     /dac  do-map-out -1 is dac-adr  ;

: fhc-map     ( -- )  fhc-offset /fhc   do-map-in     is fhc-adr  ;
: fhc-unmap   ( -- )  fhc-adr    /fhc   do-map-out -1 is fhc-adr  ;

: thc-map     ( -- )  thc-offset /thc   do-map-in     is thc-adr  ;
: thc-unmap   ( -- )  thc-adr    /thc   do-map-out -1 is thc-adr  ;

: fbc-map     ( -- )  fbc-offset  /fbc  do-map-in     is fbc-adr  ;
: fbc-unmap   ( -- )  fbc-adr     /fbc  do-map-out -1 is fbc-adr  ;

: tec-map     ( -- )  tec-offset  /tec  do-map-in     is tec-adr  ;
: tec-unmap   ( -- )  tec-adr     /tec  do-map-out -1 is tec-adr  ;

: fb-map      ( -- )  fb-offset  /frame  do-map-in    is fb-adr  ;
: fb-unmap    ( -- )  fb-adr     /frame  do-map-out -1 is fb-adr  ;
```

Code Example 7-3   Complete display device driver example

```
            \ Complete Display device driver


  : map-regs   ( -- )  dac-map    fhc-map    thc-map    fbc-map    tec-map  ;
   : unmap-regs ( -- )  tec-unmap  fbc-unmap  thc-unmap  fhc-unmap  dac-
unmap   ;


  \ Brooktree DAC interface section

  \ The Brooktree DAC has an internal address register which helps to
  \ select the internal register which is to be accessed.
  \ First, the address is written to register 0, then the data is written
  \ to one of the other registers.
  \ Ibis has 3 separate DAC chips which appear as the three least-
significant
  \ bytes of a longword.  All three chips may be simultaneously updated
  \ with a single longword write.

  : dac!  ( data reg# -- ) >r dup 2dup bljoin r> dac-adr + l!  ;
  : dac-ctl! ( data int.adr reg# -- )  swap 0 dac!  dac!  ;


  \ color! sets an overlay color register.
  \ In order to be able to use either the Brooktree 457 or 458 dacs, we
  \ set the address once, then store the color 3 times.  The chip
internally
  \ cycles each time the color register is written, selecting in turn the
  \ red color, the green color, and the blue color.
  \ The chip is used in "RGB mode".

  : color!  ( r g b c# -- )
     0 dac!        ( r g b )
     swap rot      ( b g r )
     4 dac!        ( b g )
     4 dac!        ( b )
     4 dac!        (   )
  ;


  : lego-init-dac  ( -- )

     40 06  8 dac-ctl! \ Control reg: enable off, overlay off, RGB on
     0  05  8 dac-ctl! \ Blinking off
     ff 04  8 dac-ctl! \ Read mask set to all ones
     ff ff ff 0   color! \ White in overlay background color register
     0  0  0  ff  color! \ Black in overlay foreground color register
     64 41 b4  1  color! \ SUN-blue for logo
  ;
```

Code Example 7-3   Complete display device driver example

```
              \ Complete Display device driver

   \ End of Brooktree DAC code

   \ Lego Selftest section

   : fbc!  ( value offset -- )  fbc-adr + l!  ;
   : fbc@  ( offset -- value )  fbc-adr + l@  ;
   : tec!  ( value offset -- )  tec-adr + l!  ;

   : lego-selftest ( -- failed? )  false  ;

   \ Hardware configuration register section

   : fhc!  ( value offset -- )  fhc-adr + l!  ;
   : thc!  ( value offset -- )  thc-adr + l!  ;

   : set-res-params  ( hcvd hcvs hchd hchsdvb hchs fhc-conf -- )
      0 fhc!  0 thc!  4 thc!  8 thc!  c thc!  10 thc!
   ;

  \ Resolution params:         hcvd     hcvs    hchd  hchsdvb   hchs  fhc-conf

   : r1024x768   ( -- params )  2c032c   32c0005  110051   490000   510007
3bb  ;
   : r1152x900   ( -- params )  2403a8   10005   15005d   570000   10009   bbb ;
   : r1024x1024  ( -- params )  200426   10005   180054   520000   10009   3bb ;
   : r1152x870   ( -- params )  2c0392   20005   120054   540000   10009   bbb ;
   : r1600x1280  ( -- params )  340534   534009  130045   3d0000   450007
1bbb  ;

   0 value lego-rez-width
   0 value lego-rez-height

   0 value sense-code

   : set-resolution  ( sense-code -- )
      case
         0 of  d# 1152  d#  900  endof
        12 of  d# 1024  d# 1024  endof
        13 of  d# 1600  d# 1280  endof
        drop   d# 1152  d#  900  0
      endcase
      is lego-rez-height  is lego-rez-width
   ;
```

Code Example 7-3   Complete display device driver example

```
          \ Complete Display device driver

8f value thc-misc
: lego-video-on  ( -- )  thc-misc  400 or  18  thc!  ;
: lego-video-off ( -- )  thc-misc          18  thc!  ;
: lego-blink ( -- ) lego-video-off 20 ms lego-video-on ;
: lego-init-hc  ( -- )
   sense-code  case
     0 of   r1152x900    endof
     12 of   r1024x1024   endof
     13 of   r1600x1280   endof
     drop    r1152x900    0
   endcase                  ( resolution-params )
   set-res-params

   016b 14  thc!          \ THC_HCREFRESH
   148f 18  thc!          \ THC_HCMISC

   lego-video-off\ Turn video on at install time
;

\ End of hardware configuration register section

\ Lego graphics section
: lego-install  ( -- )
   map-regs fb-map  fb-adr is frame-buffer-adr

   default-font  ( param ... )  set-font

   frame-buffer-adr xdrint    " address"   attribute

  lego-rez-width lego-rez-height  over char-width /  over char-height
/
   fb8-install
   ['] lego-blink is blink-screen
   lego-video-on
;
: lego-remove  ( -- )
   lego-video-off
   unmap-regs
   fb-unmap  -1 is frame-buffer-adr
;

\ End of Lego graphics section
```

Code Example 7-3   Complete display device driver example

```
        \ Complete Display device driver

: lego-probe   ( -- )

   map-regs

   sense-code   set-resolution

   lego-init-dac
   lego-init-hc

   unmap-regs

   lego-rez-width  xdrint   " width"   attribute
   lego-rez-height xdrint   " height" attribute
   d# 8            xdrint   " depth"   attribute
   lego-rez-width  xdrint   " linebytes"  attribute

   ['] lego-install  is-install
   ['] lego-remove   is-remove
   ['] lego-selftest is-selftest
;
lego-probe
end0
```

Hierarchical Devices

This device type generally applies to random access or memory mapped buses, for which the children of the bus can be mapped into the CPU address space and accessed like memory.

Hierarchical devices include such buses as SBus and VMEbus.

Not all bus devices fall into this category. For example, SCSI is not a memory mapped bus; SCSI targets are not accessed with load or store instructions.

Required Methods

The hierarchical device package code must implement the open, close, reset, and selftest methods, as well as the following:

decode-unit

```
( adr len -- low high )
```

Convert adr len, a text string representation, to low high, a numerical representation of a physical address within the address space defined by this package.

dma-alloc

```
( size -- virt )
```

Allocate a virtual address range of length *size* bytes that is suitable for direct memory access by a bus master device. The memory is allocated according to the most stringent alignment requirements for the bus. virt is an 32-bit address that the OpenBoot-based system can use to access the memory.

Note that dma-map-in must also be called to generate a suitable DMA address.

A child of a hierarchical device calls dma-alloc using

```
" dma-alloc" $call-parent
```

For example:

```
-1 value my-reg

: my-dma-alloc ( size -- )

    " dma-alloc"  $call-parent  is my-reg

;
```

dma-free
(virt size --)

Free *size* bytes of memory previously allocated by dma-alloc at the virtual address virt.

A child of a hierachical device calls dma-free by using

```
" dma-free" $call-parent
```

For example:

```
2000 value my-size

: my-dma-free  ( -- )

    my-reg my-size " dma-free"  $call-parent

    -1 is my-reg

;
```

dma-map-in
(virt size cacheable? -- devaddr)

Convert the virtual address range virt size, previously allocated by dma-alloc, into an address devaddr suitable for DMA on the bus. dma-map-in can also be used to map application-supplied data buffers for DMA use if the bus allows. If cacheable? is true, the calling child desires to use any available fast caches for the DMA buffer. If access to the buffer is required before the buffer is mapped out, the child must call dma-sync or dma-map-out to ensure cache coherency with memory.

A child of a hierachical device calls `dma-map-in` using

```
" dma-map-in" $call-parent
```

For example:

```
: my-reg-dma-map ( -- )

  my-reg my-size false " dma-map-in"  $call-parent   ( devaddr )

   is my-reg-dma

;
```

dma-map-out

```
                       ( virt devaddr size -- )
```

Remove the DMA mapping previously created with `dma-map-in`. Flush all caches associated with the mapping.

A child of a hierachical device calls dma-map-in by using

```
" dma-map-out" $call-parent
```

For example:

```
$call-parent

: my-reg-dma-free ( -- )

  my-reg my-reg-dma my-size " dma-map-out"  $call-parent

   -1 is my-reg-dma

;
```

dma-sync

(virt devaddr size --)

Synchronize (flush) any memory caches associated with the DMA mapping previously established by dma-map-in. You must interleave calls to this method (or dma-map-out) between DMA and CPU accesses to the memory region, or errors may result.

For example, a child of a hierachical device calls dma-sync by using $call-parent. This method is valid for FCode version 2.1 or later. Some early version 2 systems do not define this method in the /sbus node. Those systems automatically synchronize DMA and CPU access. The following example will give correct results in all cases.

```
: my-dma-sync ( virt devadr size -- )

   " dma-sync"  ['] $call-parent  catch  if

      \ Parent does not have dma-sync

      \ cleanup the stack and return

      2drop 3drop

   then

;
```

probe-self

(arg-adr arg-len reg-adr reg-len fcode-adr fcode-len --)

Probe for a child of this node. fcode-adr fcode-len is a unit-address text string that locates the FCode program for the child. reg-adr reg-len is a unit-address text string that identifies the address of the child itself. arg-adr arg-len is a string for any device arguments for the child. probe-self checks whether there is indeed FCode at the indicated location, perhaps using cpeek.

If the FCode exists, probe-self creates a new child device node and interprets the FCode. If the interpretation of the FCode fails in some way, the new device node may be empty, containing no properties or methods.

For example, to probe FCode for SBus slot #1:

```
" /sbus" select-dev

0 0 " 1,0" 2dup probe-self

unselect-dev
```

map-in
                              (low high size -- virt)

Create a mapping associating the range of physical addresses beginning at low high, extending for size bytes, within the package's physical address space, with a processor virtual address virt.

For example, a child of a hierachical device calls map-in with " map-in" $call-parent :

```
: map-reg ( -- )

   my-address xx-offset + my-space  xx-size  ( adr space size )

   " map-in" $call-parent          ( virt )

   is xx-reg                       ( )

;
```

map-out
                              (virt size --)

Destroy the mapping set by map-in at virtual address virt of length size bytes.

For example, a child of a hierachical device calls map-out with " map-out" $call-parent :

```
: unmap-reg ( virt -- )

   xx-reg xx-size  ( virt size )
```

```
    " map-out" $call-parent       ( )

    -1 is xx-reg

;
```

SBus Addressing

The SBus uses geographical addressing with numbered slots.

An SBus physical address is represented numerically by the SBus slot number as the high number and the offset from the base of that slot as the low number. The text string representation is slot#, offset, where both slot# and offset are the ASCII representations of hexadecimal numbers.

SBus Required Properties

Table 8-1   Required SBus Properties

Property Name	Sample Value
name	"SUNW,finagle"
burst-sizes	
device-type	" sbus"
ranges	
slot-address-bits	

VMEBus Addressing

VMEBus has a number of distinct address spaces represented by a subset of the 64 possible values encoded by the six "address modifier" bits. The maximum size of one of these address spaces is 32 bits. An additional bit is used to select between 16-bit and 32-bit data.

A VMEBus physical address is represented numerically as follows. The *high* number is made up of the six address modifier bits AM0-5 in bits 0-5 and the data width bit (0 = 16-bit data, 1 = 32-bit data) in bit 6. The *low* number is the offset within the selected address space. The text string representation is *as,offset*, where both *as* and *offset* are ASCII representations of a hexadecimal numbers; *as* encodes the data width and address modifier bits.

VMEBus Required Properties

Table 8-2   Required VMEbus Properties

Property Name	Sample Value
name	"SUNW,vizzy"
device-type	" vmebus"
ranges	

Device Driver Examples

The following examples of a hierarchical FCode driver are based on Sun's SBus expansion hardware called "XBox". XBox increases the number of SBus slots available in a system by providing a bus-bridge between the platform's onboard SBus and an SBus in the XBox hardware. XBox includes an SBus card called the XAdaptor card which plugs into the host platform's SBus and includes an expansion chassis called the XBox Expansion Box. Therefore XBox is an example of a hierarchical device which, in fact, implements an SBus interface to child plug-in devices.

The example is divided into three parts: the basic device driver, the extended device driver, and the complete device driver. In the case of a hierarchical device, in practice, one would only want to develop and ship a driver with the complete functionality. Otherwise, plug-in cards which rely on a full set of parent services generally would not be able to function. The three stage presentation of the driver simply shows how a driver might grow through the development cycle.

Basic Hierarchical Device Driver

The basic driver simply declares most of the important properties of the device, particularly the addresses of the various registers. A driver in this state might be used to support the develoment of the OS driver which would attach to the device name and configure itself based on the device properties published by the FCode driver.

Code Example 8-1   Basic hierarchical device driver sample

```
hex
fcode-version2

" SUNW,xbox"  name
" 501-1840"   model

\ XBox Registers
\ XAdaptor card registers
h#       0 constant write0-offset    h# 4 constant /write0
h#  2.0000 constant xac-err-offset    h# c constant /xac-err
h# 10.0000 constant xac-ctl0-offset   h# 4 constant /xac-ctl0
h# 11.0000 constant xac-ctl1-offset   h# 4 constant /xac-ctl1
h# 12.0000 constant xac-elua-offset   h# 4 constant /xac-elua
h# 13.0000 constant xac-ella-offset   h# 4 constant /xac-ella
h# 14.0000 constant xac-ele-offset    h# 4 constant /xac-ele

\ XBox Exapnsion box registers
h# 42.0000 constant xbc-err-offset    h# c constant /xbc-err
h# 50.0000 constant xbc-ctl0-offset   h# 4 constant /xbc-ctl0
h# 51.0000 constant xbc-ctl1-offset   h# 4 constant /xbc-ctl1
h# 52.0000 constant xbc-elua-offset   h# 4 constant /xbc-elua
h# 53.0000 constant xbc-ella-offset   h# 4 constant /xbc-ella
h# 54.0000 constant xbc-ele-offset    h# 4 constant /xbc-ele

 : >reg-spec ( offset size -- xdrreg )
    >r my-address + my-space xdrphys r> xdrint xdr+
 ;

write0-offset    /write0    >reg-spec
xac-err-offset   /xac-err   >reg-spec   xdr+
xac-ctl0-offset  /xac-ctl0  >reg-spec   xdr+
xac-ctl1-offset  /xac-ctl1  >reg-spec   xdr+
xac-elua-offset  /xac-elua  >reg-spec   xdr+
xac-ella-offset  /xac-ella  >reg-spec   xdr+
xac-ele-offset   /xac-ele   >reg-spec   xdr+
xbc-err-offset   /xbc-err   >reg-spec   xdr+
xbc-ctl0-offset  /xbc-ctl0  >reg-spec   xdr+
```

Code Example 8-1   Basic hierarchical device driver sample

```
xbc-ctl1-offset   /xbc-ctl1  >reg-spec  xdr+
xbc-elua-offset   /xbc-elua  >reg-spec  xdr+
xbc-ella-offset   /xbc-ella  >reg-spec  xdr+
xbc-ele-offset    /xbc-ele   >reg-spec  xdr+
" reg" attribute

\ Xbox can interrupt on any SBus level

1 xdrint       2 xdrint xdr+  3 xdrint xdr+  4 xdrint xdr+
5 xdrint xdr+  6 xdrint xdr+  7 xdrint xdr+
" interrupts"  attribute

1 sbus-intr>cpu xdrint       0 xdrint xdr+
2 sbus-intr>cpu xdrint xdr+  0 xdrint xdr+
3 sbus-intr>cpu xdrint xdr+  0 xdrint xdr+
4 sbus-intr>cpu xdrint xdr+  0 xdrint xdr+
5 sbus-intr>cpu xdrint xdr+  0 xdrint xdr+
6 sbus-intr>cpu xdrint xdr+  0 xdrint xdr+
7 sbus-intr>cpu xdrint xdr+  0 xdrint xdr+
" intr" attribute

\ XBox bus clock speed
d# 25.000.000 xdrint  " clock-frequency"  attribute

\ Burst sizes 64,32,16,8,4,2,1 bursts.
h# 7f xdrint  " burst-sizes"  attribute

\ XBox has no slave-only slots
0 xdrint  " slave-only" attribute

\ Get the number of address bits for this SBus slot from the parent SBus
\ node without inheritance .  OpenBoot 2.5 doesn't publish slot-address-
bits.
\ However 2.5 is only on 4m machines, which are all 28 bits per slot.

: $=  ( addr1 len1 addr2 len2 -- equal? )        \ string compare
   rot over -  if
      drop 2drop  false                          \ different lengths
   else  comp 0=
   then
;
: 4mhack  ( -- n )
   " compatible" get-inherited-attribute  if
      d# 25                                 \ no "compatible" prop; assume 4c
```

Code Example 8-1   Basic hierarchical device driver sample

```
    else  xdrtostring  " sun4m" $=  if
        d# 28
      else
        d# 25                                  \ not sun4m
      then
      nip nip
    then
;
: #bits  ( -- n )
   " slot-address-bits"  my-parent ihandle>phandle
   get-package-attribute  if
      4mhack
   else
      xdrtoint  nip nip
   then
;
#bits constant  host-slot-size
host-slot-size xdrint  " slot-address-bits" attribute

end0
```

Extended Hierarchical Device Driver

The extended driver adds methods allowing access to various device registers in addtion to the functions of the basic driver. It provides methods to:

* map in the registers
* fetch from and store to the registers
* program one of the registers which control the allocation of address space across the various SBus slots.

Such an extended driver provides methods that a developer can use to read and write registers and verify correct hardware responses. Note that the complete driver does not use all of the device registers; read/write access methods were included for all of them to allow easy testing during development.

Code Example 8-2   Extended hierarchical device driver sample

```
\ extended hierarchical device driver sample

hex
fcode-version2
```

Code Example 8-2   Extended hierarchical device driver sample

```
\ extended hierarchical device driver sample

" SUNW,xbox"  name
" 501-1840"   model

\ XBox Registers

h#       0 constant write0-offset    h# 4 constant /write0
h#  2.0000 constant xac-err-offset   h# c constant /xac-err
h# 10.0000 constant xac-ctl0-offset  h# 4 constant /xac-ctl0
h# 11.0000 constant xac-ctl1-offset  h# 4 constant /xac-ctl1
h# 12.0000 constant xac-elua-offset  h# 4 constant /xac-elua
h# 13.0000 constant xac-ella-offset  h# 4 constant /xac-ella
h# 14.0000 constant xac-ele-offset   h# 4 constant /xac-ele

h# 42.0000 constant xbc-err-offset   h# c constant /xbc-err
h# 50.0000 constant xbc-ctl0-offset  h# 4 constant /xbc-ctl0
h# 51.0000 constant xbc-ctl1-offset  h# 4 constant /xbc-ctl1
h# 52.0000 constant xbc-elua-offset  h# 4 constant /xbc-elua
h# 53.0000 constant xbc-ella-offset  h# 4 constant /xbc-ella
h# 54.0000 constant xbc-ele-offset   h# 4 constant /xbc-ele

: >reg-spec ( offset size -- xdrreg )
   >r my-address + my-space xdrphys r> xdrint xdr+
;

write0-offset    /write0    >reg-spec
xac-err-offset   /xac-err   >reg-spec  xdr+
xac-ctl0-offset  /xac-ctl0  >reg-spec  xdr+
xac-ctl1-offset  /xac-ctl1  >reg-spec  xdr+
xac-elua-offset  /xac-elua  >reg-spec  xdr+
xac-ella-offset  /xac-ella  >reg-spec  xdr+
xac-ele-offset   /xac-ele   >reg-spec  xdr+
xbc-err-offset   /xbc-err   >reg-spec  xdr+
xbc-ctl0-offset  /xbc-ctl0  >reg-spec  xdr+
xbc-ctl1-offset  /xbc-ctl1  >reg-spec  xdr+
xbc-elua-offset  /xbc-elua  >reg-spec  xdr+
xbc-ella-offset  /xbc-ella  >reg-spec  xdr+
xbc-ele-offset   /xbc-ele   >reg-spec  xdr+
" reg" attribute

\ Xbox can interrupt on any SBus level

1 xdrint       2 xdrint xdr+  3 xdrint xdr+  4 xdrint xdr+
5 xdrint xdr+  6 xdrint xdr+  7 xdrint xdr+
```

Code Example 8-2   Extended hierarchical device driver sample

```
\ extended hierarchical device driver sample
" interrupts"  attribute

1 sbus-intr>cpu xdrint        0 xdrint xdr+
2 sbus-intr>cpu xdrint xdr+  0 xdrint xdr+
3 sbus-intr>cpu xdrint xdr+  0 xdrint xdr+
4 sbus-intr>cpu xdrint xdr+  0 xdrint xdr+
5 sbus-intr>cpu xdrint xdr+  0 xdrint xdr+
6 sbus-intr>cpu xdrint xdr+  0 xdrint xdr+
7 sbus-intr>cpu xdrint xdr+  0 xdrint xdr+
" intr" attribute

\ XBox bus clock speed
d# 25.000.000 xdrint  " clock-frequency"  attribute

\ Burst sizes 64,32,16,8,4,2,1 bursts.
h# 7f xdrint  " burst-sizes"  attribute

\ XBox has no slave-only slots
0 xdrint  " slave-only" attribute

\ Get the number of address bits for this SBus slot from the parent SBus
\ node without inheritance .  OpenBoot 2.5 doesn't publish slot-address-
bits.
\ However 2.5 is only on 4m machines, which are all 28 bits per slot.

: $=  ( addr1 len1 addr2 len2 -- equal? )        \ string compare
   rot over -  if
      drop 2drop  false                          \ different lengths
   else  comp 0=
   then
;
: 4mhack  ( -- n )
   " compatible" get-inherited-attribute  if
      d# 25                                       \ no "compatible" prop; assume 4c
   else xdrtostring  " sun4m" $=  if
        d# 28
      else
        d# 25                                     \ not sun4m
      then
      nip nip
   then
;
: #bits  ( -- n )
   " slot-address-bits"  my-parent ihandle>phandle
```

Code Example 8-2   Extended hierarchical device driver sample

```
\ extended hierarchical device driver sample
   get-package-attribute  if
      4mhack
   else
      xdrtoint  nip nip
   then
;
#bits constant  host-slot-size
host-slot-size xdrint  " slot-address-bits" attribute

\ Utility display string
: .me  ( -- )  ." SBus "  my-space .d  ." XBox "  ;


\ The XBox device has two modes opaque and transparent.

\ Upon reset the device is set to opaque mode.  In this mode all
\ accesses to address space of the device are directed to the XBox H/W
\ (ie. XAdaptor Card or the XBox Expansion Box) itself.

\ In the transparent mode all accesses are mapped to the SBus cards
\ which are plugged into the XBox.  In transparent mode the XBox H/W is
\ accessible only via the "write-0" register. To allow another bus
\ bridge to be plugged into the XBox all writes to the write-0 register
\ must contain a "key" which is programmed into the XBox H/W at boot
\ time. If the key field of a write to write-0 matches that programmed
\ at boot time the H/W intercepts the write.  Otherwise the H/W passes
\ the write along.

\ The XBox has two sets of registers. Those of the XAdaptor card and
\ and those of the XBox Expansion Box.

\ Opaque mode host adapter registers
-1  value xac-err-regs
-1  value xac-ctl0     -1  value xac-ctl1
-1  value xac-elua     -1  value xac-ella
-1  value xac-ele
\ Opaque mode expansion box registers
-1  value xbc-err-regs
-1  value xbc-ctl0     -1  value xbc-ctl1
-1  value xbc-elua     -1  value xbc-ella
-1  value xbc-ele
\ Transparent mode register
-1  value write0-reg
```

Code Example 8-2   Extended hierarchical device driver sample

```
\ extended hierarchical device driver sample
: xbox-map-in  ( offset space size -- virt ) " map-in"  $call-parent ;
: xbox-map-out ( virt size -- )                " map-out" $call-parent ;
: map-regs   ( -- )
   write0-offset  my-address + my-space /write0   xbox-map-in  is write0-
reg
   xac-err-offset  my-address + my-space /xac-err  xbox-map-in  is xac-
err-regs
  xac-ctl0-offset my-address + my-space /xac-ctl0 xbox-map-in  is xac-ctl0
  xac-ctl1-offset my-address + my-space /xac-ctl1 xbox-map-in  is xac-ctl1
  xac-elua-offset my-address + my-space /xac-elua xbox-map-in  is xac-elua
  xac-ella-offset my-address + my-space /xac-ella xbox-map-in  is xac-ella
   xac-ele-offset  my-address + my-space /xac-ele  xbox-map-in  is xac-ele
   xbc-err-offset  my-address + my-space /xbc-err  xbox-map-in  is xbc-
err-regs
  xbc-ctl0-offset my-address + my-space /xbc-ctl0 xbox-map-in  is xbc-ctl0
  xbc-ctl1-offset my-address + my-space /xbc-ctl1 xbox-map-in  is xbc-ctl1
  xbc-elua-offset my-address + my-space /xbc-elua xbox-map-in  is xbc-elua
  xbc-ella-offset my-address + my-space /xbc-ella xbox-map-in  is xbc-ella
   xbc-ele-offset  my-address + my-space /xbc-ele  xbox-map-in  is xbc-ele
;
: unmap-regs  ( -- )
   write0-reg   /write0   xbox-map-out   -1 is write0-reg
   xac-err-regs /xac-err   xbox-map-out   -1 is xac-err-regs
   xac-ctl0    /xac-ctl0  xbox-map-out   -1 is xac-ctl0
   xac-ctl1    /xac-ctl1  xbox-map-out   -1 is xac-ctl1
   xac-elua    /xac-elua  xbox-map-out   -1 is xac-elua
   xac-ella    /xac-ella  xbox-map-out   -1 is xac-ella
   xac-ele     /xac-ele   xbox-map-out   -1 is xac-ele
   xbc-err-regs /xbc-err   xbox-map-out   -1 is xbc-err-regs
   xbc-ctl0    /xbc-ctl0  xbox-map-out   -1 is xbc-ctl0
   xbc-ctl1    /xbc-ctl1  xbox-map-out   -1 is xbc-ctl1
   xbc-elua    /xbc-elua  xbox-map-out   -1 is xbc-elua
   xbc-ella    /xbc-ella  xbox-map-out   -1 is xbc-ella
   xbc-ele     /xbc-ele   xbox-map-out   -1 is xbc-ele
;

\ Opaque mode register access words

: xac-errd@  ( -- l )  xac-err-regs     rl@ ;
: xac-erra@  ( -- l )  xac-err-regs 4 + rl@ ;
: xac-errs@  ( -- l )  xac-err-regs 8 + rl@ ;
: xac-ctl0@  ( -- w )  xac-ctl0 rl@ ;
: xac-ctl0!  ( w -- )  xac-ctl0 rl! ;
: xac-ctl1@  ( -- w )  xac-ctl1 rl@ ;
```

Code Example 8-2   Extended hierarchical device driver sample

```
\ extended hierarchical device driver sample
: xac-ctl1!  ( w -- )  xac-ctl1 rl!  ;
: xac-elua@  ( -- l )  xac-elua rl@  ;
: xac-elua!  ( l -- )  xac-elua rl!  ;
: xac-ella@  ( -- w )  xac-ella rl@  ;
: xac-ella!  ( w -- )  xac-ella rl!  ;

: xbc-errd@  ( -- l )  xbc-err-regs rl@  ;
: xbc-erra@  ( -- l )  xbc-err-regs 4 + rl@  ;
: xbc-errs@  ( -- l )  xbc-err-regs 8 + rl@  ;
: xbc-ctl0@  ( -- w )  xbc-ctl0 rl@  ;
: xbc-ctl0!  ( w -- )  xbc-ctl0 rl!  ;
: xbc-ctl1@  ( -- w )  xbc-ctl1 rl@  ;
: xbc-ctl1!  ( w -- )  xbc-ctl1 rl!  ;
: xbc-elua@  ( -- l )  xbc-elua rl@  ;
: xbc-elua!  ( l -- )  xbc-elua rl!  ;
: xbc-ella@  ( -- w )  xbc-ella rl@  ;
: xbc-ella!  ( w -- )  xbc-ella rl!  ;

\ Transparent Mode register access words

external
: unique-key  ( -- n )  " unique-key" $call-parent  ;
headers
unique-key constant my-key
my-key xdrint  " write0-key" attribute

: xbox!  ( w offset -- )  my-key h# 18 << or or   write0-reg rl!  ;

: write-xac-ctl0  ( w -- )  xac-ctl0-offset xbox! ;
: write-xac-ctl1  ( w -- )  xac-ctl1-offset xbox! ;
: write-xbc-ctl0  ( w -- )  xbc-ctl0-offset xbox! ;
: write-xbc-ctl1  ( w -- )  xbc-ctl1-offset xbox! ;

\ Some functionally oriented words

: set-key        ( -- )  my-key 8 <<  xac-ctl0!  ;
: transparent    ( -- )            1 xac-ctl1!  ;
: opaque         ( -- )        0 write-xac-ctl1  ;
: enable-slaves  ( -- )    h# 38 write-xbc-ctl1  ;

: xbox-errors  ( -- xbc-err xac-err )
   opaque  xbc-errd@ xac-errd@  transparent
;
```

Code Example 8-2   Extended hierarchical device driver sample

```
\ extended hierarchical device driver sample
: ?.errors  ( xbc-err xac-err -- )
   dup h# 8000.0000 and  if
      cr .me  ." xac-error " .h cr
   else  drop
   then
   dup h# 8000.0000 and  if
      cr .me  ." xbc-error " .h cr
   else drop
   then
;

\ The address space of the XBox in transparent mode may be dynamically
\ allocated across its plug-in slots.  This is called the
\ upper-address-decode-map (uadm).  Below is a table which relates the
\ slot configuration code which is programmed in hardware to the
\ allocation of address space for each slot.  The number in each cell is
\ the number of address bits needed for the slot.

decimal
create slot-sizes-array
\ slot0 slot1 slot2 slot3     slot-config
  23 c, 23 c, 23 c, 23 c,     \ 00
  23 c, 23 c, 23 c, 23 c,     \ 01
  23 c, 23 c, 23 c, 23 c,     \ 02
  23 c, 23 c, 23 c, 23 c,     \ 03
  25 c,  0 c,  0 c,  0 c,     \ 04
   0 c, 25 c,  0 c,  0 c,     \ 05
   0 c,  0 c, 25 c,  0 c,     \ 06
   0 c,  0 c,  0 c, 25 c,     \ 07
  24 c, 24 c,  0 c,  0 c,     \ 08
  24 c,  0 c, 24 c,  0 c,     \ 09
   0 c, 24 c, 24 c,  0 c,     \ 0a
   0 c,  0 c,  0 c,  0 c,     \ 0b
  24 c, 23 c, 23 c,  0 c,     \ 0c
  23 c, 24 c, 23 c,  0 c,     \ 0d  \ Overridden in code
  23 c, 23 c, 24 c,  0 c,     \ 0e  \ Overridden in code
  25 c,  0 c,  0 c,  0 c,     \ 0f
  26 c, 26 c, 26 c, 26 c,     \ 10
  26 c, 26 c, 26 c, 26 c,     \ 11
  26 c, 26 c, 26 c, 26 c,     \ 12
  26 c, 26 c, 26 c, 26 c,     \ 13
  28 c,  0 c,  0 c,  0 c,     \ 14
   0 c, 28 c,  0 c,  0 c,     \ 15
   0 c,  0 c, 28 c,  0 c,     \ 16
```

Code Example 8-2   Extended hierarchical device driver sample

```
\ extended hierarchical device driver sample
   0 c,   0 c,   0 c,  28 c,       \ 17
  28 c,  28 c,  28 c,  28 c,       \ 18
  28 c,  28 c,  28 c,  28 c,       \ 19
  28 c,  28 c,  28 c,  28 c,       \ 1a
  28 c,  28 c,  28 c,  28 c,       \ 1b
   0 c,   0 c,   0 c,   0 c,       \ 1c
   0 c,   0 c,   0 c,   0 c,       \ 1d
   0 c,   0 c,   0 c,   0 c,       \ 1e
   0 c,   0 c,   0 c,   0 c,       \ 1f
hex

20 constant /slot-sizes-array
-1 value slot-config

: >slot-size  ( slot# -- size )
   slot-sizes-array  slot-config 1a+  swap ca+ c@  1 swap <<
   1 not and         \ Could have slot size of 0.
;

\ This array is to be filled with offsets for each slot.
\ Eg. 0, 100.0000, 180.0000, 200.0000
create host-offsets  0 , 0 , 0 , 0 ,

: >host-offset  ( child-slot# -- adr )  host-offsets swap na+ @  ;

create config-d-offsets  h# 100.0000 , 0            ,  h# 180.0000 ,  0 ,
create config-e-offsets  h# 100.0000 , h# 180.0000 ,  0            ,  0 ,

: set-host-offsets  ( -- )
   slot-config  case
      h# d of  config-d-offsets host-offsets 4 /n* move  exit  endof
      h# e of  config-e-offsets host-offsets 4 /n* move  exit  endof
   endcase
   0                                 ( initial-offset )
   4 0  do                           ( offset )
      dup host-offsets i na+ !       ( offset )
      i >slot-size +                 ( offset' )
   loop                              ( final-offset )
   drop
;

: set-configuration  ( config-code -- )
   is slot-config
   set-host-offsets
```

Code Example 8-2   Extended hierarchical device driver sample

```
\ extended hierarchical device driver sample
   slot-config 3 <<  my-key 8 << or
   dup write-xac-ctl0                   \ set XAC
       write-xbc-ctl0                   \ set XBC
   slot-config xdrint  " uadm" attribute    \ publish slot configuration
;

end0
```

Complete Hierarchical Device Driver

The complete driver includes all the required device node methods. It also includes code
to initalize the hardware at system reset. In particular, it configures the allocation of
address space across slots. It does this by either performing an autoconfiguration or by
accepting a manual override via a property in its parent. During the configuration
process, the driver interprets the FCode of any SBus card plugged into the XBox. This
results in devices being added to the device tree.

Code Example 8-3   Complete hierarchical device driver sample

```
\ complete hierarchical device driver sample
hex
fcode-version2

" SUNW,xbox"  name
" 501-1840"   model
" sbus"       device-type

\ XBox Registers

h#       0 constant write0-offset    h# 4 constant /write0
h#  2.0000 constant xac-err-offset    h# c constant /xac-err
h# 10.0000 constant xac-ctl0-offset   h# 4 constant /xac-ctl0
h# 11.0000 constant xac-ctl1-offset   h# 4 constant /xac-ctl1
h# 12.0000 constant xac-elua-offset   h# 4 constant /xac-elua
h# 13.0000 constant xac-ella-offset   h# 4 constant /xac-ella
h# 14.0000 constant xac-ele-offset    h# 4 constant /xac-ele

h# 42.0000 constant xbc-err-offset    h# c constant /xbc-err
h# 50.0000 constant xbc-ctl0-offset   h# 4 constant /xbc-ctl0
h# 51.0000 constant xbc-ctl1-offset   h# 4 constant /xbc-ctl1
h# 52.0000 constant xbc-elua-offset   h# 4 constant /xbc-elua
h# 53.0000 constant xbc-ella-offset   h# 4 constant /xbc-ella
h# 54.0000 constant xbc-ele-offset    h# 4 constant /xbc-ele
```

Code Example 8-3   Complete hierarchical device driver sample

```
\ complete hierarchical device driver sample

: >reg-spec ( offset size -- xdrreg )
   >r my-address + my-space xdrphys r> xdrint xdr+
;

write0-offset    /write0    >reg-spec
xac-err-offset   /xac-err   >reg-spec   xdr+
xac-ctl0-offset  /xac-ctl0  >reg-spec   xdr+
xac-ctl1-offset  /xac-ctl1  >reg-spec   xdr+
xac-elua-offset  /xac-elua  >reg-spec   xdr+
xac-ella-offset  /xac-ella  >reg-spec   xdr+
xac-ele-offset   /xac-ele   >reg-spec   xdr+
xbc-err-offset   /xbc-err   >reg-spec   xdr+
xbc-ctl0-offset  /xbc-ctl0  >reg-spec   xdr+
xbc-ctl1-offset  /xbc-ctl1  >reg-spec   xdr+
xbc-elua-offset  /xbc-elua  >reg-spec   xdr+
xbc-ella-offset  /xbc-ella  >reg-spec   xdr+
xbc-ele-offset   /xbc-ele   >reg-spec   xdr+
" reg" attribute

\ Xbox can interrupt on any SBus level

1 xdrint       2 xdrint xdr+  3 xdrint xdr+  4 xdrint xdr+
5 xdrint xdr+  6 xdrint xdr+  7 xdrint xdr+
" interrupts"  attribute

1 sbus-intr>cpu xdrint       0 xdrint xdr+
2 sbus-intr>cpu xdrint xdr+  0 xdrint xdr+
3 sbus-intr>cpu xdrint xdr+  0 xdrint xdr+
4 sbus-intr>cpu xdrint xdr+  0 xdrint xdr+
5 sbus-intr>cpu xdrint xdr+  0 xdrint xdr+
6 sbus-intr>cpu xdrint xdr+  0 xdrint xdr+
7 sbus-intr>cpu xdrint xdr+  0 xdrint xdr+
" intr" attribute

\ XBox bus clock speed
d# 25.000.000 xdrint  " clock-frequency"  attribute

\ Burst sizes 64,32,16,8,4,2,1 bursts.
h# 7f xdrint  " burst-sizes"  attribute

\ XBox has no slave-only slots
0 xdrint  " slave-only" attribute
```

Code Example 8-3   Complete hierarchical device driver sample

```
\ complete hierarchical device driver sample
\ Get the number of address bits for this SBus slot from the parent SBus
\ node without inheritance .  OpenBoot 2.5 doesn't publish slot-address-
bits.
\ However 2.5 is only on 4m machines, which are all 28 bits per slot.

: $=  ( addr1 len1 addr2 len2 -- equal? )           \ string compare
   rot over -  if
      drop 2drop  false                             \ different lengths
   else  comp 0=
   then
;
: 4mhack  ( -- n )
   " compatible" get-inherited-attribute  if
      d# 25                                  \ no "compatible" prop; assume 4c
   else  xdrtostring  " sun4m" $=  if
         d# 28
      else
         d# 25                                       \ not sun4m
      then
      nip nip
   then
;
: #bits  ( -- n )
   " slot-address-bits"  my-parent ihandle>phandle
   get-package-attribute  if
      4mhack
   else
      xdrtoint  nip nip
   then
;
#bits constant  host-slot-size
host-slot-size xdrint  " slot-address-bits" attribute

\ Utility display string
: .me  ( -- )  ." SBus "  my-space .d  ." XBox "  ;


\ The XBox device has two modes opaque and transparent.

\ Upon reset the device is set to opaque mode.  In this mode all
\ accesses to address space of the device are directed to the XBox H/W
\ (ie. XAdaptor Card or the XBox Expansion Box) itself.

\ In the transparent mode all accesses are mapped to the SBus cards
```

Code Example 8-3   Complete hierarchical device driver sample

```
\ complete hierarchical device driver sample
\ which are plugged into the XBox.  In transparent mode the XBox H/W is
\ accessible only via the "write-0" register. To allow another bus
\ bridge to be plugged into the XBox all writes to the write-0 register
\ must contain a "key" which is programmed into the XBox H/W at boot
\ time. If the key field of a write to write-0 matches that programmed
\ at boot time the H/W intercepts the write.  Otherwise the H/W passes
\ the write along.

\ The XBox has two sets of registers. Those of the XAdaptor card and
\ and those of the XBox Expansion Box.

\ Opaque mode host adapter registers
-1  value xac-err-regs
-1  value xac-ctl0     -1  value xac-ctl1
-1  value xac-elua     -1  value xac-ella
-1  value xac-ele
\ Opaque mode expansion box registers
-1  value xbc-err-regs
-1  value xbc-ctl0     -1  value xbc-ctl1
-1  value xbc-elua     -1  value xbc-ella
-1  value xbc-ele
\ Transparent mode register
-1  value write0-reg

: xbox-map-in  ( offset space size -- virt ) " map-in"  $call-parent ;
: xbox-map-out ( virt size -- )               " map-out" $call-parent ;
: map-regs  ( -- )
   write0-offset   my-address + my-space /write0   xbox-map-in  is write0-
reg
    xac-err-offset  my-address + my-space /xac-err  xbox-map-in  is xac-
err-regs
   xac-ctl0-offset my-address + my-space /xac-ctl0 xbox-map-in is xac-ctl0
   xac-ctl1-offset my-address + my-space /xac-ctl1 xbox-map-in is xac-ctl1
   xac-elua-offset my-address + my-space /xac-elua xbox-map-in is xac-elua
   xac-ella-offset my-address + my-space /xac-ella xbox-map-in is xac-ella
   xac-ele-offset  my-address + my-space /xac-ele  xbox-map-in  is xac-ele
    xbc-err-offset  my-address + my-space /xbc-err  xbox-map-in  is xbc-
err-regs
   xbc-ctl0-offset my-address + my-space /xbc-ctl0 xbox-map-in is xbc-ctl0
   xbc-ctl1-offset my-address + my-space /xbc-ctl1 xbox-map-in is xbc-ctl1
   xbc-elua-offset my-address + my-space /xbc-elua xbox-map-in is xbc-elua
   xbc-ella-offset my-address + my-space /xbc-ella xbox-map-in is xbc-ella
   xbc-ele-offset  my-address + my-space /xbc-ele  xbox-map-in  is xbc-ele
 ;
```

Code Example 8-3   Complete hierarchical device driver sample

```
\ complete hierarchical device driver sample
: unmap-regs  ( -- )
   write0-reg   /write0    xbox-map-out    -1 is write0-reg
   xac-err-regs /xac-err   xbox-map-out    -1 is xac-err-regs
   xac-ctl0     /xac-ctl0  xbox-map-out    -1 is xac-ctl0
   xac-ctl1     /xac-ctl1  xbox-map-out    -1 is xac-ctl1
   xac-elua     /xac-elua  xbox-map-out    -1 is xac-elua
   xac-ella     /xac-ella  xbox-map-out    -1 is xac-ella
   xac-ele      /xac-ele   xbox-map-out    -1 is xac-ele
   xbc-err-regs /xbc-err   xbox-map-out    -1 is xbc-err-regs
   xbc-ctl0     /xbc-ctl0  xbox-map-out    -1 is xbc-ctl0
   xbc-ctl1     /xbc-ctl1  xbox-map-out    -1 is xbc-ctl1
   xbc-elua     /xbc-elua  xbox-map-out    -1 is xbc-elua
   xbc-ella     /xbc-ella  xbox-map-out    -1 is xbc-ella
   xbc-ele      /xbc-ele   xbox-map-out    -1 is xbc-ele
;

\ Opaque mode register access words

: xac-errd@  ( -- l )  xac-err-regs      rl@  ;
: xac-erra@  ( -- l )  xac-err-regs 4 + rl@  ;
: xac-errs@  ( -- l )  xac-err-regs 8 + rl@  ;
: xac-ctl0@  ( -- w )  xac-ctl0 rl@  ;
: xac-ctl0!  ( w -- )  xac-ctl0 rl!  ;
: xac-ctl1@  ( -- w )  xac-ctl1 rl@  ;
: xac-ctl1!  ( w -- )  xac-ctl1 rl!  ;
: xac-elua@  ( -- l )  xac-elua rl@  ;
: xac-elua!  ( l -- )  xac-elua rl!  ;
: xac-ella@  ( -- w )  xac-ella rl@  ;
: xac-ella!  ( w -- )  xac-ella rl!  ;

: xbc-errd@  ( -- l )  xbc-err-regs rl@  ;
: xbc-erra@  ( -- l )  xbc-err-regs 4 + rl@  ;
: xbc-errs@  ( -- l )  xbc-err-regs 8 + rl@  ;
: xbc-ctl0@  ( -- w )  xbc-ctl0 rl@  ;
: xbc-ctl0!  ( w -- )  xbc-ctl0 rl!  ;
: xbc-ctl1@  ( -- w )  xbc-ctl1 rl@  ;
: xbc-ctl1!  ( w -- )  xbc-ctl1 rl!  ;
: xbc-elua@  ( -- l )  xbc-elua rl@  ;
: xbc-elua!  ( l -- )  xbc-elua rl!  ;
: xbc-ella@  ( -- w )  xbc-ella rl@  ;
: xbc-ella!  ( w -- )  xbc-ella rl!  ;

\ Transparent Mode register access words
```

Code Example 8-3   Complete hierarchical device driver sample

```
\ complete hierarchical device driver sample
external
: unique-key  ( -- n )  " unique-key" $call-parent  ;
headers
unique-key constant my-key
my-key xdrint  " write0-key" attribute

: xbox!  ( w offset -- )  my-key h# 18 << or or   write0-reg rl!  ;

: write-xac-ctl0  ( w -- )  xac-ctl0-offset xbox! ;
: write-xac-ctl1  ( w -- )  xac-ctl1-offset xbox! ;
: write-xbc-ctl0  ( w -- )  xbc-ctl0-offset xbox! ;
: write-xbc-ctl1  ( w -- )  xbc-ctl1-offset xbox! ;

\ Some functionally oriented words

: set-key         ( -- )  my-key 8 <<  xac-ctl0!  ;
: transparent     ( -- )            1 xac-ctl1!  ;
: opaque          ( -- )          0 write-xac-ctl1  ;
: enable-slaves  ( -- )     h# 38 write-xbc-ctl1  ;

: xbox-errors  ( -- xbc-err xac-err )
   opaque  xbc-errd@ xac-errd@  transparent
;

: ?.errors  ( xbc-err xac-err -- )
   dup h# 8000.0000 and  if
     cr .me  ." xac-error " .h cr
   else  drop
   then
   dup h# 8000.0000 and  if
     cr .me  ." xbc-error " .h cr
   else drop
   then
;

\ The address space of the XBox in transparent mode may be dynamically
\ allocated across its plug-in slots.  This is called the
\ upper-address-decode-map (uadm).  Below is a table which relates the
\ slot configuration code which is programmed in hardware to the
\ allocation of address space for each slot.  The number in each cell is
\ the number of address bits needed for the slot.

decimal
create slot-sizes-array
```

Code Example 8-3   Complete hierarchical device driver sample

```
\ complete hierarchical device driver sample
\ slot0 slot1 slot2 slot3    slot-config
  23 c, 23 c, 23 c, 23 c,     \ 00
  23 c, 23 c, 23 c, 23 c,     \ 01
  23 c, 23 c, 23 c, 23 c,     \ 02
  23 c, 23 c, 23 c, 23 c,     \ 03
  25 c,  0 c,  0 c,  0 c,     \ 04
   0 c, 25 c,  0 c,  0 c,     \ 05
   0 c,  0 c, 25 c,  0 c,     \ 06
   0 c,  0 c,  0 c, 25 c,     \ 07
  24 c, 24 c,  0 c,  0 c,     \ 08
  24 c,  0 c, 24 c,  0 c,     \ 09
   0 c, 24 c, 24 c,  0 c,     \ 0a
   0 c,  0 c,  0 c,  0 c,     \ 0b
  24 c, 23 c, 23 c,  0 c,     \ 0c
  23 c, 24 c, 23 c,  0 c,     \ 0d  \ Overridden in code
  23 c, 23 c, 24 c,  0 c,     \ 0e  \ Overridden in code
  25 c,  0 c,  0 c,  0 c,     \ 0f
  26 c, 26 c, 26 c, 26 c,     \ 10
  26 c, 26 c, 26 c, 26 c,     \ 11
  26 c, 26 c, 26 c, 26 c,     \ 12
  26 c, 26 c, 26 c, 26 c,     \ 13
  28 c,  0 c,  0 c,  0 c,     \ 14
   0 c, 28 c,  0 c,  0 c,     \ 15
   0 c,  0 c, 28 c,  0 c,     \ 16
   0 c,  0 c,  0 c, 28 c,     \ 17
  28 c, 28 c, 28 c, 28 c,     \ 18
  28 c, 28 c, 28 c, 28 c,     \ 19
  28 c, 28 c, 28 c, 28 c,     \ 1a
  28 c, 28 c, 28 c, 28 c,     \ 1b
   0 c,  0 c,  0 c,  0 c,     \ 1c
   0 c,  0 c,  0 c,  0 c,     \ 1d
   0 c,  0 c,  0 c,  0 c,     \ 1e
   0 c,  0 c,  0 c,  0 c,     \ 1f
hex

20 constant /slot-sizes-array
-1 value slot-config

: >slot-size  ( slot# -- size )
   slot-sizes-array  slot-config 1a+  swap ca+ c@  1 swap <<
   1 not and         \ Could have slot size of 0.
;

\ This array is to be filled with offsets for each slot.
```

Code Example 8-3   Complete hierarchical device driver sample

```
\ complete hierarchical device driver sample
\ Eg. 0, 100.0000, 180.0000, 200.0000
create host-offsets  0 , 0 , 0 , 0 ,

: >host-offset  ( child-slot# -- adr )  host-offsets swap na+ @  ;

create config-d-offsets  h# 100.0000 , 0          , h# 180.0000 ,  0 ,
create config-e-offsets  h# 100.0000 , h# 180.0000 ,  0          ,  0 ,

: set-host-offsets  ( -- )
  slot-config  case
    h# d of  config-d-offsets host-offsets 4 /n* move  exit  endof
    h# e of  config-e-offsets host-offsets 4 /n* move  exit  endof
  endcase
  0                             ( initial-offset )
  4 0  do                       ( offset )
    dup host-offsets i na+ !    ( offset )
    i >slot-size +              ( offset' )
  loop                          ( final-offset )
  drop
;

: set-configuration  ( config-code -- )
  is slot-config
  set-host-offsets
  slot-config 3 <<  my-key 8 << or
  dup write-xac-ctl0                   \ set XAC
      write-xbc-ctl0                   \ set XBC
  slot-config xdrint  " uadm" attribute    \ publish slot configuration
;

\ Required package methods

external

: dma-alloc   ( #bytes -- )                     " dma-alloc" $call-parent  ;
: dma-free    ( #bytes -- )                      " dma-free" $call-parent  ;
: dma-map-in ( vaddr #bytes cache? -- devaddr ) " dma-map-in" $call-parent
;
: dma-map-out ( vaddr devaddr #bytes -- )        " dma-map-out" $call-
parent  ;
: dma-sync    ( virt devaddr #bytes -- )        " dma-sync" $call-parent  ;

: map-in  ( offset slot# size -- virtual )
    >r                            ( offset xbox-slot# )
```

Code Example 8-3   Complete hierarchical device driver sample

```
\ complete hierarchical device driver sample
  >host-offset +  my-space        ( parent-offset parent-slot# )
  r>  " map-in" $call-parent      ( virtual )
;


: map-out  ( virt size -- )  " map-out" $call-parent  ;

: decode-unit    ( adr len -- address space )
  decode-2int                                       ( offset slot# )
  dup 0 3 between 0=  if
     ." Invalid XBox slot number " .d cr
     1 abort
  then                                              ( offset slot# )
;


\ Hack because set-args and byte-load are not FCodes
: byte-load ( adr len -- )             " byte-load" $find drop execute  ;
: set-args  ( adr len adr len -- )    " set-args"  $find drop execute  ;

: probe-self  ( arg-adr arg-len reg-adr reg-len fcode-adr fcode-len -- )

   ['] decode-unit catch  if
      2drop 2drop 2drop 2drop
      exit
   then                                   ( arg-str reg-str fcode-offs,space )

   h# 10000 map-in                             ( arg-str reg-str fcode-vaddr )

   dup cpeek  if                      ( arg-str reg-str fcode-vaddr byte )
      dup h# f0 =  swap h# fd =  or  if    ( arg-str reg-str fcode-vaddr )
         new-device                        ( arg-str reg-str fcode-vaddr )
            >r  set-args r>                 ( fcode-vaddr )
            dup 1 byte-load                 ( fcode-vaddr )
         finish-device
      else                                  ( arg-str reg-str fcode-vaddr )
         nip nip nip nip                    ( fcode-vaddr )
         ." Invalid FCode start byte in " .me cr
      then                                  ( fcode-vaddr )
   else                                     ( arg-str reg-str fcode-vaddr )
      nip nip nip nip                       ( fcode-vaddr )
   then

   h# 10000 map-out
;
```

Code Example 8-3   Complete hierarchical device driver sample

```
\ complete hierarchical device driver sample
: open  ( -- ok? )  true ;
: close  ( -- ) ;

headers

\ The XBox slot configuration may be forced by the user. The mechanism
\ for doing this is a string which specifies megs/slot (eg. "16,8,8,0").

\ This string is processed into the config bits array.  Then the
\ slot-sizes-array is searched for a configuration which matches or
\ exceeds the requested number for each slot.  If the request is
\ unreasonable the default-slot-config is used.
\ Then the configuration is set in the XBox hardware.
\ Finally each slot is probed based on the config.

: default-slot-config  ( -- n )
   host-slot-size  d# 25 = if
      h# c                   \ 1x24 bits, 2x23 bits
   else  h# 10               \ 4x26 bits
   then
;

\ This array to be filled with bit sizes for each slot.
\ Eg. 24, 23, 23, 0
create config-bits  0 c, 0 c, 0 c, 0 c,

: config-ok?  ( config -- ok? )
   true
   slot-sizes-array rot 4 * ca+     ( ok? slot-adr )
   4 0 do
      config-bits i ca+  c@
      over i ca+  c@                ( ok? slot-adr conf-bits slot-bits )
      > if
         nip false swap  leave
      then
   loop
   drop
;

: fit-config  ( -- config )
   default-slot-config
   /slot-sizes-array  0 do
      i config-ok? if
         drop i leave
```

Code Example 8-3   Complete hierarchical device driver sample

```
\ complete hierarchical device driver sample
      then
   loop
;

: megs>bits  ( megs -- bits )      \ Convert requested megs to # of address
bits
   ?dup       0= if           0  exit  then
   dup        9 < if  drop d# 23  exit  then
   dup d#  17 < if  drop d# 24  exit  then
   dup d#  33 < if  drop d# 25  exit  then
   dup d#  65 < if  drop d# 26  exit  then
   dup d# 129 < if  drop d# 27  exit  then
      d# 257 < if        d# 28  exit  then
   d# 29                           \ d#29 is too many bits => error
;

: request-megs  ( adr len -- )      \ Fill config-bits table
   base @ >r  decimal
   4 0 do
      ascii , left-parse-string
      $number  0= if
         megs>bits  config-bits i ca+ c!
      then
   loop
   2drop
   r> base !
;

: find-config  ( adr len -- config )
   request-megs  fit-config
;

create slot-string  ascii # c, ascii , c,  ascii 0 c,

: probe-slot  ( slot# -- )
   dup >slot-size 0=  if  drop exit  then  ( slot# )
   ascii 0 +  slot-string c!
   " " slot-string 3                 ( arg-str reg-str )
   2dup                              ( arg-str reg-str fcode-str )
   probe-self
;

: probe-children  ( -- )
   4 0  do
```

Code Example 8-3   Complete hierarchical device driver sample

```
\ complete hierarchical device driver sample
      config-bits i ca+ c@  if
          i probe-slot
      then
   loop
;

: forced-configuration  ( adr len  -- )
   find-config           ( config-code )
   set-configuration
   probe-children
;



\ The Xbox slot configuration may be autoconfigured by the driver.  The
\ autoconfiguration mechanism uses the following state transition table.
\ The table basically loops through each XBox slot with a current guess
\ at the slot config.  With each slot the code then probes the slot's
\ FCode and uses the reg property information of the slot's new device
\ node to determine the amount of address space required by the slot.
\ The slot config guess is updated and a state transition is made.

\ This is the state transition table.  Each entry in the table consists
\ of 16 bits.  The most significant 8 bits is the XBox configuration
\ code for the next state, and the least 8 bits is the next state.

create states
\ Empty       min       mid
\ Empty       23        24          for 25 bit host SBus slot
   0501 w,   0d04 w,   0803 w,   \ 0                              testing slot 0
   0602 w,   0a05 w,   0a0f w,   \ 1  Slot 0 empty,              testing slot 1
   0706 w,   000f w,   060e w,   \ 2  Slots 0,1 empty,           testing slot 2
   090f w,   0c0f w,   080e w,   \ 3  Slot 0 is 24 bit,          testing slot 1
   0e05 w,   0e05 w,   0d0f w,   \ 4  Slot 0 23 bit,             testing slot 1
   000f w,   000f w,   0e0e w,   \ 5  Slot 0 empty and Slot1 23 bit,
                                 \ or Slot 0,1 are 23 bit        testing slot 2
   0c0e w,   070e w,   070e w,   \ 6  Slots 0,1,2 empty,         testing slot 3
\ Empty       notused   26          for 28 bit host SBus slot
   1508 w,   100e w,   100b w,   \ 7                             testing slot 0
   1609 w,   100e w,   100c w,   \ 8  Slot  0 empty,             testing slot 1
   170a w,   100e w,   100d w,   \ 9  Slots 0,1 empty,           testing slot 2
   100e w,   100e w,   170e w,   \ a  Slots 0,1,2 empty,         testing slot 3
   100c w,   100e w,   100c w,   \ b  Slot 0 is 26 bit,          testing slot 1
   100d w,   100e w,   100d w,   \ c  Slots 0,1 are 26 bit,      testing slot 2
   100e w,   100e w,   100e w,   \ d  Slots 0,1,2 are 26 bit,testing slot 3
```

Code Example 8-3   Complete hierarchical device driver sample

```
\ complete hierarchical device driver sample
                              \ e
                              \ f
0           value slot#
0           value start-state        \ for auto-config state machine
4           value start-config
h# 100.0000 value max-card           \ 25 bit default
h# 080.0000 value mid-card           \ 25 bit default


: configure25  ( -- )                \ 25 bit host SBus slots
   0           is start-state
   4           is start-config
   h# 100.0000 is max-card           \ 25 bits for one Xbox slot
   h# 080.0000 is mid-card           \ 24 bits per XBox slot
;
: configure28  ( -- )                \ 28 bit host SBus slots
   7           is start-state
   h# 14       is start-config
   h# 800.0000 is max-card           \ 28 bits for one XBox slot
   h# 0        is mid-card           \ 26 bits per Xbox slot
;

0 value child-node

\ Since child and peer do not appear until 2.3,
\ we include the following workarounds.
: next-peer  ( phandle -- phandle' )
   fcode-version 2.0003 >=  if
      peer
   else
      " romvec" $find drop execute    1c + @   0 + @
      " call"   $find drop execute    nip
   then
;
: first-child  ( phandle -- phandle' )
   fcode-version 2.0003 >=  if
      child
   else
      " romvec" $find drop execute    1c + @   4 + @
      " call"   $find drop execute    nip
   then
;

0 value extent                \ 1 if card exists, but no reg prop or 0 reg
```

Code Example 8-3   Complete hierarchical device driver sample

```
\ complete hierarchical device driver sample

: bump-extent  ( n -- )   extent max  is extent ;

: max-reg-extent  ( adr len -- )
   begin  dup  while
      xdrtoint drop xdrtoint >r   xdrtoint r> +   ( adr' len' extent)
      bump-extent
   repeat
   2drop
   extent 0=  if           \ reg prop is 0 -- fake it
      1 bump-extent
   then
;

: find-extent  ( -- )
   0 is extent
   begin
      child-node  if
         child-node next-peer
      else
         my-self ihandle>phandle first-child
      then                    ( next-child )
   ?dup while
      is child-node
      " reg" child-node get-package-attribute  0=  if  ( adr len )
         max-reg-extent
      else                 \ card has no reg prop -- fake it
         1 bump-extent
      then
   repeat
;

: evaluate-size  ( -- size-code )
   find-extent
   extent  slot# >slot-size >  if
      ." The card in slot "  slot# .
      ." of "  .me
      ." uses too much address space." cr
      abort
   then
   extent                                 ( max-extent )
   dup max-card > if  drop 3  exit  then  ( max-extent )  \ max-size card
   dup mid-card > if  drop 2  exit  then  ( max-extent )  \ mid-size card?
            0 > if     1  exit  then  ( )            \ 25-small card?
```

Code Example 8-3   Complete hierarchical device driver sample

```
\ complete hierarchical device driver sample
    0                                              \ null for 28
;

: test-slot  ( xbox-config -- size-code )
    set-configuration    ( )
    slot# probe-slot     ( )
    evaluate-size        ( size-code )
;

: autoconfigure  ( -- )
    0  is child-node
    -1 is slot#

    host-slot-size d# 25 =  if  configure25   else  configure28   then

    start-state  start-config                  ( state# xbox-config )
    begin                                      ( state# xbox-config )
        slot# 1+ is slot#  test-slot           ( state# size-code )
        dup 3 =      if  2drop  exit  then     ( state# size-code )
        over h# f =  if  2drop  exit  then     ( state# size-code )
        states  rot 3 * wa+  swap wa+  w@ wbsplit ( state#' xbox-config' )
    over h# e =  until                         ( state#' xbox-config' )

    2drop
;

\ Initialize the XBox H/W.  If the XAdaptor H/W detects that XBox
\ Expansion H/W is connected and powered-up it puts the H/W into
\ transparent mode and sets the XBox slot configuraton based on either a
\ forced configruation or the autoconfiguration algorithm.

: configuration  ( -- )
    " xbox-slot-config" get-inherited-attribute  0=  if
        xdrtostring     ( adr len adr len )
        find-config forced-configuration
        2drop
    else
        2drop
        autoconfigure
    then
;

: null-xdr  ( -- adr len )
    fcode-version 2.0001 >=  if
```

Code Example 8-3   Complete hierarchical device driver sample

```
\ complete hierarchical device driver sample
     0 0 xdrbytes
   else
     here 0
   then
;

: make-ranges  ( -- )
   null-xdr                                      ( adr len )
   4 0  do
     i >slot-size  if                           ( adr len )
     0                 i         xdrphys xdr+    ( adr len )
     i >host-offset  my-space  xdrphys xdr+    ( adr len )
        i >slot-size            xdrint  xdr+    ( adr len )
     then
   loop
   " ranges" attribute
;

\ Because we go transparent in the middle and therefore the fcode prom
\ disappears the following must be in a definition.

: init-pkg  ( -- )
   map-regs
   set-key                     \ opaque already
   xac-errs@ h# 40 and  if  \ Child ready?
     transparent              \ Go transparent, then enable-slaves
     enable-slaves
     configuration
     make-ranges
     xbox-errors
     ?.errors
     " true"
   else
     cr .me
     ." child not ready --"  cr
     ." perhaps the cable is not plugged in"  cr
     ." or the expansion box is not turned on."  cr
     " false"
   then                            ( adr len )
   xdrstring  " child-present"  attribute
   unmap-regs
   ['] end0 execute
;
```

Code Example 8-3   Complete hierarchical device driver sample

```
\ complete hierarchical device driver sample
init-pkg

end0
```

Network Devices 9

Network devices are packet-oriented devices capable of sending and receiving packets addressed according to IEEE 802.2 (Ethernet). OpenBoot firmware typically uses network devices for diskless booting. The standard obp-tftp *support package assists in the implementation of the* load *method for this device type.*

This chapter describes how to implement network device drivers. First, the developer of a network driver needs to cooperate with the developers of OS driver to agree on the structure of the device tree, based on the functionalities of the drivers. Then they need to define all necessary properties used by OS or OpenBoot firmware.

Normally the network device driver could have a one level tree or a two level tree. While it is unlikely it will have more than two level tree, if necessary, the user can create more than a two level tree by applying new-device *and* finish-device.

A one level tree could have several nodes, depending on how many net channels the SBus card can support, each node corresponds to one net channel.

For a two level tree, it could have one "control" node on the top level, one or more nodes at the bottom level, depending on the number of net channels it supports. The simplest driver is to support has only one net channel and will only create one node, all properties and all methods being under this node.

This chapter shows three sample network device drivers for the Quad Ethernet device card. The structure of the device tree for the examples is as follows:

Each QED SBus card defines two levels:

- *one* qec *device node*
- *four* qe *device nodes*

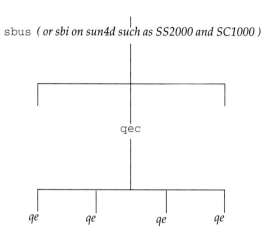

sbus (or sbi on sun4d such as SS2000 and SC1000)

Figure 9-1   QED Device Tree

The general pathname (after sbus *or* sbi*) for a* qe *node is*

```
qec@S,20000/qe@C,0
```

where S *is the SBus slot number,* C *is the network channel number.*

Required Methods

The network device FCode must declare the network device-type, and must implement
the methods open and close, as well as the following methods:

load

(adr -- len)

Read the default stand-alone program into memory starting at adr using the default
network booting protocol. len is the size in bytes of the program read in.

read

(adr len -- actual)

Receive a network packet, placing at most the first `len` bytes in memory at `adr`. Return the `actual` number of bytes received (not the number copied), or 0 if no packet is currently available. Packets with hardware-detected errors are discarded as though they were not received. Do not wait for a packet (non-blocking).

write

`( adr len -- actual )`

Transmit the network packet of size `len` bytes starting at memory address `adr`. Return the number of bytes actually transmitted. The packet must be complete with all addressing information, including source hardware address.

Required Device Properties

The required properties for a network device are

Table 9-1   Required Network Device Properties

Name	Typical Value
name	"SUNW,my-net" *{any name chosen by the manufacturer}*
reg	list of registers *{depends on the device}*
device_type	"network"
mac-address	8 0 0x20 0x0c 0xea 0x41 *{the currently using MAC address.}*

Optional Device Properties

Several other properties may be declared for network devices:

Table 9-2   Optional Network Device Properties

Property Name	Typical Property Value
max-frame-size	0x4000
address-bits	48
slave-burst-sizes	0x7f *{depends on the number of entries in the reg property}*
local-mac-address	8 0 0x20 0x0c 0xea 0x41 *{the built-in Media Access Control addr.}*

Device Driver Examples

If the network device is not to be bootable, it likely needs only one level tree. The examples below, however, show device drivers for two-level trees.

Simple Network Device Example

At minimum, a network device driver need only provide the desired tree structure and to publish all the necessary properties to identify the devices.

Code Example 9-1   QED Identification PROM Sample

```
\ QED identification PROM
\ qed-idprom.fth

fcode-version1

   fload board.fth
   headers
   : copyright ( -- )
      ." Two-level QED-IDPROM 1.1 " cr
    ." Copyright 1992-1993 Sun Microsystems, Inc.  All Rights Reserved" cr
   ;


   : identify-qed  ( -- )
      create-qec-attributes
      4 0  do
         new-device
         i create-qe-attributes
         finish-device
      loop
   ;
   identify-qed

end0



\ ----------------------------------------------------------------
\ board.fth
\ To define required properties for QED devices.

   headers
   my-address    constant my-sbus-addr
   my-space      constant my-sbus-space
   headerless

\ Define the address map.
\ MED Address Map PA[18:0] (totally 512KB address space).
\  h# 00.0000   constant eprom-pa
\  h# 00.8000   constant /eprom                 \ 32KB used, 64KB total
   h# 01.0000   constant mace-regs-offset
```

Code Example 9-1   QED Identification PROM Sample

```
\ QED identification PROM
  h# 01.0000    constant mace0-base
  h# 01.4000    constant mace1-base
  h# 01.8000    constant mace2-base
  h# 01.c000    constant mace3-base
  h# 00.4000    constant /mace-regs          \ 16KB per channel, 64KB total
  h# 02.0000    constant global-regs-offset
  h# 01.0000    constant /global-regs          \ 64KB total
  h# 03.0000    constant channel-regs-offset
  h# 03.0000    constant channel0-base
  h# 03.4000    constant channel1-base
  h# 03.8000    constant channel2-base
  h# 03.c000    constant channel3-base
  h# 00.4000    constant /channel-regs        \ 16KB per channel, 64KB total
  h# 04.0000    constant locmem-pa
  h# 01.0000    constant /locmem              \ 64KB used, 256KB total

\ Real size of mace/qec-global/qec-channel registers.
  20 constant /qec-mace-regs
  14 constant /qec-global-regs
  34 constant /qec-channel-regs

\ Miscellaneous constant definitions.
  1            constant #channels
  h# 4000      constant max-frame-size        ( d# 1536 for le )
  d# 48        constant address-bits
\ Hardwired SBus interrupt level for MED.
  4  constant sbus-qe-intr

  : xdrreg  ( addr space size -- adr len )  >r xdrphys  r> xdrint  xdr+  ;
  : xdrranges  ( offs bustype  phys offset size -- adr len )
    >r >r >r  xdrphys  r> r> r> xdrreg  xdr+
  ;
  : offset>physical-addr  ( offset -- paddr.lo paddr.hi )
    my-sbus-addr + my-sbus-space
  ;

headers
  : create-qec-attributes  ( -- )
    " qec"        name
    " SUNW,595-3198" xdrstring " model" attribute    \ 595-3198-01
    global-regs-offset offset>physical-addr /global-regs xdrreg
    locmem-pa  offset>physical-addr /locmem xdrreg xdr+
    " reg" attribute
```

Code Example 9-1   QED Identification PROM Sample

```
\ QED identification PROM
    0 0 channel0-base  offset>physical-addr /channel-regs xdrranges
    0 1 channel1-base  offset>physical-addr /channel-regs xdrranges xdr+
    0 2 channel2-base  offset>physical-addr /channel-regs xdrranges xdr+
    0 3 channel3-base  offset>physical-addr /channel-regs xdrranges xdr+
    0 h# 10 mace0-base offset>physical-addr /mace-regs    xdrranges xdr+
    0 h# 11 mace1-base offset>physical-addr /mace-regs    xdrranges xdr+
    0 h# 12 mace2-base offset>physical-addr /mace-regs    xdrranges xdr+
    0 h# 13 mace3-base offset>physical-addr /mace-regs    xdrranges xdr+
    " ranges" attribute

    #channels xdrint " #channels" attribute
  \ One interrupt per qec, not one interrupt per channel.
    sbus-qe-intr  xdrint  " interrupts"  attribute
    sbus-qe-intr 0 intr       \ Create intr property.
 ;
 : create-qe-attributes  ( chan# -- )
    >r
    " qe" xdrstring  " name"   attribute
    r@ xdrint " channel#" attribute
    max-frame-size xdrint " max-frame-size" attribute
    address-bits xdrint " address-bits" attribute
    0 r@ /channel-regs xdrreg
      0 r@ h# 10 + /mace-regs xdrreg xdr+
      " reg" attribute
    r> drop
 ;
```

Sample Driver With Test and Debugging Methods

This version of a network device driver is still non-bootable, but it shows how an intermediate step of driver can be used to debug and test the device during or after development.

The coding techniques shown in this and the following examples are:

- Each qe node has exactly the same set of instance variables as each of the other qe nodes.
- All the qe nodes share the same qe driver source code defined in the first qe node (qe0).

Code Example 9-2   QED test PROM Sample

```
\ QED test PROM.
\ qed-test.fth

fcode-version2
   headers
   fload board.fth
   : copyright ( -- )
      ." QED-TEST 1.1 " cr
     ." Copyright 1992-1993 Sun Microsystems, Inc.  All Rights Reserved" cr
   ;


\
\ ***** The following is the FCode driver for version2 CPU PROMs. *****
\
   \ Tokenizer 2.1 or later has the word 'instance'
   : instance ( -- ) version 20001 >=  if  instance  then  ;

\ Create qec device node.
   create-qec-attributes
   fload qec-test.fth   \ qec test code.

\ Create qe0 device node.
   new-device
      0 create-qe-attributes
     : dma-sync ( virt-addr dev-addr size -- )  " dma-sync" $call-parent  ;

      \ ***** qe0 instance variables *****
      0 instance value mace  \ virtual address of Mace registers base
    0 instance value qecc  \ virtual address of Qec channel registers base
      instance variable my-channel# \ qe channel#
      my-channel# off
      fload qe-test.fth      \ qe test code.

      \ ***** qe0 external methods *****
      external
      : selftest  ( -- fail? )
        qe0-selftest
      ;
      : open  ( -- okay? )
        qe0-open
      ;
      : close  ( -- )
        qe0-close
```

Code Example 9-2   QED test PROM Sample

```
\ QED test PROM.
    ;
    : reset  ( -- )
      qe0-reset
    ;
    headers
  finish-device

\ Create qe1 device node.
  new-device
    1 create-qe-attributes

    \ ***** qe1 instance variables *****
    0 instance value mace   \ virtual address of Mace registers base
  0 instance value qecc  \ virtual address of Qec channel registers base
    instance variable my-channel# \ qe channel#
    my-channel# off

    \ ***** qe1 external methods *****
    external
    : selftest  ( -- fail? )
      qe0-selftest
    ;
    : open  ( -- okay? )
      qe0-open
    ;
    : close  ( -- )
      qe0-close
    ;
    : reset  ( -- )
      qe0-reset
    ;
    headers
  finish-device

\ Create qe2 device node.
  new-device
    2 create-qe-attributes

    \ ***** qe2 instance variables *****
    0 instance value mace   \ virtual address of Mace registers base
  0 instance value qecc  \ virtual address of Qec channel registers base
    instance variable my-channel# \ qe channel#
    my-channel# off
```

Code Example 9-2   QED test PROM Sample

```
\ QED test PROM.
      \ ***** qe2 external methods *****
      external
      : selftest  ( -- fail? )
         qe0-selftest
      ;
      : open  ( -- okay? )
         qe0-open
      ;
      : close  ( -- )
         qe0-close
      ;
      : reset  ( -- )
         qe0-reset
      ;
      headers
   finish-device

\ Create qe3 device node.
   new-device
      3 create-qe-attributes

      \ ***** qe3 instance variables *****
      0 instance value mace   \ virtual address of Mace registers base
    0 instance value qecc  \ virtual address of Qec channel registers base
      instance variable my-channel# \ qe channel#
      my-channel# off

      \ ***** qe3 external methods *****
      external
      : selftest  ( -- fail? )
         qe0-selftest
      ;
      : open  ( -- okay? )
         qe0-open
      ;
      : close  ( -- )
         qe0-close
      ;
      : reset  ( -- )
         qe0-reset
      ;
      headers
   finish-device
```

Code Example 9-2   QED test PROM Sample

```
\ QED test PROM.
end0

\ -------------------------------------------------------------------
\ qec-test.fth
\ Test code for the qec node.

/locmem #channels / value chmem
chmem 2/ value rxbufsize

\ ***** qed utility (from qed-util.fth) *****

: lwrt-rd-cmp ( mask data adr -- success? )
   2dup rl! rl@ rot and =
;
: cwrt-rd-cmp ( mask data adr -- success? )
   2dup rb! rb@ rot and =
;
instance defer wrt-rd-cmp
' lwrt-rd-cmp is wrt-rd-cmp
d# 32 instance value #bits

external
: wlk-test ( mask adr #bits -- success? )
   dup is #bits
   d# 32 =  if  ['] lwrt-rd-cmp  else  ['] cwrt-rd-cmp  then  is wrt-rd-cmp
   true -rot     ( true mask adr )
   #bits 0
   do      ( flag0 mask adr )
      over 1 i << and ?dup  if   ( flag0 mask adr data )
         >r 2dup r> swap wrt-rd-cmp false =     ( flag0 mask adr flag )
         if  rot drop false -rot leave  then
      then
   loop
   2drop
;

headers
instance variable ms-timeout

external
: set-ms-timeout  ( #ms -- ) ms-timeout !  ;
: ms-timeout?  ( -- flag )
   ms-timeout @ dup  if
      1- ms-timeout ! 1 ms false
```

Code Example 9-2   QED test PROM Sample

```
\ QED test PROM.
   else
      drop true
   then
;
headers

\ ***** qec global register (from global.h.fth) *****
\
\ QEC Global register set.
\

\ Virtual addresses of QEC global registers.
\ The actual addresses will be assigned later.
0 instance value qecg

hex
\ global control register (RW)
: qecg-control  ( -- vaddr )  qecg  ;
: qecg-control@ ( -- data )  qecg-control rl@  ;
: qecg-control! ( data -- )  qecg-control rl!  ;

headerless
\ For Global Control Register.
f000.0000 constant gcr-mode     \ Mode mask
4000.0000 constant gcr-mace     \ Mace mode
1 constant gcr-reset    \ Reset bit (0), 1 to enable reset.

headers

\ ***** qec map (from qecmap.fth ) *****

0 instance value locmem-base
false value dma-sync?
0 value dma-sync-adr

: find-dma-sync  ( -- )
   " dma-sync" my-parent ihandle>phandle find-method  if
      true is dma-sync?
      is dma-sync-adr
   then
;
find-dma-sync

external
```

Code Example 9-2   QED test PROM Sample

```
\ QED test PROM.
: decode-unit   ( adr len -- address space )  decode-2int   ;
: map-in ( offset slot# #bytes -- virtual ) " map-in" $call-parent   ;
: map-out   ( adr len -- )  " map-out" $call-parent   ;
: dma-map-in  ( vaddr n cache? -- devaddr ) " dma-map-in" $call-parent   ;
: dma-map-out  ( vaddr devaddr n -- )  " dma-map-out" $call-parent   ;
: dma-alloc ( size -- addr )  " dma-alloc" $call-parent   ;
: dma-free ( addr size -- )  " dma-free" $call-parent   ;

\ Dma-sync could be dummy routine if parent device doesn't support.
\ sun4c Proms may not support it.
: dma-sync   ( virt-adr dev-adr size -- )
   dma-sync?  if
      dma-sync-adr my-parent call-package
   else
      3drop
   then
;

headers

: map-qec-regs   ( -- )
   global-regs-offset my-sbus-addr + my-sbus-space /qec-global-regs
   " map-in" $call-parent is qecg
;
: unmap-qec-regs   ( -- )
   qecg /qec-global-regs " map-out" $call-parent
   0 is qecg
;

: map-locmem   ( -- )
   locmem-pa my-sbus-addr + my-sbus-space /locmem
   " map-in" $call-parent is locmem-base
;
: unmap-locmem   ( -- )
   locmem-base /locmem " map-out" $call-parent
   0 is locmem-base
;


\ ***** qec test (from qectest.fth) *****
hex

headerless
\ 18 constant /qec-global-regs
```

Code Example 9-2   QED test PROM Sample

```
\ QED test PROM.
\ Define the mask bits that can be tested for each global register.
create gl-reg-masks
        0000.001e , 0000.0000 , 0000.0000 , 0001.e000 ,
        0000.f000 , 0000.f000 ,

\ Test Qec global registers.
: gl-reg-test  ( -- success? )
   true
   /qec-global-regs 0  do                      ( flag0 )
      gl-reg-masks i + @
      qecg i + d# 32 wlk-test                  ( flag0 flag )
      false =  if  drop false leave  then      ( flag0 )
   4  +loop
;

\ Perform register test for the qec node.
: qec-reg-test ( -- success? )
   diagnostic-mode?  if
      ."  Qec register test -- "
   then
   gl-reg-test
   diagnostic-mode?  if
      dup  if  ." succeeded."  else  ." failed."  then  cr
   then
;

headers

\ ***** qec package *****

: reset-qec-global  ( -- fail? )
   gcr-reset qecg-control!            \ Issue global reset.
   d# 100 set-ms-timeout
   begin
      qecg-control@ gcr-reset and
   while
      ms-timeout?  if ." Global reset failed" cr true exit then
   repeat
   false
;
: identify-chip  ( -- okay? )
   qecg-control@ gcr-mode and gcr-mace =
;
```

Code Example 9-2   QED test PROM Sample

```
\ QED test PROM.
external
: open  ( -- true )
   map-qec-regs
   identify-chip dup 0=  if
      unmap-qec-regs
   then
;
: close ( -- )
   qecg  if unmap-qec-regs then
;

: selftest ( -- fail? )
   qecg                ( qecg )
   map-qec-regs
   qec-reg-test        ( qecg success? )
   unmap-qec-regs
   swap is qecg        ( success? )
   0=                  ( fail? )
;

: reset  ( -- )
   qecg
   map-qec-regs
   reset-qec-global drop
   unmap-qec-regs
   is qecg
;

headers

\ ----------------------------------------------------------------
\ qe-test.fth
\ Test code for the qe node.

: wlk-test ( mask adr #bits -- success? )  " wlk-test" $call-parent  ;
: set-ms-timeout ( #ms -- )  " set-ms-timeout" $call-parent  ;
: ms-timeout? ( -- flag )  " ms-timeout?" $call-parent  ;

\ ***** qe map (from qemap.fth) *****

headers
\ instance variable my-channel# my-channel# off
: my-channel#! ( channel# -- )  my-channel# !  ;
```

Code Example 9-2   QED test PROM Sample

```
\ QED test PROM.
: my-chan#  ( -- channel# )
   my-channel# @
;
: mace-regs  ( -- devaddr space size )
   my-sbus-addr mace-regs-offset + /mace-regs my-chan# * +
   my-sbus-space /qec-mace-regs
;

: map-mace    ( -- )
   mace-regs " map-in" my-parent $call-method is mace
;
: unmap-mace  ( -- )
   mace /qec-mace-regs " map-out" my-parent $call-method
   0 is mace
;

: channel-regs  ( -- devaddr space size )
   my-sbus-addr channel-regs-offset + /channel-regs my-chan# * +
   my-sbus-space /qec-channel-regs
;

: map-channel    ( -- )
   channel-regs " map-in" my-parent $call-method is qecc
;
: unmap-channel  ( -- )
   qecc /qec-channel-regs " map-out" my-parent $call-method
   0 is qecc
;

: map-chips  ( -- )
   mace 0=  if          \  Do mapping if it is unmapped.
      map-mace
      map-channel
   then
;
: unmap-chips  ( -- )
   mace  if             \ Do unmapping if it is mapped.
      unmap-channel
      unmap-mace
   then
;

\ ***** qe test (from qeregtst.fth) *****
```

Code Example 9-2   QED test PROM Sample

```
\ QED test PROM.
hex

\ Define the mask bits that can be tested for each register.
create ch-reg-masks
        0000.0004 , 0000.0000 , ffff.f800 , ffff.f800 ,
        0000.0001 , 0000.0001 , 001f.001f , 1fc0.3fc0 ,
        0000.fffe , 0000.fffe , 0000.fffe , 0000.fffe ,
        0000.00ff ,
create mace-reg-masks
        00 c, 00 c, 89 c, 00 c, 00 c, 0d c, 00 c, 00 c,
        00 c, 67 c, 00 c, 70 c, f3 c, ef c, 04 c, 5f c,
        00 c, 00 c, 00 c, 00 c, 00 c, 00 c, 00 c, 00 c,
        00 c, 00 c, 00 c, 00 c, 00 c, 00 c, 00 c, 00 c,

\ Test Qec per channel registers.
: ch-reg-test   ( -- flag )
    true
    /qec-channel-regs 0 do                      ( flag0 )
      ch-reg-masks i + @
      qecc i + d# 32 wlk-test                   ( flag0 flag )
      false =  if  drop false leave  then       ( flag0 )
    4 +loop
;
\ Test Mace registers.
: mace-reg-test   ( -- flag )
    true
    /qec-mace-regs 0 do                         ( flag0 )
      mace-reg-masks i + c@
      mace i + 8 wlk-test                        ( flag0 flag )
      false =  if  drop false leave  then       ( flag0 )
    loop
;

\ Perform register test for the qe node.
:  qe-reg-test ( -- success? )
   diagnostic-mode?  if
     ."  Qe register test -- "
   then
   ch-reg-test
   mace-reg-test and
   diagnostic-mode?  if
     dup  if  ." succeeded."  else  ." failed."  then  cr
   then
;
```

Code Example 9-2   QED test PROM Sample

```
\ QED test PROM.

\ ***** qe0 package *****

headerless
\ For MACE BIU Configuration Control (R11). (RW)
01 constant m-swrst                \ software reset
: mace-biucc   ( -- vaddr )  h# 0b mace +  ;
: mace-biucc@   ( -- data )  mace-biucc rb@  ;
: mace-biucc!   ( data -- )  mace-biucc rb!  ;
\ For QEC per channel control reg. (RW)
02 constant c-rst
: qecc-control  ( -- vaddr ) qecc  ;
: qecc-control@           ( -- data ) qecc-control rl@  ;
: qecc-control!           ( data -- ) qecc-control rl!  ;


headers
: set-my-channel#  ( -- )
\ If don't find the channel attribute, use 0.
   " channel#" get-my-attribute  if  0  else  xdrtoint nip nip  then
   my-channel#!
;
\ Reset (or stop) the qec channel.
\      Issue a soft reset to the desired Mace.
\      Then issue a soft reset to the desired channel in QEC.
\ Chip reset algorithm:
\      Set the reset bit then wait until the reset bit cleared.
\ Timeout in 0.1 sec if fail.
\
: channel-reset  ( -- fail? )
   m-swrst mace-biucc!          \ Issue Mace reset.
   d# 100 set-ms-timeout
   begin
      mace-biucc@ m-swrst and
   while
      ms-timeout? if ." Cannot reset Mace" cr true exit then
   repeat
   c-rst qecc-control!          \ Reset QEC channel registers.
   d# 100 set-ms-timeout
   begin
      qecc-control@ c-rst and
   while
      ms-timeout?  if  ." Cannot reset QEC channel" cr true exit  then
   repeat
   false
```

Code Example 9-2   QED test PROM Sample

```
\ QED test PROM.
;

external
: qe0-selftest  ( -- flag )      \ Flag 0 if passes test.
   set-my-channel#
   map-chips
   qe-reg-test             ( success? )
   unmap-chips
   0=                      ( fail? )
;

: qe0-open  ( -- okay? )
   set-my-channel#
   mac-address drop 6 xdrstring  " mac-address" attribute
   true
;
: qe0-close  ( -- )
;
: qe0-reset  ( -- )
   set-my-channel#
   map-chips channel-reset drop unmap-chips
;
headers
```

Bootable Network Device Driver Example

The example below shows a complete version of a bootable network driver. It implements the selftest *method callable by OpenBoot* test *and* test-all *commands and the* watch-net *method callable by OpenBoot* watch-net *and* watch-net-all *commands.*

Code Example 9-3   QED bootable driver sample

```
\ QED bootable driver
\ qed.fth

fcode-version1
   headers
   fload board.fth
   : copyright ( -- )
      ." QED 1.1 " cr
    ." Copyright 1992-1993 Sun Microsystems, Inc.  All Rights Reserved" cr
```

Code Example 9-3   QED bootable driver sample

```
\ QED bootable driver
  ;


\
\ ***** The following is the FCode driver for version2 CPU PROMs. *****
\
  \ Tokenizer 2.1 or later has the word 'instance'
  : instance ( -- ) version 20001 >=  if  instance  then  ;

\ Create qec device node.
  create-qec-attributes
  fload qec.fth               \ qec driver.

\ Create qe0 device node.
  new-device
     0 create-qe-attributes
     " network" device-type
     fload qeinstance.fth      \ qe instance variables.
    : dma-sync  ( virt-addr dev-addr size -- )  " dma-sync" $call-parent  ;
     fload qe.fth              \ qe driver.
     fload qe-package.fth      \ qe external methods.
  finish-device

\ Create qe1 device node.
  new-device
     1 create-qe-attributes
     " network" device-type
     fload qeinstance.fth      \ qe instance variables.
     fload qe-package.fth      \ qe external methods.
  finish-device

\ Create qe2 device node.
  new-device
     2 create-qe-attributes
     " network" device-type
     fload qeinstance.fth      \ qe instance variables.
     fload qe-package.fth      \ qe external methods.
  finish-device

\ Create qe3 device node.
  new-device
     3 create-qe-attributes
     " network" device-type
     fload qeinstance.fth      \ qe instance variables.
     fload qe-package.fth      \ qe external methods.
```

Code Example 9-3   QED bootable driver sample

```
\ QED bootable driver
   finish-device

end0


\ -------------------------------------------------------------
\ qec.fth

/locmem #channels / value chmem
chmem 2/ value rxbufsize

fload qed-util.fth      \ Not included, refer to example 2.
fload global.h.fth      \ Not included.
fload qecmap.fth        \ Not included, refer to example 2.
fload qectest.fth       \ Not included, refer to example 2.

: reset-qec-global  ( -- fail? )
   gcr-reset qecg-control!      \ Issue global reset.
   d# 100 set-ms-timeout
   begin
      qecg-control@ gcr-reset and
   while
      ms-timeout?  if ." Global reset failed" cr true exit then
   repeat
   false
;
: qec-init  ( -- )
   chmem qecg-memsize!
   rxbufsize qecg-rxsize!
   chmem rxbufsize - qecg-txsize!
   gcr-burst16 qecg-control!    \ SBus parity disabled, Rx/Tx equal
priority.
;
: identify-chip  ( -- okay? )
   qecg-control@ gcr-mode and gcr-mace =
;

external
: open  ( -- true )
   map-qec-regs
   identify-chip dup  if
      qec-init
   else unmap-qec-regs
   then
;
```

Code Example 9-3   QED bootable driver sample

```
\ QED bootable driver
: close ( -- )
   qecg  if unmap-qec-regs then
;

: selftest ( -- fail? )
   qecg                   ( qecg )
   map-qec-regs
   qec-reg-test           ( qecg success? )
   unmap-qec-regs
   swap is qecg           ( success? )
   0=                     ( fail? )
;

: reset  ( -- )
   qecg
   map-qec-regs
   reset-qec-global drop
   unmap-qec-regs
   is qecg
;

headers

\ -------------------------------------------------------------
\ qeinstance.fth
\ Define instance words for qe driver.

\ headerless
\ mace.h.fth:
0 instance value mace          \ virtual address of Mace registers base
\ channel.h.fth:
0 instance value qecc          \ virtual address of Qec channel registers
base
\ qemap.fth:
instance variable my-channel#  \ qe channel#
        my-channel# off
\ qecore.fth:
\ CPU base address of tmd, rmd, tbuf, rbuf rings.
0 instance value cpu-dma-base  \ base address of dma memory object viewed
by cpu
0 instance value tmd0          \ transmit message descriptor#0
0 instance value rmd0          \ receive message descriptor#0
0 instance value tbuf0         \ base address of transmit buffer
0 instance value rbuf0         \ base address of receive buffers
```

Code Example 9-3   QED bootable driver sample

```
\ QED bootable driver
\ IO (or dvice) base address of tmd, rmd, tbuf, rbuf rings.
0 instance value io-dma-base    \ base addr of dma memory object viewed by
device
0 instance value io-tmd0            \ transmit message descriptor#0
0 instance value io-rmd0            \ receive message descriptor#0
0 instance value io-tbuf0           \ base address of transmit buffer
0 instance value io-rbuf0           \ base address of receive buffers
\ Required total Dma buffer size for all rings.
0 instance value qe-dma-size    \ Amount of memory mapped
\ *** Define required variables ***
instance variable status            \ Accumulated channel status word.
instance variable restart?          \ Restart? flag on after serious error.
instance variable nextrmd           \ Point to next rmd.
instance variable nexttmd           \ tmd0 nexttmd !, never changes presently
instance variable mode            \ To store loopback control & promiscuous
info.
6 instance buffer: this-en-addr \ Contain ethernet address
instance defer .receive-error
instance defer .error
instance defer .transmit-error
\ timed-receive.fth:
instance variable alarmtime
instance defer handle-broadcast-packet
\ qetest.fth:
instance variable qe-verbose?     \ Flag for displaying diagnostic message.
        qe-verbose? off
instance variable ext-lbt?        \ Flag for execution of external loopback
test.
        ext-lbt? off
\ qe0-package.fth:
6 instance buffer: macbuf          \ Contain mac address.
0 instance value obp-tftp          \ Contain ihandle of TFTP package.
instance variable qe-nbytes        \ Buffer size of higher layer receiver.
instance variable qe-buf           \ Buffer address of higher layer receiver.

headers
\ ---------------------------------------------------------------
\ qe.fth

: wlk-test ( mask adr #bits -- success? )  " wlk-test" $call-parent   ;
: set-ms-timeout  ( #ms -- )  " set-ms-timeout" $call-parent   ;
: ms-timeout?  ( -- flag )  " ms-timeout?" $call-parent   ;

fload mace.h.fth        \ Not included.
```

Code Example 9-3   QED bootable driver sample

```
\ QED bootable driver
fload channel.h.fth      \ Not included.
fload qemap.fth          \ Not included, refer to example 2.
fload qecore.fth
fload timed-receive.fth
fload qeregtest.fth      \ Not included, refer to example 2.
fload qetest.fth
fload qe0-package.fth


\ ----------------------------------------------------------------
\ qe0-package.fth
\ Define the required methods for the network qe driver

set-my-channel#
external
: read  ( buf len -- -2 | actual-len )
   qe0-read
;
: write  ( buf len -- actual-len )
   qe0-write
;
: selftest  ( -- flag ) \ Flag 0 if passes test.
   qe0-selftest
;
: watch-net  ( -- )
   qe0-watch-net
;
: load  ( adr -- len )
   qe0-load
;
: open  ( -- okay? )
   qe0-open
;
: close  ( -- )
   qe0-close
;
: reset  ( -- )
   qe0-reset
;
headers
\ ----------------------------------------------------------------
\ qecore.fth
\ Main core of QEC/MACE per channel Tx/Rx drivers.

\
```

Code Example 9-3   QED bootable driver sample

```
\ QED bootable driver
\ SQEC has the following features:
\       - Supports four independent IEEE 802.3 10BASE-T twisted pair
interfaces.
\       - Supports SBus parity checking.
\       - Supports 32 bit of DVMA addressing.
\       - Automatic rejection/discard of receive/transmit packets
\         when receive/transmit suffers from errors.
\


headerless
\ *** Rx/Tx Ring Descriptor Layout ***

struct ( Rx/Tx Descriptor )
4 field >flags                  \ OWN, SOP, EOP, size/length
4 field >addr                   \ buffer address
( total-length )  constant /md

hex
\ Definition for >flag field.
\ Bit[10:0] - Rx for W is buffer size, Rx for R is byte count, Tx for W is
byte count.
8000.0000       constant own    \ For both Rx & Tx.
4000.0000       constant stp    \ For Tx only.
2000.0000       constant enp    \ For Tx only.
     07ff       constant lenmask
\ Value to write to message descriptor to enable it for use
enp stp or own or       constant ready

\ *** buffer sizes and counts ***

\ Xmit/receive buffer structure.
\ This structure is organized to meet the following requirements:
\       - starts on an QEBURSTSIZE (64) boundary.
\       - qebuf is an even multiple of QEBURSTSIZE.
\       - qebuf is large enough to contain max frame (1518) plus
\               QEBURSTSIZE for alignment adjustments.
\
\ Similar to the 7990 ethernet controller, the QEC and the Software driver
\ communicate via ring descriptors. There are separate Rx & Tx descriptor
\ rings of 256 entries. Unlike 7990 the number of descriptor entries
\ is not programmable (fixed at 256 entries).

decimal
 /md constant /rmd       \ rmd size = 8
```

Code Example 9-3   QED bootable driver sample

```
\ QED bootable driver
 /md constant /tmd      \ tmd size = 8
1792 constant /rbuf     \ 7*256 receive buffer size at least 1518+128=1636
1600 constant /tbuf     \ transmit buffer size
 256 constant #rmds
 256 constant #tmds
\  1 constant #tbufs    \ Just allocate one buffer for transmiter buffer
pool.
  32 constant #rbufs    \ # buffers allocated for receiver buffer pool.

#rmds /rmd *        value /rmds
#tmds /tmd *        value /tmds

headers

: restart?-on  ( -- ) restart? on  ;

\ Conversion between cpu dma address and io dma address.
: cpu>io-adr  ( cpu-adr -- io-adr )  cpu-dma-base - io-dma-base +  ;
: io>cpu-adr  ( io-adr -- cpu-adr )  io-dma-base - cpu-dma-base +  ;

\ buffer# to address calculations
: rmd#>rmdaddr  ( n -- addr )  /rmd * rmd0 +  ;
: rbuf#>rbufaddr  ( n -- addr )  #rbufs mod /rbuf * io-rbuf0 +  ;
: tmd#>tmdaddr  ( n -- addr )  /tmd * tmd0 +  ;
\ address to buffer# calculations
: rmdaddr>rmd#  ( addr -- n )  rmd0 - /rmd /  ;

\ *** Qe message descriptor ring access ***

\ Get current rx/tx message descriptor ring pointer (on CPU side).
: nextrmd@  ( -- cpu-rmd-addr )  nextrmd @  ;
: nexttmd@  ( -- cpu-tmd-addr )  nexttmd @  ;

\ get location of buffer
: addr@  ( rmd/tmd-addr -- buff-addr )
   >addr rl@
;

: status@  ( rmd/tmd-addr -- statusflag ) >flags rl@  ;

\ gets length of incoming message, receive only
: length@  ( rmdaddr -- messagelength )  >flags rl@ lenmask and  ;

\ Set current rx/tx message descriptor ring pointer (on CPU side).
```

Code Example 9-3   QED bootable driver sample

```
\ QED bootable driver
: nextrmd!  ( cpu-rmd-addr -- )  nextrmd ! ;
: nexttmd!  ( cpu-tmd-addr -- )  nexttmd ! ;

\ Store buffer address into message descriptor
: addr!  ( buff-addr  rmd/tmd-addr -- )
   >addr rl!
;

\ Set length of message to be sent - transmit only
: length!  ( length rmd/tmd-addr -- )  >flags rl! ;

\ *** Qe synchronization ***

\ Sync the message descriptor after cpu or device writes it.
: qesynciopb ( md -- )
   dup cpu>io-adr /md            ( cpu-addr io-addr size )
   dma-sync
;
\ Sync the transmitting/received buffer after cpu/device writes it.
: qesyncbuf  ( md -- )
   dup addr@ dup io>cpu-adr swap       ( md cpu-buf-addr io-buf-addr )
   rot length@                  ( cpu-buf-addr io-buf-addr size )
   dma-sync
;

\ The buffer was already put back, put the descriptor in the chip's ready
list
: give-buffer  ( rmd/tmd-addr -- )
   dup >flags dup rl@ ready or swap rl!      ( md )
   \ Sync the descriptor so the device sees it.
   qesynciopb                        ( )
;

\ *** Qe error handling ***

: get-qe-status  ( -- channel-status )
   qecc-status@ status @ or dup status !
;

\ get receive errors, receive only
: rerrors@  ( -- errorsflag )  get-qe-status c-rerr-mask and ;

\ gets transmit errors, transmit only
: xerrors@  ( -- errorsflag )  get-qe-status c-terr-mask and ;
```

Code Example 9-3   QED bootable driver sample

```
\ QED bootable driver

\ Clear transmit/receive/all error flags
: clear-terrors  ( -- ) status @ c-terr-mask not and status !  ;
: clear-rerrors  ( -- )  status @ c-rerr-mask not and status !  ;
: clear-errors  ( -- )  status off restart? off  ;
: clear-tint   ( -- ) status @ c-tint not and status !  ;


\ *** Basic initialization routines ***

\ words to set loopback control mode in UTR(R29) & promiscuous mode in
MACCC(R13)
\ Bit<7> to control promiscuous mode, Bits<2:1> to control loopback mode,
\ Bit<0> to test the cable connection.
1 constant m-cable

: set-loop-mode  ( -- )  mode @ m-loop-mask and m-rpa or mace-utr!  ;
: set-prom-mode  ( -- ) mode @ m-prom and mace-maccc!  ;
: check-cable-mode?  ( -- flag )  mode @ m-cable =  ;
: external-loopback?  ( -- flag )  mode @ m-loop-mask and m-loop-ext =  ;

\ Check existence of no-tpe-test property to initialize disable-tpe-link-
test bit.
\ Enable tpe-link-test if the property doesn't exist,
\      or disable tpe-link-test if the property exists.
: init-link-test  ( -- )
  \ Disable link test for external loopback mode.
   external-loopback?  if m-dlnktst mace-phycc! exit  then
   " no-tpe-test" get-my-attribute  if  0
   else  2drop m-dlnktst  then
   mace-phycc!
;
\ Enable/disable tpe-link-test
: setup-link-test  ( enable-flag -- )
   " no-tpe-test" " get-attribute" eval  if
            \ Property doesn't exist, already enabled.
    0=  if  0 0 " no-tpe-test" attribute  then
   else  2drop                   \ Currently disabled.
     if  " no-tpe-test" delete-attribute  then
   then
;
\
\ After doing a port select of the twisted pair port, the
\ driver needs to give ample time for the MACE to start
\ sending pulses to the hub to mark the link state up.
```

Code Example 9-3   QED bootable driver sample

```
\ QED bootable driver
\ Loop here and check of the link state has gone into a
\ pass state.
\
: link-state-fail?  ( -- fail? )
   d# 1000 set-ms-timeout
   begin
      mace-phycc@ m-lnkst and
   while
      ms-timeout?  if
         check-cable-mode?  if
            ." failed, transceiver cable problem? or check the hub." cr
            true
         else
\           m-dlnktst mace-phycc!
            false
         then
         exit
      then
   repeat
   check-cable-mode?  if  ." passed."  cr  then
   false
;

: set-physical-address  ( -- )
   m-addrchg mace-iac!
   begin  mace-iac@ m-addrchg and 0=  until
   m-phyaddr mace-iac!
  \ Store least significant byte first.
   this-en-addr 6 bounds  do  i c@ mace-padr!  loop
   0 mace-iac!
;

: set-address  ( en-addr len -- )
  drop  this-en-addr 6 cmove  ;

: set-logaddr-filter  ( -- )
   m-addrchg mace-iac!
   begin  mace-iac@ m-addrchg and 0=  until
   m-logaddr mace-iac!
   8 0  do  0 mace-ladrf!  loop
   0 mace-iac!
;

\ Reset (or stop) the qec channel.
```

Code Example 9-3   QED bootable driver sample

```
\ QED bootable driver
\       Issue a soft reset to the desired Mace.
\       Then issue a soft reset to the desired channel in QEC.
\ Chip reset algorithm:
\       Set the reset bit then wait until the reset bit cleared.
\ Timeout in 0.1 sec if fail.
\
: channel-reset  ( -- fail? )
   m-swrst mace-biucc!          \ Issue Mace reset.
   d# 100 set-ms-timeout
   begin
      mace-biucc@ m-swrst and
   while
      ms-timeout? if ." Cannot reset Mace" cr true exit then
   repeat
   c-rst qecc-control!          \ Reset QEC channel registers.
   d# 100 set-ms-timeout
   begin
      qecc-control@ c-rst and
   while
      ms-timeout?  if  ." Cannot reset QEC channel" cr true exit  then
   repeat
   false
;

\ Initialize a single message descriptor
: rmd-init  ( rbufaddr rmdaddr -- )
   /rbuf over length!            \ Buffer length
   addr!                         \ Buffer address
;

\ Set up the data structures necessary to receive a packet
: init-rxring  ( -- )
   rmd0 nextrmd!
   #rmds 0  do   i rbuf#>rbufaddr  i rmd#>rmdaddr  rmd-init  loop
;
\
\ Initially first N=#rbufs descriptors with one-to-one association with a
\ buffer are made ready, the rest (256-N) not ready, then turn on receiver.
\ Whenever a receive buffer is processed, the information is copied out,
\ the buffer will be linked to the ((current+N)%256) entry then make the
\ entry is ready. Ie. The window of N ready descriptor/buffer pair is
\ moving around the ring.
\
: enable-rxring  ( -- )
```

Code Example 9-3   QED bootable driver sample

```
\ QED bootable driver
   #rbufs 0  do  i rmd#>rmdaddr give-buffer  loop
;

\ transmit buffer initialize routine
: init-txring ( -- )
   tmd0 nexttmd!
   #tmds 0  do io-tbuf0 i tmd#>tmdaddr addr!  loop
;

\ *** Receive packet routines ***

\ Utility words used in .rerr-text & .terr-text.
: bits   ( mask #right-bits -- mask' right-bits )
   >r dup d# 32 r@ - tuck << swap >>    ( mask bits ; RS: #bits )
   swap r> >> swap                      ( mask' bits )
;
: 1bit   ( mask -- mask' rightest-bit-value )
   1 bits
;

: .rerr-text  ( -- )
   rerrors@
   1bit  if  ." SBus Rx Error Ack  " restart?-on  then
   1bit  if  ." SBus Rx Parity  " restart?-on  then
   1bit  if  ." SBus Rx Late  " restart?-on  then
   1bit  if  ." Data Buffer Too Small  " then
\  1bit  if  ." Rx packet Dropped  " then
   1bit drop                          \ Skip drop error, happens all the time
   1bit drop                             \ Skip receive interrupt bit.
   1bit  if  ." CRC error  " then
   1bit  if  ." Framing error  " then
   1bit  if  ." MACE Rx Late Collision  " then
   1bit  if  ." MACE FIFO overflow " then
   1bit  if  ." MACE Missed Counter Overflow  " then
   1bit  if  ." MACE Runt Counter Overflow  " then
   1bit  if  ." MACE Rx Coll Counter Overflow  " then
   1bit  if  ." Collision error " then
   drop cr
;

: (.receive-error  ( -- )
   rerrors@  if  .rerr-text  then
;
' (.receive-error is .receive-error
```

Code Example 9-3   QED bootable driver sample

```
\ QED bootable driver
' (.receive-error is .error

: to-next-rmd  ( -- )
   /rmd nextrmd +!
   nextrmd@ rmd0 - /rmds >=  if  rmd0 nextrmd!  then
;


\  *** Transmit packet routines ***

: to-next-tmd  ( -- )
   /tmd nexttmd +!
   nexttmd@ tmd0 - /tmds >=  if  tmd0 nexttmd!  then
;

\ Ignores the size argument, and uses the standard buffer.
: get-buffer  ( dummysize -- buffer )
   drop  nexttmd@ addr@         ( io-tbuf )
   io>cpu-adr                           ( cpu-tbuf )
;

\ Display time domain reflectometry information
\ : .tdr  ( -- )  ;

: .terr-text  ( -- )
   xerrors@
   d# 16 bits drop                      \ Skip the receiver bits.
   1bit  if  ." SBus Tx Error Ack  " restart?-on  then
   1bit  if  ." SBus Tx Parity  " restart?-on  then
   1bit  if  ." SBus Tx Late  " restart?-on  then
   1bit  if  ." QEC Chained Tx Descriptor Error  " restart?-on  then
   1bit  if  ." QEC Tx Retry Counter Overflow  " then
   1bit drop                            \ Skip transmit interrupt bit
   1bit  if  ." MACE >1518 Babble  " then
   1bit  if  ." MACE Jabber  " then
   1bit  if  ." MACE FIFO Underflow  " then
   1bit  if  ." Tx Late Collision  " then
   1bit  if  ." Too Many Retries  " then
   1bit  if  ." Lost Carrier  (transceiver cable problem?)  "  then
   1bit  if  ." Excessive Defer  " then
   drop cr
;

\ print summary of any HARD errors
: (.transmit-error  ( -- )
```

Code Example 9-3   QED bootable driver sample

```
\ QED bootable driver
   xerrors@  if  .terr-text  then
;
' (.transmit-error is .transmit-error

\ Set up CPU page maps
: map-qe-buffers  ( -- )
   #rbufs /rbuf *
\ 2KB (8*256) for tmds & 2KB (8*256) for rmds & 4KB for tbuf
\ ie. one page for tmds & rmds, one page for tbuf, the rest for rbufs.
   h# 2000 +
   is qe-dma-size

   \ Allocate and map that space
   qe-dma-size dma-alloc                  ( dma-adr )

   \ Set the addresses of the various DMA regions used by the cpu.
   dup  is cpu-dma-base
   dup  is tmd0     h# 800 +  ( next-address )
   dup  is rmd0     h# 800 +  ( next-address ) \ Enough for 256 entries
   dup  is tbuf0    h# 1000 + ( next-address ) \ Enough for max packet
        is rbuf0              ( )
   tmd0 qe-dma-size false dma-map-in    ( io-dma-adr )
   \ Set the addresses of the various DMA regions used by the qec chip.
   dup  is io-dma-base
   dup  is io-tmd0    h# 800 +  ( next-address )
   dup  is io-rmd0    h# 800 +  ( next-address ) \ Enough for 256 entries
   dup  is io-tbuf0   h# 1000 + ( next-address ) \ Enough for max packet
        is io-rbuf0            ( )

;
: unmap-qe-buffers  ( -- )
   tmd0 io-tmd0 qe-dma-size dma-map-out
   tmd0 qe-dma-size dma-free
   0 is tmd0
;

\ *** Chips initialization routines ***

\ Initializes the QEC/Mace chips.
: channel-init ( -- fail? )
   \ *** Initialize QEC per channel registers.
   io-rmd0 qecc-rxring!
   io-tmd0 qecc-txring!
   c-rintmask qecc-rintmask!                \ Mask RINT.
```

Code Example 9-3   QED bootable driver sample

```
\ QED bootable driver
  c-tintmask qecc-tintmask!              \ Mask XINT.
  my-chan# chmem * dup qecc-lmrxwrite! dup qecc-lmrxread!
  rxbufsize + dup qecc-lmtxwrite! qecc-lmtxread!
  c-qecerrmask qecc-qecerrmask!
  c-macerrmask qecc-macerrmask!
  \ *** Initialize MACE registers.
\   0 mace-xmtfc!
  m-apadxmt mace-xmtfc!            \ Set auto pad transmit for transmit frame
control
  0 mace-rcvfc!                    \ Init. receive frame control.
  \ Init. Interrupt Mask Register to mask rcvint & cerr and unmask xmtint
  \     according QEC spec.
  m-cerrm m-rcvintm or mace-imr!
  \ Init. Bus Interface Unit Configuration Control to transmit after 64
bytes
  \       have been loaded & byte swap.
  m-xmtsp64 m-xmtspshift << m-bswp or mace-biucc!
  \ Init. FIFO Conf Control to set transmit/receive fifo watermark update
  m-xmtfw16 m-rcvfw32 or m-xmtfwu or m-rcvfwu or mace-fifocc!
  m-10base-t mace-plscc!          \ Select twisted pair mode.
  init-link-test                  \ Init. tpe link test mode.
  set-physical-address            \ Set mac address.
  set-logaddr-filter              \ Set logical address filter.
  0 mace-iac!
  link-state-fail?                \ Wait and check the link state marked up.
  mace-mpc@ drop      \ Read to reset counter and to prevent an invalid int.
  set-loop-mode          \ Set UTR
  set-prom-mode          \ Set MACCC
  m-apadxmt not mace-xmtfc@ and mace-xmtfc!
  m-astrprcv not mace-rcvfc@ and mace-rcvfc!
;

\ Turn on the Mace, ready to tx/rx packets.
: enable-mace  ( -- )
  m-enxmt m-enrcv or mace-maccc@ or mace-maccc!
;

\ *** Ethernet on/off routines ***

\ Initializes the QEC/Mace chips, allocating the necessary memory,
\ and enabling the transmitter and receiver.
: net-on  ( -- flag )            \ true if net-on succeeds
  clear-errors
  mac-address set-address
```

Code Example 9-3   QED bootable driver sample

```
\ QED bootable driver
  channel-reset 0=  if
     init-txring
     init-rxring
     channel-init 0= dup  if
        enable-rxring
        enable-mace
     then
  else  false
  then
;

\ Stop the activity of this net channel.
: net-off  ( -- )  channel-reset drop init-link-test  ;

\ *** Main receive routines ***

\
\ Whenver a receive buffer is processed, the information is copied out,
\ the buffer will be linked to the ((current+N)%256)th entry then make the
\ entry is ready. Ie. The window of N ready descriptor/buffer pair is
\ moving around the ring.
\
\ If 256 (#rmds) is multiples of N (#rbufs=32), we don't need to link the
\ next-ready-rmd with the current processed rx buffer dynamically. They can
\ be set at the initialization time statically. For run time, we just need
\ to make the ((current+N)%256)th rmd ready.
\
: return-buffer ( buf-handle -- )
  rmdaddr>rmd#                      ( [io-rbuf] rmd# )
  #rbufs + #rmds mod                ( [io-rbuf] next-ready-rmd# )
  rmd#>rmdaddr                      ( [io-rbuf] next-ready-rmd )
  dup addr@ over rmd-init           ( next-ready-rmd ; Set length )
  give-buffer                       ( ; Make it ready )
  to-next-rmd                       \ Bump SW nextrmd to next one
;

: receive-ready? ( -- packet-waiting? )
  restart? @  if  net-on drop  then
  nextrmd@                          ( rmd )
  \ Sync RMD before CPU looking at it.
  dup qesynciopb                    ( rmd )
  status@ own and 0=                ( flag )
;
```

Code Example 9-3   QED bootable driver sample

```
\ QED bootable driver
: receive  ( -- buf-handle buffer len )        \ len non-zero if packet ok
  nextrmd@ dup addr@                   ( rmd io-rbuf-addr )
  io>cpu-adr                           ( rmd cpu-rbuf-addr )
  over length@                         ( rmd cpu-rbuf-addr len )
  rerrors@  if
     .receive-error clear-rerrors
  then
  dup  if                              ( rmd cpu-rbuf-addr len )
  \ Sync the received buffer before CPU looking at it.
     nextrmd@ qesyncbuf                ( rmd cpu-rbuf-addr len )
  then
;

\ *** Main transmit routines ***

: set-timeout  ( interval -- )  get-msecs  +  alarmtime !  ;
: timeout?  ( -- flag )  get-msecs  alarmtime @ >=  ;
: 10us-wait  ( -- )  d# 10 begin 1- dup 0= until drop  ;

\ Wait until transmission completed
: send-wait  ( -- )
\ Wait the packet to get to the local memory, ready for MACE to xmit.
  d# 2000 set-timeout         \ 2 second timeout.
  begin
     get-qe-status
     c-tint and               \ Transmit interrupt bit set?
     timeout? or              \ Or timeout?
  until
  timeout?  if
     ." TINT was not set!" cr true exit
  then
  \ Transmit completion, sync TMD before looking at it.
  nexttmd@ dup qesynciopb      ( tmd )
  status@ own and  if          ( flag )
     ." Tx descriptor still owned by QEC!" cr
  then
\ Wait the packet to get to net, make sure at most one xmit packet in MACE
FIFO.
  d# 1000 set-timeout         \ 1 second timeout.
  begin
     10us-wait
     qecc-lmtxwrite@ qecc-lmtxread@ =
     timeout? or
  until
```

Code Example 9-3   QED bootable driver sample

```
\ QED bootable driver
   timeout?  if
      ." Tx packet not out to net!" cr
   then
   false
;


\ This send routine does not enforce the minimum packet length.  It is
\ used by the loopback test routines.
:  short-send  ( buffer length -- error? )
   clear-tint                      \ Erase tint status bit.
   \ discard buffer address, assumes using nexttmd
   nip nexttmd@                    ( length tmd )
   tuck length!                    ( tmd ; Set length )
   \ Sync the transmit buffer so the device sees it.
   dup qesyncbuf                   ( tmd )
   give-buffer                     ( ; Give tmd to chip )
   c-tdmd qecc-control!         \ Bang the chip, let chip look at it right
away
   send-wait                    ( fail? )        \ wait for completion
   xerrors@ dup  if             ( fail? error? )
      .transmit-error clear-terrors
   then  or                     ( error? )
   to-next-tmd                  ( error? )
   restart? @  if  net-on drop  then    ( error? )
   c-hard-terr-mask and         ( hard-error? )
;


\ Transmit packet routine, no S/W retry on this layer.
: net-send  ( buffer length -- error? )  \ error? is contents of chan-status
   d# 64 max                     \ force minimum length to be 64
   short-send                    ( error? )
;


\ -------------------------------------------------------------------
\ timed-receive.fth
\ Implements a network receive that will timeout after a certain interval.

decimal

: multicast? ( handle data-address length -- handle data-address length
flag )
   \ Check for multicast/broadcast packets
   over                          ( ... data-address )
   c@ h# 80 and dup  if          \ Look at the multicast bit
```

Code Example 9-3   QED bootable driver sample

```
\ QED bootable driver
        ( handle data-address length multicast? )
        handle-broadcast-packet
   then
;

: receive-good-packet  ( -- [ buffer-handle data-address length ]  | 0 )
   begin
      begin
         timeout?  if  false exit  then
         receive-ready?
      until
      receive dup 0=
   while
      .error  2drop return-buffer
   repeat
;
: receive-unicast-packet  ( -- [ buffer-handle data-address length ] | 0 )
   begin
      receive-good-packet  dup 0=  if  exit  then
      multicast?
   while
      2drop return-buffer
   repeat
;
\ Receive a packet, filtering out broadcast packets and timing
\ out if no packet comes in within a certain time.
: timed-receive ( timeout-msecs -- [ buffer-handle data-address length ]
err?)
   set-timeout  receive-unicast-packet ?dup 0=
;


\ -------------------------------------------------------------
\ qetest.fth
\ Define Qec/Mace loopback-test, net-init & watch-test routines.

\ This file contains Qec/Mace selftest routines.
\ It defines the following external words:
\      loopback-test  ( internal/external-flag -- success? )
\      net-init  ( -- success? )
\      watch-test ( -- )
\ Also it defines the following external variable.
\      qe-verbose?     - Flag to indicate if want the test messages
displayed.
\      ext-lbt?      - Flag to indicate if run the external loopback test.
```

Code Example 9-3   QED bootable driver sample

```
\ QED bootable driver
\
\ The algorithme for the loopback test:
\       Set internal or external loopback with no promiscuous mode.
\       Turn on the Qec/Mace Ethernet port.
\       If it succeeds, send out a short packet containing walking 0/1
patterns.
\       If it succeeds, wait for a period, check if receive the loopback
packet.
\       If so, verify the length of the received packet is right.
\       Also check if the data of the received packet is right.
\       Return true if everything is fine, otherwise return false.
\

hex
headerless
create loopback-prototype
    ff c, 00 c,                                       \ Ones and zeroes
    01 c, 02 c, 04 c, 08 c, 10 c, 20 c, 40 c, 80 c,  \ Walking ones
    fe c, fd c, fb c, f7 c, ef c, 0df c, 0bf c, 7f c,  \ Walking zeroes
    55 c, aa c,

: loopback-buffer  ( -- adr len )
    d# 32 get-buffer  ( adr )
    mac-address drop    over               6 cmove   \ Set source address
    mac-address drop    over 6 +        6 cmove   \ Set destination address
    loopback-prototype  over d# 12 +  d# 20 cmove   \ Set buffer contents
    d# 32
;

: pdump  ( adr -- )
    base @ >r  hex
    dup      d# 10  bounds  do  i c@  3 u.r  loop  cr
    d# 10 +  d# 10  bounds  do  i c@  3 u.r  loop  cr
    r> base !
;

\ Print loopback control type for verbose mode.
: .loopback  ( -- )
    mode @  m-loop-mask and
    ?dup  if
       dup m-loop-ext =  if  ." External " drop
       else ." Internal " m-loop-intmen =  if  ." (including Mendec) "  then
       then
       ." loopback test -- "
```

Code Example 9-3   QED bootable driver sample

```
\ QED bootable driver
  then
;

\ Print loopback control type for non-verbose mode,
\ it is used after any error occurs.
: ?.loopback  ( -- )
  qe-verbose? @  0=  if  .loopback  then  ;

: switch-off  ( -- false )
  qe-verbose? off  false
;

: bad-rx-data  ( buf-handle data-address -- false )
  ?.loopback
  ." Received packet contained incorrect data.  Expected: " cr
  loopback-prototype pdump
  ." Observed:" cr
  d# 12 + pdump
  switch-off
;

\ Check the data of the received packet, return true if data is ok.
: check-data  ( buf-handle data-address length -- ok? )
  drop  ( buf-handle data-address )
  dup d# 12 +  loopback-prototype  d# 20 comp
  if  bad-rx-data
  else  drop  ( buf-handle )
    return-buffer
    qe-verbose? @  if  ." succeeded." cr  then
    mode off  true
  then
;

\ Check the length & data of the received packet, return true if data &
len ok.
: check-len&data  ( buf-handle data-address length -- ok? )
  \ The CRC is appended to the packet, thus it is 4 bytes longer than
  \ the packet we sent.
  dup d# 36 <>
  if  ?.loopback
    ." Wrong packet length; expected 36, observed " .d cr
    switch-off
  else  check-data
  then
```

Code Example 9-3   QED bootable driver sample

```
\ QED bootable driver
;

headers
\ Run internal or external loopback test, return true if the test passes.
: loopback-test   ( internal/external -- pass? )
   mode !
   qe-verbose? @  if  ." "  " .loopback   then
   net-on  if
      loopback-buffer short-send  if
         ?.loopback  ." send failed." cr
         switch-off
      else
         d# 2000 timed-receive  if
            ?.loopback
            ." Did not receive expected loopback packet." cr
            switch-off
         else           ( buf-handle data-address length )
            check-len&data
         then
      then
   else
      switch-off
   then
   net-off  mode off
;

\ If there is a normal external loopback test, then we don't need this.
\ MACE external loopback test requires a special cable. Don't run external
\ loopback test for selftest & watch-net.
: check-cable?  ( -- ok? )
   m-cable mode !
   ."  Link state check -- "
   net-on                 ( success? )
   net-off mode off
;

\ Turn on the Ethernet port after pass loopback test.
\ Return true if net-init succeeds, otherwise return false if it fails.
: net-init  ( -- flag )
   mode @                 \ Save requested mode because loopback changes it.
   m-loop-int loopback-test
   if                     ( mode-saved ; Pass internal loopback test. )
      ext-lbt? @          \ Run external loopback test if the ext-lbt? flag
is set.
```

Writing FCode Programs

Code Example 9-3   QED bootable driver sample

```
\ QED bootable driver
   \ qe internal loopback with mendec is equivalent to external loopback
of le.
      if  m-loop-intmen loopback-test  else  true  then ( mode-saved )
      swap mode !       \ Restore the mode.
      if  net-on        \ Pass loopback test, turn on the ethernet port.
      else  false
      then
   else  mode ! false
   then
;

headerless
: wait-for-packet  ( -- )
   begin  key?  receive-ready?  or  until
;

headers
\ Check for incoming Ethernet packets.
\ Use promiscuous mode to check for all incoming packets.
: watch-test  ( -- )
   ." Looking for Ethernet packets." cr
   ." '.' is a good packet.  'X' is a bad packet."  cr
   ." Type any key to stop."  cr
   begin
      wait-for-packet
      receive-ready?
      if  receive
        if   ." ." else  ." X"  then
           drop   return-buffer
      then
      key? dup  if  key drop  then
   until
;

\ ---------------------------------------------------------------
\ qe0-package.fth
\ Implement the architectural interface for the qe driver

headerless
\
\ The network driver uses the standard "obp-tftp" support package for
\ implementation. The "obp-ftfp" package implements the Internet Trivial
File
```

Code Example 9-3   QED bootable driver sample

```
\ QED bootable driver
\ Transfer Protocol (TFTP) for use in network booting. The "obp-tftp"
package
\ defines the following methods to be used by the network driver:
\       open    ( -- okay? )
\       close   ( -- )
\       load    ( addr -- size )
\ The "obp-tftp" package uses the read and write methods of the network
driver
\ for receiving and transmitting packets. The package assums the size of
the
\ maximum transfer packet is 1518 bytes. If the network driver needs bigger
\ maximum packet size, then it requires the method "max-transfer" defined,
\ the method will be called by the obp-tftp package to define the maximum
\ transfer packet size.
\
: init-obp-tftp  ( -- okay? )
   " obp-tftp" find-package  if        ( phandle )
      my-args rot open-package         ( ihandle )
   else  0
   then
   dup is obp-tftp                      ( ihandle | 0 )
   dup 0=  if
      ." Can't open OBP standard TFTP package"  cr
   then
;
: set-my-channel#  ( -- )
\ If don't find the channel attribute, use 0.
   " channel#" get-my-attribute  if  0  else  xdrtoint nip nip  then
   my-channel#!
;

headers
: qe-xmit  ( bufaddr nbytes -- #sent )
   tuck get-buffer                      ( nbytes bufaddr ether-buffer )
   tuck  3 pick  cmove                  ( nbytes ether-buffer )
   over net-send  if  drop 0  then      ( #sent )
;

: qe-poll  ( bufaddr nbytes -- #received )
   qe-nbytes ! qe-buf !                 ( )
   receive-ready?  0=  if  0 exit  then    \ Bail out if no packet ready
   receive ?dup  if                     ( rmd ether-buffer length )
      dup >r                            ( rmd ether-buffer length )
      qe-nbytes @ min                   ( rmd ether-buffer length' )
```

Code Example 9-3   QED bootable driver sample

```
\ QED bootable driver
     qe-buf @ swap cmove              ( rmd )
     return-buffer  r>                ( #received )
   else
     drop return-buffer 0             ( 0 )
   then
;

: set-vectors  ( -- )
   ['] (.receive-error  is .error
   ['] (.transmit-error is .transmit-error
   ['] noop is handle-broadcast-packet
;
: map-qe  ( -- )
   mace 0=  if          \ Do mapping if it is unmapped.
      map-chips
      map-qe-buffers
   then
;
: unmap-qe  ( -- )
   mace  if             \ Do unmapping if it is mapped.
      unmap-qe-buffers
      unmap-chips
   then
;

: qe-loopback-test  ( -- flag )        \ flag true if passes test
   set-vectors
   mode off  qe-verbose? on
   ext-lbt? on
   net-init
   ext-lbt? off
   dup  if  net-off drop check-cable?  then
   qe-verbose? off
;
: (watch-net) ( -- )
   map-qe
   set-vectors
   m-prom mode !
   qe-verbose? off
   ext-lbt? off
   net-init  if  watch-test net-off  then
   unmap-qe
;
```

Code Example 9-3   QED bootable driver sample

```
\ QED bootable driver
external
: qe0-read  ( buf len -- -2 | actual-len )
   qe-poll  ?dup  0=  if  -2  then
;
: qe0-write  ( buf len -- actual-len )  qe-xmit  ;
: qe0-selftest  ( -- flag )      \ Flag 0 if passes test.
   map-qe
   qe-reg-test        ( success? )
   if
      qe-loopback-test 0=        \ Alternate the return flag.
   else
      true
   then            ( failure? )
   unmap-qe
;
: qe0-watch-net  ( -- )
   qe0-selftest 0=  if  (watch-net)  then
;

: qe0-load  ( adr -- len ) " load" obp-tftp $call-method  ;
: qe0-open  ( -- okay? )
   map-qe
   set-vectors
   mode off  qe-verbose? off
   net-init 0=  if  unmap-qe false exit  then

   mac-address drop macbuf 6 cmove      \ Update macbuf.
   macbuf 6 xdrstring  " mac-address" attribute

   init-obp-tftp 0=  if  close false exit  then
   true
;
: qe0-close  ( -- )
   obp-tftp ?dup  if  close-package  then
   mace  if  net-off  then
   unmap-qe
;
: qe0-reset  ( -- )
   mace  if  net-off
   else  map-chips net-off unmap-chips  then
;
headers
```

Serial Devices

Serial devices are byte-oriented, sequentially-accessed devices such as asynchronous communication lines (often attached to a "dumb" terminal).

Required Methods

The `serial` device driver must declare the `serial` device-type, and must implement the methods `open` and `close`, as well as the following:

install-abort

```
( -- )
```

Instruct the driver to begin periodic polling for a keyboard abort sequence. `install-abort` is executed when the device is selected as the console input device.

read

```
( adr len -- actual )
```

Read `len` bytes of data from the device into memory starting at `adr`. Return the number of bytes actually read, `actual`, or -2 if no bytes are currently available from the device. -1 is returned if other errors occur.

remove-abort

```
( -- )
```

Instruct the driver to cease periodic polling for a keyboard abort sequence. `remove-abort` is executed when the console input device is changed from this device to another.

write

```
( adr len -- actual )
```

Write `len` bytes of data to the device from memory starting at *adr*. Return the number of bytes actually written, `actual`.

Required Properties

The standard properties of a serial driver are:

Table 10-1 Serial Driver Required Properties

Property Name	Value
name	" SUNW,thingy"
reg	{ device-dependent}
device_type	" serial"

Device Driver Examples

The three examples that follow are serial device drivers for the Zilog 8530 SCC (UART) chip.

- The first sample is a short driver which simply creates a device node and declare the properties for the device.
- The second sample is a more sophisticated driver that defines methods to control and access the device.
- The third sample shows the complete serial device driver.

Simple Serial FCode Program

```
fcode-version1

   hex

   " SUNW,zs"           name

   my-address 10.0000 + my-space 8 reg

   7 xdrint           " interrupts"  attribute

   7 0 intr

end0
```

Extended Serial FCode Program

Code Example 10-1   Extended Serial FCode Program

```
\ Extended Serial FCode Program
\ In addition to publishing the properties, this sample driver
\ provides methods to access and control the serial ports.
\
\ The following main methods are provided:
\ - usea   ( -- )
\    Selects serial port A. All subsequent operations will
\        be directed to port A
\ - useb   ( -- )
\        Selects serial port B. All subsequent operations will
\        be directed to port B
\ - uemit  ( char -- )
\ Emits a given character to the selected serial port.
\ - ukey   ( -- key )
\ Retrieves a character from the selected serial port.
\ - read   ( adr len -- #read )
\  Reads "len" number of characters from the selected port,
\    and store them at "adr".
\ - write  ( adr len -- #written )
\  Writes "len" number of characters from the buffer located
\      at "adr" to the selected serial port.

fcode-version2
hex

   my-address 10.0000 + constant phys-addr
   my-space   constant  my-sbus-space
   my-address constant  my-sbus-address

   " SUNW,zs"                name
   phys-addr my-sbus-space 8 reg
   7 xdrint " interrupts"    attribute
   7 0                  intr

   : >phys-adr  ( offset -- adr space )
     my-sbus-address +  my-sbus-space
   ;
   : do-map-in  ( offset size -- va )
     >r >phys-adr r>  " map-in" $call-parent
   ;
   : do-map-out ( va size -- )  " map-out" $call-parent  ;
   : rc! c! ;
   : rc@ c@ ;
```

Code Example 10-1 Extended Serial FCode Program

```
\ Extended Serial FCode Program
  : /string  ( adr len n -- adr+n len-n )  tuck  -  -rot  +  swap  ;

  1 constant RXREADY  \ received character available
  4 constant TXREADY  \ transmit buffer empty

  : instance  ( -- )   \ verify that "instance" is defined
    ['] instance ['] ferror < > if
        instance
    then
  ;

  0 instance value  uart                \ define uart as an "per-instance"
value.
  0 instance value  uartbase
  h# ff instance value  mask-#data    \ mask for #data bits
  h# 10 instance buffer: mode-buf

  \ The following line assumes that A2 selects the channel within the chip
  : usea  ( -- )     uartbase 4 + is uart  ;
  : useb  ( -- )     uartbase is uart  ;
  : uctl!  ( c -- )  uart  rc!  ;
  : uctl@  ( -- c )  uart  rc@  ;

  \ The following line assumes that A1 chooses the command vs. data port
  : udata!  ( c -- )  uart  2 + rc!  ;
  : udata@  ( -- c )  uart  2 + rc@  ;


  \ Test for "break" character received.
  : ubreak?  ( -- flag )  10 uctl!  uctl@  h# 80 and  0<>  ;

  \ Clear the break flag
  : clear-break  ( -- )
    begin  ubreak? 0=  until    \ Let break finish
    udata@ drop                 \ Eat the null character
    30 uctl!                    \ Reset errors
  ;

  : uemit? ( -- flag )  uctl@ TXREADY and  ;
  : uemit  ( char -- )  begin  uemit?  until  udata!  ;

  : ukey? ( -- flag )  uctl@ RXREADY and  ;
  : ukey  ( -- key )   begin  ukey?  until  udata@  ;
```

Code Example 10-1 Extended Serial FCode Program

```
\ Extended Serial FCode Program
  : uwrite              ( adr len -- #written )
    tuck  bounds ?do    ( len )
    i c@  uemit         ( len )
    loop                ( len )
  ;
  : uread  ( adr len -- #read )           \ -2 for none available right now
    ukey? 0=  if  2drop -2  exit  then     ( adr len )
    tuck                                   ( len adr len )
    begin  dup 0<>   ukey? 0<>  and  while ( len adr len )
      over  ukey mask-#data and swap c!    ( len adr len )
      1 /string                            ( len adr' len' )
    repeat                                 ( len adr' len' )
    nip -                                  ( #read )
  ;

external
  : read   ( adr len -- #read )     uread   ;
  : write  ( adr len -- #written )  uwrite  ;

end0
```

Complete Serial FCode Program

Code Example 10-2   Complete Serial FCode Program

```
\ Complete Serial driver.
\ In addition to the methods defined in the above driver sample,
\ this version defines more methods to initialize, test, and access
\ the serial ports.
\ The new main methods are:
\ - inituarts      ( -- )
\     Initializes both serial ports A and B.
\ - open           ( -- okay? )
\     Maps in the uart chip.  Selects port A on default, then check
\     my-args, if port B was specified, then selects port B instead.
\ - close          ( -- )
\     Unmap the uart chip.
\ - selftest       ( -- )
\     Performs selftest on both Port A and B.
\ - install-abort  ( -- )
\     Sets up alarm to do poll-tty every 10 miliseconds.
\ - remove-abort   ( -- )
\     Removes the poll-tty alarm.

fcode-version2
hex

   my-address 10.0000 +       constant  phys-adr
   my-space                   constant  my-sbus-space
   my-address                 constant  my-sbus-address
   " SUNW,zs"                 name
   phys-addr my-sbus-space 8 reg
   7 xdrint " interrupts" attribute
   7 0                   intr
   " serial"             device-type

   : >phys-adr  ( offset -- adr space )
       my-sbus-address +  my-sbus-space
   ;
   : do-map-in  ( offset size -- va )
       >r >phys-adr r>  " map-in" $call-parent
   ;
   : do-map-out ( va size -- )  " map-out" $call-parent  ;
   : rc! c! ;
   : rc@ c@ ;
   : /string  ( adr len n -- adr+n len-n )  tuck  -  -rot  +  swap  ;
 : instance  ( -- )   \ verify that "instance" is defined
   ['] instance ['] ferror < > if
```

Code Example 10-2   Complete Serial FCode Program

```
\ Complete Serial driver.
        instance
    then
  ;

    fload inituarts.fth
    fload ttydriver.fth
end0


\-------------------------------------------------------------------
-----
\ inituarts.fth

hex
headerless
create uart-init-table
\ 9 c, c0 c,     \ Master reset channel a (80), channel b (40)

 9 c,  2 c,      \ Don't respond to intack cycles (02)

 4 c, 44 c,      \ No parity (00), 1 stop bit (04), x16 clock (40)

 3 c, c0 c,      \ receive 8 bit characters (c0)
 5 c, 60 c,      \ transmit 8 bits (60)
 e c, 82 c,      \ Processor clock is baud rate source (02)

 b c, 55 c,     \ TRxC = xmit clk (01), enable TRxC (04), Tx clk is baud (10),
                 \ Rx clk is baud (40)
 c c,  e c,      \ Time constant low
 d c,  0 c,      \ Time constant high

 3 c, c1 c,      \ receive 8 bit characters (c0), enable (01)
 5 c, 68 c,      \ transmit 8 bits (60), enable (08)
 e c, 83 c,     \ Processor clock is baud rate source (02), Tx enable (01)

 0 c, 10 c,      \ Reset status bit latches

ff c, ff c,      \ Mark end of data

 \-------------------------------------------------------------------
-----
\ ttydriver.fth - Driver for Zilog 8530 SCC (UART) chips.

hex
0 instance value uartbase
```

Code Example 10-2   Complete Serial FCode Program

```
\ Complete Serial driver.

create default-mode
\   0      1      2      3      4      5      6      7
   00 c,   00 c,   00 c,   c1 c,   44 c,   68 c,   00 c,   00 c,

\   8      9      a      b      c      d      e      f
   00 c,   02 c,   00 c,   55 c,   0e c,   00 c,   83 c,   00 c,

      0 instance value uart        \ define uart as an "per-instance" value.
   h# ff instance value  mask-#data  \ mask for #data bits
   h# 10 instance buffer: mode-buf

   create masks    1f c,   7f c,   3f c,   ff c,

   \ The following line assumes that A2 selects the channel within the chip
   : usea   ( -- )     uartbase 4 + is uart  ;
   : useb   ( -- )     uartbase is uart  ;
   : uctl!  ( c -- )  uart  rc!  ;
   : uctl@  ( -- c )  uart  rc@  ;

   \ The following line assumes that A1 chooses the command vs. data port
   : udata!  ( c -- )  uart  2 + rc!  ;
   : udata@  ( -- c )  uart  2 + rc@  ;

   \ Write all the initialization sequence to both uarts
   : inituart  ( -- )
     uart-init-table
     begin   dup c@ ff <>   while
       dup c@ uctl!   dup ca1+ c@ uctl!
       /c 2* +
     repeat
     drop
   ;

   : inituarts  ( -- )   usea inituart   useb inituart   usea  ;

   \ Test for "break" character received.
   : ubreak?  ( -- break? )  10 uctl!   uctl@  h# 80 and  0<>  ;

   \ Clear the break flag
   : clear-break  ( -- )
     begin  ubreak? 0=  until  \ Let break finish
     udata@ drop                \ Eat the null character
     30 uctl!                   \ Reset errors
```

Code Example 10-2   Complete Serial FCode Program

```
\ Complete Serial driver.
  ;

  1 constant RXREADY            \ received character available
  4 constant TXREADY            \ transmit buffer empty

  : uemit? ( -- emit? ) uctl@ TXREADY and  ;
  : uemit ( char -- )  begin  uemit?  until  udata!  ;

  : ukey? ( -- key? )  uctl@ RXREADY and  ;
  : ukey  ( -- key )  begin  ukey?  until  udata@  ;

  : uwrite  ( adr len -- #written )
    tuck  bounds ?do   ( len )
      i c@  uemit      ( len )
    loop               ( len )
  ;
  : uread ( adr len -- #read )          \ -2 for none available right now
    ukey? 0=  if  2drop -2  exit  then   ( adr len )
    tuck                                 ( len adr len )
    begin  dup 0<>   ukey? 0<>  and  while  ( len adr len )
      over  ukey mask-#data and swap c!   ( len adr len )
      1 /string                          ( len adr' len' )
    repeat                               ( len adr' len' )
    nip -                                ( #read )
  ;

  : poll-tty  ( -- )
    ttylock @ if  exit  then
    ubreak?  if  clear-break  user-abort  then
  ;


external
  : open  ( -- okay? )
    phys-adr 8 do-map-in is uartbase
    usea
    my-args                             ( arg-str )
    ascii , left-parse-string  if       ( rem adr )
      c@  ascii b = if                  ( rem )
        2drop                           ( )
        useb                            ( )
      then                              ( rem )
    else                                ( rem adr )
      drop 2drop                        ( )
```

Code Example 10-2 Complete Serial FCode Program

```
\ Complete Serial driver.
      then                                         ( )

      true
   ;
   : close  ( -- )   uartbase 8 do-map-out  ;
headers
   : utest  ( -- 0 )  h# 7f  bl  ?do  i uemit  loop 0  ;
external
   : selftest  ( -- error? )
      open  0=  if  ." Can't open device" true exit  then
      my-args  if       ( adr )
        c@  case
          ascii a  of usea  endof
          ascii b  of useb  endof
          ( default ) ." Bad zs port letter" drop false exit
        endcase
      else  \ No port letter so test both ports.
        drop
        usea utest
        useb utest
        or close exit          ( fail? )
      then
      utest                    ( fail? )
      close
   ;
   : read    ( adr len -- #read )     uread   ;
   : write   ( adr len -- #written )  uwrite  ;
   : install-abort  ( -- )  ['] poll-tty d# 10 alarm  ;
   : remove-abort   ( -- )  ['] poll-tty 0 alarm  ;

   \ "seek" might be implemented to select a load file name
   \ Implement "load" ( optional )

headers
```

FCode Dictionary

This dictionary describes the pre-defined FCode words that you can use as part of FCode source code programs. Appendix A, "FCode Reference", contains a command summary, with words grouped by function.

The words are given alphabetically in this chapter, sorted by the first alphabetic character in the word's name. For example, the words mod and */mod are adjacent to each other. Words having no alphabetic characters in their names are placed at the beginning of the chapter, in ASCII order.

The boot PROM and tokenizer are case-insensitive (all Forth words are converted to lowercase internally). The only exceptions are literal text, such as text inside " strings and text arguments to the ascii command, which are left in the original form. In general, you may use either uppercase or lowercase.

All arithmetic uses 32-bit signed values, unless otherwise specified.

Defining words create a header by calling external-token, named-token, or new-token. See these words for more details.

All FCode byte values listed in this chapter are given in hexadecimal. Version 2 FCodes cannot be used OpenBoot 1 systems, they are called out in the dictionary definitions by "Version 2".

The rest of this chapter contains definitions of the FCodes and tokenizer macros defined for use in the SPARCstation OpenBoot PROM.

!

                              (n adr --)   **code#** 72

Store n at adr. For more portable code, use 1! if you explicitly want a 32-bit access. adr must be aligned as given by variable.

"

                    (text)"   (-- adr len)**code#** 12 len xx xx xx
                    ...
                    generates: b(") len text

11

This word is used to compile a text string, delimited by a " . At execution time, the address and length of the string is left on the stack. For example:

```
" SUNW,new-model" xdrstring " model" attribute
```

You can embed control characters and 8-bit binary numbers within strings. This is similar in principle to the \n convention in C, but syntactically tuned for Forth. This feature applies to the string arguments of the words " and ."

The escape character is '"'. Here is the list of escapes:

Table 11-1 Escape Sequences in Text Strings

Syntax	Function
""	quote (")
"n	newline
"r	carret
"t	tab
"f	formfeed
"l	linefeed
"b	backspace
"!	bell
"^x	control x, where x is any printable character
"(hh hh)	Sequence of bytes, one byte for each pair of hex digits hh . Non-hex characters will be ignored

"<whitespace> terminates the string, as usual.

" followed by any other printable character not mentioned above is equivalent to that character. This syntax is completely backwards compatible with old code, since the only legal previous usage was "<whitespace>

For example:

```
" This is "(01 32 8e)abc"nA test xyzzy "!"! abcdefg""hijk"^bl"

           ^^^^^^        ^            ^ ^        "        ^
           3 bytes     newline      2 bells      "     control b
```

The "(hh hh hh hh) form is useful for entering binary data.

Any non-hex characters (such as space or comma) are ignored within the data field of "(
...), and thus make useful delimiters. The "makearray" tool can be used in conjunction
with this syntax to easily incorporate large binary data fields into any FCode program.

Note – The use of "n for line breaks is discouraged. The preferred method is to use cr ,
rather than embedding the line break character inside a string. Use of cr results in more
accurate display formatting, because Forth updates its internal line counter when cr is
executed.

When " is used outside a colon definition, current implementations permit only two
interpreted strings to be active at any given time, a third interpreted string overwrites the
first one. This limitation does not apply in colon definitions.

#

```
                              (  +L1  --  +L2  )                    code#  99
```

The remainder of +L1 divided by the value of base is converted to an ASCII character
and appended to the output string toward lower memory addresses. +L2 is the quotient
and is maintained for further processing. Typically used between <# and #>.

#>

```
                              (  L  --  adr  +n  )                  code#  97
```

Pictured numeric output conversion is ended dropping L. adr is the address of the
resulting output array. +n is the number of characters in the output array. adr and +n
together are suitable for type. See (.) and (u.) for typical usages.

'

```
                     name     (  --  acf  )    code#  11  FCode(name)
                     generates:   b(')
```

Used to generate the code field address (acf) of the word immediately following the ' .
' should only be used *outside* of definitions. See ['] for more details.

For example:

```
    defer opt-word    ( -- ) ' noop is opt-word
```

(

```
                     text)    (  --  )                             code#  none
```

Ignore subsequent text after the "(" up to a delimiting ")" . Note that a space is required
after the (. Although either (or \ may be used equally well for documentation, by
common convention we use (...) for stack comments and \ ... for all other text
comments and documentation. See also (s .

For example:

```
: 4drop          ( a b c d -- )

   2drop          ( a b )

   2drop          ( )

;
```

(.)

               (n -- adr len)**code#** 47 2d 96 9a 49   98 97

               generates: dup abs <# #s swap sign #>

This is the numeric conversion primitive, used to implement display words such as "." It converts a number into a string. If n is negative, the first character in the array will be a minus (-) sign.

For example:

```
: show-version ( -- )

   ." CPU bootprom version is " base @  d# 16 base !  ( old-base )

   firmware-version  ( old-base version )

   lwsplit (.) type ascii . emit .h cr base !          ( )

;
```

*

               (n1 n2 -- n3)   **code#** 20

n3 is the arithmetic product of n1 times n2. If the result cannot be represented in one stack entry, the least significant bits are kept.

*/

               (n1 n2 n3 -- n4)   **code#** 30 20 31 21

               generates: >r * r> /

Calculates n1*n2/n3. The inputs, outputs and intermediate products are all 32-bit.

+

(n1 n2 -- n3)   **code#** 1e

n3 is the arithmetic sum of n1 plus n2.

+!

(n adr --)   **code#** 6c

n is added to the value stored at adr. This sum replaces the original value at adr. adr must be aligned as given by variable.

,

(n --)   **code#** d3

Compile a number into the dictionary. In current systems, the number of bytes compiled is 4 (same as l,). See c, for limitations. The dictionary pointer must be two-byte aligned.

For example, to create an array containing integers 40004000 23 45 6734:

```
create my-array 40004000 , 23 , 45 , 6734 ,
```

-

(n1 n2 -- n3)   **code#** 1f

n3 is the result of subtracting n1 minus n2.

-1

(-- -1)   **code#** a4

Leave the value -1 on the stack. The only numbers that are not encoded using b(lit) are the values -1, 0, 1, 2, or 3. Because these numbers occur so frequently, these values are assigned individual FCodes to save space.

.

(n --)   **code#** 9d

The absolute value of n is displayed in a free field format with a leading minus sign if n is negative, and a trailing space.

If the base is hexadecimal, . displays the number in unsigned format, since signed hex display is hardly ever wanted. Use s. to display signed hex numbers. See also s. .

."

text"   (--)**code#** 12 len xx xx xx ... 90
generates: b(") len text type

This word compiles a text string, delimited by " . At execution time, the string is displayed, for example, in ." hello world"

This word is equivalent to using `" text" type`

`. "` is normally used only within a definition. The text string will be displayed later when that definition is called. You may wish to follow it with `cr` to flush out the text buffer immediately.

Use `. (` to print anything while the FCode PROM is being interpreted.

See `tokenizer [` for details about printing at tokenize time.

.(text)

```
( -- )                                    code# none
generates:  b(")  len text typecode# 12 len
xx xx xx ... 90
```

Gathers a text string, delimited by `)` , to be immediately displayed during probe time. For example:

```
.( hello world)
```

This word is equivalent to: `" text" type`

Use this to print out text at the time the FCode PROM is being interpreted (you may wish to follow it with a `cr` to flush out the text buffer immediately). This word may be called either inside or outside of definitions; the text is immediately displayed in either case.

Note that the string will typically be printed out of serial port A, since any framebuffer present may not yet be activated at the time that SBus slots are being probed. Use `. "` for any printing to be done when new words are later executed.

See `tokenizer [` for details about printing at tokenize time.

/

```
( n1 n2 -- quot )                         code# 21
```

Calculates n1 divided by n2. An error condition results if the divisor (n2) is zero. See `/mod`.

0

```
( -- 0 )                                  code# a5
```

Leave the value 0 on the stack. The only numbers that are not encoded using `b(lit)` are the values -1, 0, 1, 2, or 3. Because these numbers occur so frequently, they are assigned individual FCodes to save space.

0<

```
( n -- flag )                             code# 36
```

Flag is true if n is less than zero (negative).

0<=

                       (n -- flag)   **code#** 37

Flag is true if n is less than or equal to zero.

0=

                       (n -- flag)   **code#** 34

Flag is true if n is zero. This word will invert any flag.

0<>

                       (n -- flag)   **code#** 35

Flag is true if n is not zero.

0>

                       (n -- flag)   **code#** 38

Flag is true if n is greater than zero.

0>=

                       (n -- flag)   **code#** 39

Flag is true if n is greater than or equal to zero.

1

                       (-- 1)   **code#** a6

Leave the value 1 on the stack. The only numbers that are not encoded using b(lit) are the values -1, 0, 1, 2, or 3. Because these numbers occur so frequently, these values are assigned individual FCodes to save space.

1+

                       (n1 -- n2)   **code#** a6 1e
                       generates: 1 +

n2 is the result of adding one to n1.

1-

                       (n1 -- n2)   **code#** a6 1f
                       generates: 1 -

n2 is the result of subtracting one from n1.

2

                       (-- 2)   **code#** a7

Leaves the value 2 on the stack. The only numbers that are not encoded using `b(lit)` are the values -1, 0, 1, 2, or 3. Because these numbers occur so frequently, these values are assigned individual FCodes to save space.

2!

                        (n1 n2 adr --)   **code#** 77

n1 and n2 are stored in consecutive 32-bit locations starting at `adr`. n2 is stored at the lower address.

2*

                        (n1 -- n2)   **code#** 59

n2 is the result of shifting n1 left one bit. A zero is shifted into the vacated bit position. This is equivalent to multiplying by 2.

2+

                        (n1 -- n2)   **code#** a7 1e
                        generates: 2 +

n2 is the result of adding 2 to n1.

2-

                        (n1 -- n2)   **code#** a7 1f
                        generates: 2 -

n2 is the result of subtracting 2 from n1.

2/

                        (n1 -- n2)   **code#** 57

n2 is the result of arithmetically shifting n1 right one bit. The sign is included in the shift and remains unchanged. This is equivalent to dividing by 2.

2@

                        (adr -- n1 n2)   **code#** 76

n1 and n2 are two numbers stored in consecutive 32-bit locations starting at `adr`. n2 is the number that was stored at the lower address.

3

                        (-- 3)   **code#** a8

Leaves the value 3 on the stack. The only numbers that are not encoded using `b(lit)` are the values -1, 0, 1, 2, or 3. Because these numbers occur so frequently, these values are assigned individual FCodes to save space.

:

```
name     ( -- )at creationcode# (header) b7
                ( ?? -- ?? )at execution
generates:   new header, b(type) = b(:)
```

Begin a new definition, terminated by ; Used in the form:

```
: newname   ...   ;
```

Later usage of *newname* is equivalent to usage of the contents of the definition. See `named-token`, `new-token`, and `external-token` for more information on header formats.

;

```
( -- )                                    code# c2
generates:   b(;)
```

Ends the compilation of a colon definition. See also : .

<

```
( n1 n2 -- flag )                         code# 3a
```

Flag is true if `n1` is less than `n2`. `n1` and `n2` are signed integers.

<#

```
( -- )                                    code# 96
```

Initialize pictured numeric output conversion. You can use the words:

```
<#  #  #s  hold  sign  #>
```

to specify the conversion of a 32-bit number into an ASCII character string stored in right-to-left order. See `(.)` and `(u.)` for typical usages.

<<

```
( n1 +n -- n2 )                           code# 27
```

`n2` is the result of logically left shifting `n1` by `+n` places. Zeroes are shifted into the least-significant bits.

For example:

```
: bljoin  (  byte.low byte.lowmid byte.highmid byte.high -- L )

   8 << +  8 << +  8 << +

;
```

<=

(n1 n2 -- flag)   **code#** 43

Flag is true if n1 is less than or equal to n2. n1 and n2 are signed integers.

<>

(n1 n2 -- flag)   **code#** 3d

Flag is true if n1 is not equal to n2. n1 and n2 are signed integers.

=

(n1 n2 -- flag)   **code#** 3c

Flag is true if n1 is equal to n2. n1 and n2 are signed integers.

>

(n1 n2 -- flag)   **code#** 3b

Flag is true if n1 is greater than n2. n1 and n2 are signed integers.

>=

(n1 n2 -- flag)   **code#** 42

Flag is true if n1 is greater than or equal to n2. n1 and n2 are signed integers.

>>

(n1 +n -- n2)   **code#** 28

n2 is the result of logically right shifting n1 by +n places. Zeroes are shifted into the most-significant bits. Use >>a for signed shifting.

For example:

```
: wbsplit  ( w -- b.low b.high )
```

```
    dup   h# ff and   swap    8 >>

    h# ff and


  ;
```

?

(adr --)   **code#** 6d 9d
generates: @ .

Fetch and print the 32-bit value at the given address. An old standard Forth word, primarily used interactively.

@

(adr -- n)   **code#** 6d

n is the value stored at adr. For more portable code, use l@ if you explicitly want a 32-bit access. adr must be aligned as given by variable.

[']

name   (-- acf)   **code#** 11 FCode(name)
generates: b(')

' or ['] are used to generate the code field address (acf) of the word immediately following the ' or ['].

' should only be used *outside* definitions; ['] may be used either inside or outside definitions. Examples shown usually use ['] , since it will always generate the intended result:

```
    : my-probe... ['] my-install is-install... ;
```

or

```
    ['] my-install is-install
```

In normal Forth, ' may be used within definitions for the creation of language extensions, but such usage is not applicable to FCode programs.

****

rest-of-line   (--)   **code#** none

Ignore the rest of the input line after the \ . It can occur anywhere on an input line. Note that a space must be present after the \ . See (or (s for another form for delimiting comments.

For example:

```
0 value his-ihandle   \ place to save someone's ihandle
```

<<a

         (n1 +n -- n2)   **code#** 27
         generates: <<

Arithmetic left-shift (left-shift with sign-extend), to round out the existing words <<, >>, and >>a . This word is useless, because the carry out from an arithmetic left shift is not accessible later.

>>a

         (n1 +n -- n2)   **code#** 29

n2 is the result of arithmetically right shifting n1 by +n places. The sign bit of n1 is shifted into the most-significant bits.

For example:

```
    ffff.0000 6 >>a .h
```

shows: fffffc00 , while

```
    ffff.0000 6 >>  .h
```

shows: 3fffc00 .

abort

         (--)   **code#** 2 16
         version 2

Aborts program execution. Control returns to ok prompt. Called after encountering fatal errors.

For example:

```
: probe-loop  ( adr -- )

  \ generate a tight probe loop until any key is pressed.

  begin dup 1@ drop key?  if  abort  then  again

;
```

abs
                          (n -- u)   **code#** 2d

u is the absolute value of n. If n is the maximum negative number, u is the same value (since the maximum negative number in two's complement notation has no positive equivalent).

again
                          (--)   **code#** 13 offset
                          generates: bbranch -offset

Used in the form begin ... again to generate an infinite loop. Use Stop-A from the keyboard, or abort or exit, to exit from this loop. Use this word with caution!

For example:

```
: probe-loop  ( adr -- )

  \ generate a tight probe loop until any key is pressed.

  begin dup 1@ drop key?  if  abort  then  again

;
```

alarm
                          (acf n --)   **code#** 2 13
                          version 2

Arranges to periodically execute the package method acf at intervals of n milliseconds (to the best accuracy possible).

acf is the compilation address, as returned by [']. Each time the method is called, the current instance will be the same as the current instance at the time that alarm was executed. If n is 0, stop the periodic execution of acf within the current instance context.

A common use of alarm would be to implement a console input device's polling function.

For example:

```
: my-checker  ( -- )  test-dev-status  if  user-abort  then  ;

: install-abort  ( -- )  ['] my-checker d# 10 alarm  ;
```

alias
new-name old-name (--)   **code#** none

alias creates a new name, with the exact behavior of some other existing name. The new name can then be used interchangeably with the old name and have the same effect.

The tokenizer does *not* generate any FCode for an alias command, but instead simply updates its own lookup table of existing words. Any occurrence of the new word causes the assigned FCode value of the *old* word to be generated. One implication is that the *new* word will not appear in the OpenBoot dictionary after the FCode program is compiled.

If the original FCode source text is downloaded and interpreted directly, without being tokenized or detokenized, then any new alias words *will* show up and be usable directly.

For example:

```
alias pkg-attr get-package-attribute
```

aligned
(adr1 -- adr2)   **code#** ae

Increase adr1 to the next machine word boundary — to the next value evenly divisible by 4. The correct boundary could vary on other CPU implementations.

alloc-mem
(#bytes -- virtual)   **code#** 8b

Allocate some free physical memory from Forth, and return its virtual address. See free-mem.

For example:

```
h# 100 alloc-mem ( virt ) constant my-buff
```

and

(n1 n2 -- n3)   **code#** 23

n3 is the bit-by-bit logical and of n1 with n2.

ascii

(-- n)   **code#** 10 00 00 00 xx
generates: b(lit) value

Interpret the next letter as an ASCII code. For example:

```
ascii C (equals hex 43)

ascii c (equals hex 63)
```

attribute

(value-xdr-adr value-xdr-len name-adr name-len
--)   **code#** 1 10

attribute is the way to pass properties from an FCode program to a SunOS device
driver. A property consists of two strings: a name string and a value string. The name
string gives the name of the property, and the value string gives the value associated with
that name. For example, a framebuffer may wish to declare a property named "hres" (for
horizontal resolution) with a value of 1152.

The attribute command requires two strings on the stack — the value string and the
name string. The name string is an ordinary Forth string, such as any string created with
" . This string should be written in lower case, since the attribute name is stored only
after converting uppercase letters, if any, to lower case. For example:

```
" A21-b" xdrstring " New_verSION" attribute
```

is stored as if entered

```
" A21-b" xdrstring " new_version" attribute
```

The value string, however, *must* be in the xdr format. See Chapter 5, "Properties" for more information on creating xdr-format strings.

All properties created by an FCode program are stored in a "device tree" by OpenBoot. This tree may then be queried by a SunOS device driver, using getprop or getlongprop.

The FCode program and the SunOS device driver may agree on any arbitrary set of names and values to be passed, with virtually no restrictions. Several names, though, have special meaning. For many of them, a shorthand command also exists that makes the attribute declaration a bit simpler.

For example:

```
" SUNW,new-model" xdrstring " model" attribute
```

See also: name, reg, intr, model and Chapter 5, "Properties" for more information.

b#

> *number*   (-- n)   **code#** 10 xx xx xx xx
> generates: b(lit) value

Interpret the next number in binary (base 2), regardless of any previous settings of hex, decimal, binary or octal. Only the immediately-following number is affected, the current numeric base setting is unchanged. For example:

```
hex

b# 100 (equals decimal 4)

100    (equals decimal 256)
```

See also d#, h#, and o#.

b(")

> (-- adr len) **code#** 12 len xx xx xx ...

An internal word, generated by words such as " or . " to leave a text string on the stack. The FCode for b(") should always be followed by an 8-bit length, then by the appropriate number of bytes representing the desired test string. Never use the word b(") in source code.

b(')

> (-- acf)   **code#** 11 FCode#

An internal word, generated by   ′ or [′] to leave on the stack the code field address of the immediately following word. The FCode for b(′) should always be followed by the FCode of the desired word. Never use the word b(′) in source code.

b(+loop)

(n --)   **code#** 16 -offset

An internal word, generated by +loop . The FCode for b(+loop) should always be followed by a negative offset (either 8-bit or 16-bit, see offset16). Never use the word b(+loop) in source code.

b(:)

(--)   **code#** b7

An internal word, generated by the defining word : . This is the type entry for : needed by named-token or new-token . See these words for more details. Never use the word b(:) in source code.

b(;)

(--)   **code#** c2

An internal word, generated by ; to end a colon definition. Never use the word b(;) in source code.

b(<mark)

(--)   **code#** b1

An internal word, generated by begin . Never use the word b(<mark) in source code.

b(>resolve)

(--)   **code#** b2

An internal word, generated by repeat, else, and then . Never use the word b(>resolve) in source code.

b(?do)

(end start --)   **code#** 18 +offset

An internal word, generated by ?do . The FCode for b(?do) should always be followed by a positive offset (either 8-bit or 16-bit, see offset16). Never use the word b(?do) in source code.

b(buffer:)

(n --)   **code#** bd

An internal word, generated by the defining word buffer: . This is the type entry for buffer: needed by external-token, named-token, or new-token . See these words for more details. Never use the word b(buffer:) in source code.

b(case)
(selector -- selector)   **code#** c4

An internal word, generated by case . Never use the word b(case) in source code.

b(constant)
(n --)   **code#** ba

An internal word, generated by the defining word constant . This is the type entry for constant needed by external-token, named-token or new-token . See these words for more details. Never use the word b(constant) in source code.

b(create)
(--)   **code#** bb

An internal word, generated by the defining word create. This is the type entry for create needed by external-token, named-token or new-token . See these words for more details. Never use the word b(create) in source code.

b(defer)
(--)   **code#** bc

An internal word, generated by the defining word defer . This is the type entry for defer needed by external-token, named-token or new-token . See these words for more details. Never use the word b(defer) in source code.

b(do)
(end start --)   **code#** 17 +offset

An internal word, generated by do . The FCode for b(do) should always be followed by a positive offset (either 8-bit or 16-bit, see offset16). Never use the word b(do) in source code.

b(endcase)
(--)   **code#** c5

An internal word, generated by endcase . Never use the word b(endcase) in source code.

b(endof)
(--)   **code#** c6 +offset

An internal word, generated by endof . Never use the word b(endof) in source code.

b(field)
(offset size -- offset+size) **code#** be

An internal word, generated by the defining word field . This is the type entry for field needed by external-token, named-token or new-token . See these words for more details. Never use the word b(field) in source code.

b(is)

(n --)   **code#** c3

An internal word, generated by is .

Never use the word b(is) in source code.

b(leave)

(--)   **code#** 1b

An internal word, generated by leave .

Never use the word b(leave) in source code.

b(lit)

(-- n)   **code#** 10 xx xx xx xx

Any input number, such as 205 or -14, will create the b(lit) FCode (code#10), followed by 32-bits (4 bytes) with the actual binary value in two's-complement arithmetic. The number base (hex, decimal or any other chosen radix) is controlled by any previous uses of the tokenizer directives hex, decimal, and so on, or by numeric input control words such as h#, d#, ascii, and so on. Thus,

```
decimal ... 20
```

would be encoded as the hex bytes 10 00 00 00 14

The only numbers that are not encoded using b(lit) are the values -1, 0, 1, 2, or 3. Because these numbers occur so frequently, these values are assigned individual FCodes to save space.

Never use the word b(lit) in source code.

b(loop)

(n --)   **code#** 15 -offset

An internal word, generated by loop . The FCode for b(loop) should always be followed by a negative offset (either 8-bit or 16-bit, see offset16).

Never use the word b(loop) in source code.

b(of)

(testval --)   **code#** 1c +offset

An internal word, generated by of . The FCode for b(of) should always be followed by a positive offset (either 8-bit or 16-bit, see offset16). Never use the word b(of) in source code.

b(value)

$$(\ n \ -- \ )$$ **code#** b8

An internal word, generated by the defining word `value` . This is the type entry for `value` needed by `external-token`, `named-token` or `new-token` . See these words for more details. Never use the word `b(value)` in source code.

b(variable)

$$(\ n \ -- \ )$$ **code#** b9

An internal word, generated by the defining word `variable` . This is the type entry for `variable` needed by `external-token`, `named-token` or `new-token` . See these words for more details. Never use the word `b(variable)` in source code.

b?branch

$$(\ flag \ -- \ )$$ **code#** 14 offset

An internal word, generated by `until`, `while`, and `if` . The FCode for `b?branch` should always be followed by an offset (either 8-bit or 16-bit, see `offset16`). Never use the word `b?branch` in source code.

base

$$(\ -- \ adr \ )$$ **code#** a0

The address of a `variable` containing the current numeric conversion radix to be used when the FCode program is executing, such as 10 for decimal, 16 for hex, 8 for octal, and so on. For example, to print the current value of `base`, use:

```
base @ .d
```

The tokenizer words `binary`, `decimal`, `hex`, or `octal` are also available for changing the value in `base` as desired. However, these four words behave differently depending whether they occur within a definition or outside of a definition.

If any of `binary`, `decimal`, `hex`, or `octal` occur *within* a definition, then they will be compiled, later causing a change to the value in `base` when that definition is executed.

If any of `binary`, `decimal`, `hex`, or `octal` occur *outside* of a definition, however, then they are interpreted as commands to the tokenizer program itself, thus affecting the interpretation of all subsequent numbers in the text.

Note that changes to base affect the numeric base of the Toolkit itself, which can create much confusion for any user (the default value for base is hexadecimal). If you *must* change the base, Sun recommends that you save and then restore the original base, as in:

```
: .o ( n -- )   \ Print n in octal

  base @ swap     ( oldbase n )

  octal .         ( oldbase )

  base !
```

In general, only numeric *output* will be affected by the value in base. Fixed numbers in FCode source are interpreted by the tokenizer program. Most numeric input is controlled by binary, decimal, hex, octal, b#, d#, h#, and o#, but these words only affect the tokenizer input base; they but do *not* affect the value in base. For example:

```
            (assume initial value in base is 16, i.e. Toolkit is in hex)

            (no assumptions should be made about the initial tokenizer base)

fcode-version1

hex         (tokenizer in base 16; later execution, using base, in base 16)

20 .          (compile decimal 32, later print "20" when FCode executes)

decimal       (tokenizer is in base 10, later execution is in base 16)

20 .          (compile decimal 20, later print "14" since FCode executes
in hex)

: TEST ( -- )

   octal      (still compiling in decimal, later change base when TEST
executes)

   20 .     (compiles decimal 20, prints "24" since base was just changed)
```

```
    h# 20 .d   (compiles decimal 32, prints "32"; no permanent base changes)

    20 .       (compiles decimal 20, prints "24")


;


20 .          (compile decimal 20, later print "14"

TEST          (prints "24 32 24"; has a side-effect of changing the base)

20 .          (compile decimal 20, later print 24 since TEST changed base)

hex           (tokenizer is in base 16; later execution, using base, still
in base 8)

20 .          (compile decimal 32, later print "40")
```

If this all seems confusing, simply follow these guidelines:

Good: initially declare `hex` just after `fcode-version1`, and make liberal use of `b#`, `d#`, `o#`, `h#`, `.h` and `.d`.

Bad: changing `base` either directly or by calling `binary`, `decimal`, `hex`, or `octal` from within a definition.

bbranch

                (--)   **code#** 13 offset

An internal word, generated by `again`, `repeat`, and `else`. The FCode for `bbranch` should always be followed by an offset (either 8-bit or 16-bit, see `offset16`). Never use the word `bbranch` in source code.

begin

                (--)   **code#** b1
                generates: b(<mark)

Marks the beginning of a conditional loop, such as `begin ... until`, `begin ... while ... repeat`, or `begin ... again`. See these other words for more details.

bell

                (-- n)   **code#** ab

n is the ASCII code for the bell character; decimal 7.

between

(n min max -- flag)   **code#** 44

flag is true if n is between min and max, inclusive of both endpoints (min <= n <= max).
See within for a different form of comparison.

binary

(--)   **code#** none
generates: 2 base ! *or* **code#**   a7 a0 72

If outside of a definition, commands the tokenizer program to interpret subsequent
numbers in binary (base 2). If within a definition, change the value in base affecting later
numeric output when the FCode program is executed.   See base.

bl

(-- n)   **code#** a9

The ASCII code for the space character; decimal 32, hex 20.

blank

(adr len --)   **code#** a9 79
generates: bl fill

len bytes of memory beginning at adr are set to the ASCII character value for space (hex
20). No action is taken if len is zero.

blink-screen

(--)   **code#** 1 5b

A defer word, called by the terminal emulator when needed to flash the entire screen.

This word is initially empty, but *must* be loaded with an appropriate routine in order for
the terminal emulator to function correctly.

This may be done with is, or it may be loaded automatically with fb1-install or
fb8-install (which loads fb1-blink-screen or fb8-blink-screen, respectively).
These default routines invert the screen (twice) by xor-ing every visible pixel. This is
quite slow.

A replacement routine simply disables the video for 20 milliseconds or so, i.e.

Code Example 11-1   Video replacement routine sample

```
: my-blink-screen  ( -- )   video-off  20 ms  video-on  ;
...
   \ load default behaviors with fbx-install, then:
   ['] my-blink-screen  is blink-screen
```

Of course, this example assumes that your display hardware is able to quickly enable and disable the video without otherwise affecting the state.

bljoin

(byte.lo byte2 byte3 byte.hi -- n)**code#** 7f

Merge four bytes into a single 32-bit word. Incorrect results may be generated unless the high 24 bits of each stack item are zero.

body>

(apf -- acf)   **code#** 85

Convert the parameter field address of a word to its code field address.

>body

(acf -- apf)   **code#** 86

Convert the code field address of a word to its parameter field address.

bounds

(start cnt -- start+cnt start)**code#** ac

Convert a starting value and count into the form required for a do or ?do loop. For example, to perform a loop 20 times, counting up from 4000 to 401f inclusive, use:

```
4000 20 bounds do ... loop
```

This is equivalent to:

```
4020 4000 do ... loop
```

bs

(-- n)   **code#** aa

n is the ASCII code for the backspace character; decimal 8.

buffer:

```
name( size -- )at creation code# (header)
             ( -- adr )at execution
generates:  new header, where b(type) =
b(buffer:)
```

Allocate some memory and create a name that, when executed, leaves on the stack the virtual address of the desired memory. Create with:

```
200 buffer: name
```

bwjoin

(byte.lo byte.hi -- word)   **code#** b0

Merge two bytes into the low 16-bits of a stack entry (the upper bits are zero). Incorrect results may be generated unless the high 24 bits of each stack item are zero.

4-byte-id

(--)   **code#** fe

This byte (at location 0) followed by 3 more identifier bytes, was used during some of the early OpenBoot development as a replacement for actual FCode, by providing a single "magic" number to identify an SBus device. It was a temporary measure only, as it required the boot PROM to "know" the correct magic number for a given device.

This feature is no longer supported, and should not be used under any circumstances.

c!

(n adr --)   **code#** 75

The least significant 8 bits of n are stored in the byte at adr .

c,

(n --)   **code#** d0

Compile a byte into the dictionary. This word may be used, in conjunction with create, to create an array-type structure, as:

```
create yellow  77 c, 23 c, ff c, ff c, 47 c, 22 c, ...
```

Later execution of *yellow* leaves the address of the first byte of the array (the address of the byte '77') on the stack.

c@

(adr -- n)   **code#** 71

The byte at address adr is placed into the low 8-bits of n (the upper bits are padded with zeroes).

/c

(-- n)   **code#** 5a

n is the size in bytes of a byte, which is 1. See /w, /l, and /n.

/c*

(n1 -- n2)   **code#** 66

n2 is the result of multiplying n1 by the length in bytes of a byte. This is useful for converting an index into a byte offset.

ca+

(adr1 index -- adr2)   **code#** 5e

adr2 is the address of the index'th character after adr1 . ca+ should be used in preference to + when calculating addresses because it more clearly expresses the intent of the operation and is more portable.

ca1+

(adr1 -- adr2)   **code#** 62

adr2 is the address of the next byte after adr1 . ca1+ should be used in preference to 1+ because it more clearly expresses the intent of the operation and is more portable.

$call-method

([...] adr len ihandle -- [...])**code#** 2 0e
version 2

Executes the device interface method adr len within the open package instance ihandle . The ellipses (...) indicate that the contents of the stack before and after the method is called depend upon the particular method being called.

For example:

```
: dma-alloc  ( #bytes -- vadr )   " dma-alloc"  my-parent $call-method  ;
```

See open-package.

call-package

([...] acf ihandle -- [...])**code#** 2 08
version 2

Executes the device interface method acf within the open package instance ihandle. See find-method and open-package. The ellipses (...) indicate that the contents of the stack before and after the method is called depend upon the particular method being called.

For example:

```
0 value label-ihandle  \ place to save the ihandle of other package

0 value offset-method  \ place to save the acf of found method

: init ( -- )

   my-args " disk-label" $open-package  ( ihandle )

   is label-ihandle

   " offset" label-ihandle

   ihandle>phandle ( name-adr name-len phandle )

   find-method if

      is offset-method

   else

      ." Can't find offset method "

   then

;

init

: add-offset ( d.byte# -- d.bytes# )

   offset-method label-ihandle call-package

;
```

$call-parent

([...] adr len -- [...]) **code#** 2 09
version 2

Calls the method named by `adr len` within the parent instance. If the called package has no such method, an error is signaled with `throw`. Equivalent to:

```
my-parent $call-method
```

The ellipses (...) indicate that the contents of the stack before and after the method is called depend upon the particular method being called.

For example:

```
: my-dma-alloc  ( -- vadr )  h# 2000 " dma-alloc" $call-parent  ;
```

carret

       (-- n)   **code#** 10 00 00 00 0d
       generates: b(lit) 13(decimal)

n is the ASCII code for the carriage return character; decimal 13, hex 0d.

case

       (selector -- selector)   **code#** c4
       generates: b(case)

A case statement is started that selects its action based on the value of `selector`. Example of use:

```
: foo ( selector -- )

  case

    0 of ." It was 0" endof

    5 of ." It was 5" endof

   -2 of ." It was -2" endof

    ( selector ) ." It was " dup u.   \ default clause

  endcase

;
```

The default clause is optional. When an `of` clause is executed, the selector is *not* on the stack. When a default clause is executed, the selector *is* on the stack. The default clause may use the selector, but must not remove it from the stack (it will be automatically removed just before the `encase`). `of` tests the top of the stack against the selector at run time. If they are the same, the selector is dropped and the following Forth code is executed. If they are not the same, execution continues at the point just following the matching `endof`.

`case` statements can only be used within colon definitions.

catch

```
( [...] acf -- [...] error-code ) code# 2 17
version 2
```

Creates a new error handling context and executes `acf` in that context.

If a `throw` (see below) is called during the execution of `acf`,

1. the error handling context is removed

2. the stack depth is restored to the depth that existed prior to the execution of `acf` (not counting the `acf` stack item)

3. the error code that was passed to `throw` is pushed onto the stack

4. `catch` returns

If `throw` is not called during the execution of `acf`, the error handling context is removed and `catch` returns a `false`. The stack effect is otherwise the same as if `acf` were executed using `execute` .

For example:

```
: add-n-check-limit ( n1 n2 n3   -- n )

   + + dup h# 30  >  if  true throw  then

;

: add-me ( n1 n2 n3  -- a b c | n1+n2+n3 )

   ['] add-n-check-limit catch if

      ." Sum exceeds limit " .s
```

```
        else

          ." Sum is within limit. Sum = " .s

        then cr

    ;
```

Note that, given this definition:

```
1 2 3 add-me
```

shows

```
Sum is within limit. Sum = 6
```

while

```
10 20 30 add-me
```

may show something like:

```
Sum exceeds limit  50 9 12
```

An important thing to note is that upon a non-zero throw, only the stack depth is guaranteed to be the same as before catch, not the data stack contents.

char-height
(-- n)   **code#** 1 6c

A value, containing the standard height (in pixels) for all characters to be drawn. This number, when multiplied by #lines, determines the total height (in pixels) of the active text area.

This word *must* be set to the appropriate value if you wish to use *any* fb1- or fb8- utility routines or >font . This may be done with is, but is normally done by calling set-font .

char-width

(-- n)   **code#** 1 6d

A `value`, containing the standard width (in pixels) for all characters to be drawn. This number, when multiplied by `#columns`, determines the total width (in pixels) of the active text area.

This word *must* be set to an appropriate value if you want to use *any* `fb1-` or `fb8-` utility routines. This may be done with `is`, but is normally done by calling `set-font` .

The `fb1` and `fb8` character painting support routines in current PROMs do not support widths larger than 16 (decimal). However, it is possible to display wider characters by splitting each character bitmap into 2 halves and calling `fbx-draw-character` twice.

child

(parent-phandle -- child-phandle)**code#** 2 3b
version 2.3

Returns the `phandle` of the package that is the first child of the package `parent-phandle`.

`child` returns zero if the package `parent-phandle` has no children,.

You will generally use `child`, together with `peer`, to enumerate (possibly recursively) the children of a particular device. One common use could be for bus adapter device drivers to use the phrase `my-self ihandle>phandle` to develop the `parent-phandle` argument.

For example:

```
: my-children ( -- )  \ shows phandles of all children

   my-self ihandle>phandle child  ( first-child )

   begin  ?dup  while  dup .h peer repeat

;
```

close-package

(ihandle --)   **code#** 2 06
version 2

Closes the instance identified by `ihandle` by calling that package's `close` method and then destroying the instance.

For example:

```
: tftp-load-avail? ( -- exist? )

   0 0  " obp-tftp" $open-package  ( ihandle )

   dup ihandle>phandle " load" rot

   find-method  if  drop true  else  false  then

   close-package

;
```

cmove

                    (adr1 adr2 len --)   **code#** 78
                    generates: move

Copy `len` bytes of an array starting at `adr1` to `adr2` . This word calls `move`, which is "smart" and correctly handles overlapping arrays in either direction.

`cmove` and `cmove>` are older standard Forth words that explicitly command in which order to copy the bytes (back-to-front, or front-to-back). In most cases, the distinction is not important. This distinction is important if the arrays overlap, else the source array may be overwritten prematurely, with unexpected results.

`move` will also perform 16-bit, 32-bit or possibly even 64-bit operations (for better performance) if the alignment of the operands permit. If your hardware requires explicit 8-bit or 16-bit accesses, you will probably wish to use an explicitly-coded `do... loop` instead.

cmove>

                    (adr1 adr2 len --)   **code#** 78
                    generates: move

Copy `len` bytes of an array starting at `adr1` to `adr2` . This word simply calls `move` . See `cmove` for more information.

column#

                    (-- n)   **code#** 1 53

A `value`, set and controlled by the terminal emulator, that contains the current horizontal position of the text cursor. A value of 0 represents the leftmost cursor position (this is *not* the leftmost pixel of the framebuffer - see `window-left`).

This word can (and should) be looked at as needed if your FCode program is implementing its own set of framebuffer primitives.

For example:

```
: set-column   ( column# -- )

   0 max   #columns   1- min   is column#

;
```

#columns

(-- n)   **code#** 1 51

This is a `value` that returns the number of columns of text, i.e. the number of characters in a line, to be displayed using the boot PROM's terminal emulator. It *must* be set to a proper value in order for the terminal emulator to function correctly.

`#columns` is defined in the boot PROM with an initial value of 80 (decimal), but it should always be actively set by the FCode program. This may be done with `is`, or it may be handled automatically as one of the functions performed by `fb1-install` or `fb8-install`. The value set by `fbx-install` or is the smaller of the passed `#cols` parameter and the `screen-#columns` NVRAM parameter.

For example:

```
: set-column   ( column# -- )

   0 max   #columns   1- min   is column#

;
```

comp

(adr1 adr2 len -- n)   **code#** 7a

Compare two byte arrays starting at addresses `adr1` and `adr2` and continuing for `len` bytes. n is 0 if the arrays are the same. n is 1 if the first differing character in the array at `adr1` is numerically greater than the corresponding character in the array at `adr2`. n is -1 if the first differing character in the array at `adr1` is numerically less than the corresponding character in the array at `adr2`.

For example:

```
" this" drop " that" comp .h
```

shows 1

```
" thisismy" drop " this" comp .h
```

shows 0

```
" thin" drop " this" comp .h
```

shows ffffffff .

constant

```
name( n1 -- )  at creationcode# (header) ba
                    ( -- n1 )  at execution
           generates: new header, b(type) = b(constant)
```

Creates a named constant. The name is initially created with:

```
456 constant purple
```

where the number before `constant` is the desired value for `purple` . Later occurrences of `purple` will leave the correct value on the stack. `constant` values should never be changed by the program. If you wish to change the value of a `constant` by the program, you should declare it to be a `value` instead.

control

```
x  ( -- n )              code# 10 00 00 00 xx
   generates:  b(lit) value
```

Interpret the next letter as a control-code. For example:

```
control c  ( equals 03 )
```

count

```
( pstr -- adr len )                    code# 84
```

Convert a packed string into a byte-array format. `pstr` is the address of a packed string, where the byte at address `pstr` is the length of the string and the string itself starts at address `pstr+1` .

Packed strings are generally not used in FCode. Virtually all string operations are in the "`adr len`" format.

For example:

```
h# 100 alloc-mem constant my-buff

" This is a string" my-buff pack ( pstr ) count type
```

cpeek

               (adr -- false | byte true)   **code#** 2 20
               version 2

Tries to read the 8-bit byte at address `adr`. Returns the data and `true` if the access was successful. A `false` return indicates that a read access error occurred.

cpoke

               (byte adr -- ok?)   **code#** 2 23
               version 2

Attempts to write the 8-bit byte at address `adr`. Returns `true` if the access was successful. A `false` return indicates that a write access error occurred.

Note – cpoke may be unreliable on bus adapters that buffer write accesses.

---

cr

               (--)   **code#** 92

A `defer` word used to terminate the line on the display and go to the next line. The default implementation transmits a carriage return and line feed to the display, clears `#out` , and adds 1 to `#line` .

Use `cr` whenever you want to start a new line of output, or to force the display of any previously buffered output text. This forcing is valuable for outputting error messages, to ensure that the error message is sent *before* any system crash.

For example:

```
: show-info ( -- )

   ." This is the first line of output " cr

   ." This is the second line of output " cr

;
```

(cr

(--)   **code#** 91

Output only the carriage return character (carret, hex 0d). This word is not commonly used; see cr .

create

name (--)at creation**code#** (header) bb
(-- adr)at execution
generates: new header, b(type) = b(create)

Create a name. It returns the address of memory at run time, immediately following the name in the dictionary. You can use this word to create an array-type structure, as:

```
create green 77 c, 23 c, ff c, ff c, 47 c, 22 c, ...
```

Later execution of green leaves the address of the first byte of the array (here, the address of the byte '77') on the stack. The returned address will be two-byte aligned.

In the current implementation, create may *not* be used within definitions in an FCode program. The common Forth construct create...does> is not supported.

.d

(n --)**code#** a0 6d 49 10 00 00 00 0a a0 72 9d
a0 72
generates: base @ swap d# 10 base ! . base !

n is displayed in decimal (using .). The value of base is not permanently affected.

d#

number (-- n)   **code#** 10 value
generates: b(lit) value

Interpret the next number in decimal (base 10), regardless of any previous settings of hex, decimal, binary, or octal. Only the immediately following number is affected, the default numeric base setting is unchanged. For example:

```
hex

d# 100   ( equals decimal 100 )

100      ( equals decimal 256 )
```

See also b#, h#, and o#.

decimal

(--)   **code#** none

generates: 10 base !**code#** 10 00 00 00 0a a0 72

If outside of a definition, commands the tokenizer program to interpret subsequent numbers in decimal (base 10). If within a definition, change the value in base affecting later numeric output when the FCode program is executed.   See base .

decode-2int

(adr len -- phys space)   **code#** 1 1b

version 2

Converts a string into a physical address and space.

For example:

```
" 4,ff001200" decode-2int .s

will show: ff001200 4

" 4" decode-2int .s

will show: 0 4
```

default-font

(-- fontbase charwidth charheight fontbytes
#firstchar #chars)

                                          code# 1 6a

This function returns all necessary information about the character font that is built into the boot PROM. This font defines the appearance of every character to be displayed. To load this font, simply pass these parameters to `set-font`, with:

```
default-font set-font
```

The actual parameters returned by `default-font` are:

   `fontbase` - The address of the beginning of the built-in font table

   `charwidth` - The width of each character in pixels

   `charheight` - The height of each character in pixels

   `fontbytes` - The separation (in bytes) between each scan line entry

   `#firstchar` - The ASCII value for the first character actually stored in the font table.

   `#chars` - The total number of characters stored in the font table.

defer

name　(--)at creation**code#** (header) bc
(??? -- ?)at execution
generates:　new header, b(type) = b(defer)

Create a `defer`'d executable. This is a word that has a variable behavior, depending on the function that is later loaded into it. The name is initially created with:

```
defer blob
```

Later, after some other word *foobar* has been created, this behavior can then be loaded in, with:

```
['] foobar is blob
```

`defer`'d words are useful for generating recursive routines. Here's an example:

```
defer hold2  \ Will execute action2

: action1

  ...
```

```
   hold2 ( really action2 )

   ...  ;

: action2

   ...

   action1

   ...  ;

' action2 is hold2
```

`defer`'d words can also be used for creating words with different behaviors depending on your needs. For example:

```
defer .special ( n -- ) \ Print a value, using special techniques

: print-em-all ( -- )

   ... .special

   ... .special

   ... .special

;



( .d prints in decimal

( .h prints in hexadecimal )

( .sp prints in a custom format )

: print-all-styles
```

```
    ['] .d is  .special print-em-all

    ['] .h is  .special print-em-all

    ['] .sp is .special print-em-all


;
```

If a `defer` word is executed before being loaded with some behavior, an error message will be printed.

delete-attribute

(adr len --)   **code#** 2 1e
version 2

Deletes the property named by `adr len` in the active package, if such a property exists.

For example:

```
: unmap-me ( -- )

   my-reg my-size " map-out"  $call-parent


   " address" delete-attribute


;
```

delete-characters

(n --)   **code#** 1 5e

A `defer` word, called by the terminal emulator when needed to delete n characters to the right of the cursor. The cursor position is unchanged, the cursor character and the first n-1 characters to the right of the cursor are deleted. All remaining characters to the right of the cursor, including the highlighted character, are moved left by n places. The end of the line is filled with blanks.

This word is initially empty, but *must* be loaded with an appropriate routine in order for the terminal emulator to function correctly. This may be done with `is`, or it may be loaded automatically with `fb1-install` or `fb8-install` (which loads `fb1-delete-characters` or `fb8-delete-characters` , respectively).

delete-lines

(n --)   **code#** 1 60

A `defer` word, called by the terminal emulator to delete n lines starting with the cursor line (and deletes n-1 lines below the cursor). Lines above the cursor are unchanged. The cursor position is unchanged. All lines below the deleted lines are scrolled upwards by n lines, and n blank lines are placed at the bottom of the active text area.

Use this word for scrolling, by temporarily moving the cursor to the top of the screen and then calling `delete-lines` .

This word is initially empty, but *must* be loaded with an appropriate routine in order for the terminal emulator to function correctly. This may be done with `is`, or it may be loaded automatically with `fb1-install` or `fb8-install` (which loads `fb1-delete-lines` or `fb8-delete-lines` , respectively).

depth
(-- +n)

code# 51

+n is the number of entries contained in the data stack, not counting itself. Note that when an FCode program is called, there could be other items on the stack from the calling program.

`depth` is especially useful for before/after stack depth checking, to determine if the stack was corrupted by a particular operation.

device-name
(adr len --)
version 2

code# 2 01

Creates a `name` attribute with the given string value, for example:

```
" SUNW,zebra" device-name
```

This is equivalent to using the `name` macro or

```
xdrstring " name" attribute
```

except that `device-name` performs the same function with only 2 bytes of FCode, instead of 10 bytes. This could be useful for devices with extremely limited FCode space.

See "`name`" in Chapter 5, "Properties" for more information.

device-type
(adr len --)

code# 1 1a

This is a shorthand word for creating a "`device_type`" property. This property is essential for any plug-in SBus device that will be used during booting, as it tells the boot PROM which type of boot device it is. An example usage would be:

```
" display" device-type
```

This is exactly equivalent to the following:

```
" display" xdrstring " device_type" attribute
```

Note the spelling difference between the FCode command `device-type` (hyphen) and the `device_type` property (underscore).

The `device_type` property is looked at and used by the boot PROM as well.

See also: "device_type" in Chapter 5, "Properties".

diagnostic-mode?

(-- flag)   **code#** 1 20

Returns a `true` flag if the `diag-switch?` NVRAM parameter is set to `true` . This word enables an FCode program to optionally perform some extended selftests, based on the `diag-switch?` . For example:

```
diagnostic-mode?

if    do-extended-tests

else  do-normal-tests

then
```

FCode should not generate character output during probing unless `diagnostic-mode?` is `true`, or unless an error is encountered. Error output during probing typically goes to the system serial port.

digit

(char base -- digit true | char false)**code#** a3

If the character char is a digit in the specified base, returns the numeric value of that digit under true , else returns the character under false . Appropriate characters are hex 30-39 (for digits 0-9) and hex 61-66 (for digits a-f), depending on base.

For example:

```
: probe-slot ( slot# -- ) ... ;

: probe-slots  ( adr cnt -- )

   bounds  ?do

      i c@  d# 16  digit  if  probe-slot  else  drop  then

   loop

;
```

display-status

(n --)   **code#** 1 21

Display the results of some test. The method of display is system-dependent. This FCode is obsolete and should not be used.

do

(limit start --)   **code#** 17 +offset
generates: b(do) +offset

Begin a counted loop in the form do ... loop or do ... +loop. The loop index begins at start , and terminates based on limit . See loop and +loop for details on how the loop is terminated. The loop is always executed at least once. For example:

```
8 3 do i . loop    \ would print 3 4 5 6 7

9 3 do i . 2 +loop \ would print 3 5 7
```

?do

(limit start --)   **code#** 18 +offset
generates: b(?do) +offset

Begin a counted loop in the form ?do ... loop or ?do ... +loop . The loop index begins at start , and terminates based on limit . See loop and +loop for details on how the loop is terminated. Unlike do , if start is equal to limit the loop is executed zero times. For example:

```
8 1 ?do i . loop      \ would print 1 2 3 4 5 6 7

2 1 ?do i . loop      \ would print 1

1 1 ?do i . loop      \ would print nothing

1 1  do i . loop      \ would print 1 2 3 4 5 6 7 8 9...

...
```

?do may be used in place of do in nearly all circumstances.

dma-alloc

(#bytes -- virtual)   **code#** 1 01

Used to allocate memory for DMA usae. The allocated memory may be returned to the system with free-virtual.

This FCode is obsolete on OpenBoot 2 PROMs. For use under OpenBoot 1, see Appendix D, "Changes in Version 1 FCode Usage".

For version 2 OpenBoot systems, use " dma-alloc" method of parent:

```
" dma-alloc" $call-parent

" dma-map-in" $call-parent
```

For example:

```
: my-dma-alloc  ( -- )

   my-size " dma-alloc" $call-parent   ( vaddr )

   is my-reg

;
```

draw-character

(char --)   **code#** 1 57

A `defer` word, called by the boot PROM's terminal emulator in order to display a single character on the screen at the current cursor location.

This word is initially empty, but *must* be loaded with an appropriate routine in order for the terminal emulator to function correctly. This may be done with `is`, or it may be loaded automatically with `fb1-install` or `fb8-install` (which loads `fb1-draw-character` or `fb8-draw-character` , respectively).

draw-logo

(line# laddr lwidth lheight --)**code#** 1 61

A `defer` word, called by the system to display the power-on logo (the graphic displayed on the left side during power-up, or by the `banner` Toolkit command).

This word is initially empty, but *must* be loaded with an appropriate routine in order for the terminal emulator to function correctly. This may be done with `is`, or it may be loaded automatically with `fb1-install` or `fb8-install` (which loads `fb1-draw-logo` or `fb8-draw-logo` , respectively).

It is possible to pack a custom logo into the FCode PROM and then reinitialize `draw-logo` to output the custom logo instead.

`draw-logo` is called by the system using the following parameters:

> `line#` - The text line number at which to draw the logo. See Appendix D, "Changes in Version 1 FCode Usage". For general use, also see Appendix C, "FCode Memory Allocation".

> `laddr` - The address of the logo template to be drawn. In practice, this will always be either the address of the `oem-logo` field in NVRAM, the address of a custom logo in the FCode PROM, or the address of a built-in Sun logo. In either case, the logo is a bit array of 64x64 (decimal) pixels (512 bytes). The most significant bit (msb) of the first byte represents the upper-left pixel; msb-1 represents the next pixel to the right, and so on. A bit value of 1 means that pixel will be painted.

> `lwidth` - The width of the passed-in logo (in pixels).

> `lheight`- The height of the passed-in logo (in pixels).

driver

(adr len --)   **code#** 1 18

This is an obsolete word for creating a `name` property.

`driver` is no longer supported and should not be used in FCode programs.

drop

     (n --)   **code#** 46

Removes one item from the stack.

2drop

     (n1 n2 --)   **code#** 52

Removes two items from the stack.

3drop

     (n1 n2 n3 --)   **code#** 46 52
     generates: drop 2drop

Removes three items from the stack.

dup

     (n1 -- n1 n1)   **code#** 47

Duplicates the top stack item.

?dup

     (n1 -- 0 | n1 n1)   **code#** 50

Duplicate the top stack item unless it is zero.

2dup

     (n1 n2 -- n1 n2 n1 n2) **code#** 53

Duplicates the top two stack items.

3dup

     (n1 n2 n3 -- n1 n2 n3 n1 n2 n3)**code#** a7 4e
     a7 4e a7 4e
     generates: 2 pick 2 pick 2 pick

Duplicates the top three stack items.

else

     (--)   **code#** 13 +offset b2
     generates: bbranch +offset b(>resolve)

Begin the else clause of an if ... else ... then statement. See if for more
details.

emit

     (char --)   **code#** 8f

A defer word that outputs the indicated ASCII character. For example, (hex) 41 emit
outputs an "A", 62 emit outputs a "b", 34 emit outputs a "4".

emit-byte

(n --)   **code#** n

generates: n

A tokenizer command used to manually output a desired byte of FCode. Use it together
with tokenizer[as follows:

```
tokenizer[

  44 emit-byte 20 emit-byte

]tokenizer
```

emit-byte would be useful, for example, if you wished to generate a new FCode
command that the tokenizer did not understand. This command should be used with
caution or else an invalid FCode program will result.

end0

(--)   **code#** 00

A word that marks the end of an FCode program. This word must be present at the end
of your program, or erroneous results may occur.

If you want to use end0 inside a colon definition, for example in a conditional clause, use
something like:

```
: exit-if-version1  version  h# 20000 <  if  ['] end0 execute  then  ;
```

end1

(--)   **code#** ff

An alternate word for end0 , to mark the end of an FCode program. end0 is
recommended.

endcase

(selector|<null> --)   **code#** c5

generates: b(endcase)

Marks the end of a case statement. See case for more details.

endof

(--)   **code#** c6 +offset

generates: b(endof) +offset

Marks the end of an of clause within a case statement. See case for more details.

erase

```
( adr len -- )                              code# a5 79
generates: 0 fill
```

Sets `len` bytes of memory beginning at `adr` to zero. No action is taken if `len` is zero.

erase-screen

```
( -- )                                      code# 1 5a
```

A `defer` word, called once during the terminal emulator initialization sequence in order to completely clear all pixels on the display. This word is called just *before* `reset-screen`, so that the user doesn't actually see the framebuffer data until it has been properly scrubbed.

This word is initially empty, but *must* be loaded with an appropriate routine in order for the terminal emulator to function correctly. This may be done with `is`, or it may be loaded automatically with `fb1-install` or `fb8-install` (which loads `fb1-erase-screen` or `fb8-erase-screen`, respectively).

eval

```
( ??? adr len -- ? )                        code# cd
version 2
```

Executes Forth commands within a string. The overall stack effect depends on the commands being executed. For example:

```
" 4000 20 dump" eval
```

You can use `eval` like `$find`, to find and execute Forth commands that are not FCodes.

The same cautions apply to `eval` as for `$find`, in that programs executing Forth commands are likely to encounter portability problems when moved to other systems.

execute

```
( acf -- )                                  code# 1d
```

Executes the word definition whose compilation address is `acf`. An error condition exists if `acf` is not a compilation address.

For example:

```
: my-word ( adr len -- )

   ." Given string is: " type cr

;

" great" ['] my-word execute
```

exit

(--)   **code#** 33

Compiled within a colon definition. When encountered, execution leaves the current word and returns control to the calling word. May not be used within a do loop.

For example:

```
: probe-loop  ( adr -- )

   \ generate a tight probe loop until any key is pressed.

   begin dup l@ drop key?  if  drop exit  then  again

;
```

expect

(adr len --)   **code#** 8a

A defer word that receives a line of characters from the keyboard and stores them into memory, performing line editing as the characters are typed.   Displays all characters actually received and stored into memory. The number of received characters is stored in span .

The transfer begins at adr proceeding towards higher addresses one byte per character until either a return is received or until len characters have been transferred. No more than len characters will be stored. The return is not stored into memory. No characters are received or transferred if len is zero.

For example:

```
h# 10 buffer: my-name-buff

: hello ( -- )

   ." Enter Your First name " my-name-buff h# 10 expect

   ." Sun Microsystems Welcomes " my-name-buff span @ type cr

;
```

external
            (--)   **code#** none
            version 2

After issuing external, all subsequent definitions are created so that names are later compiled into RAM, regardless of the value of the NVRAM variable fcode-debug?. external is used to define the package methods that may be called from other software external to the package, and whose names must therefore be present.

external stays in effect until headers or headerless is encountered.

For example:

```
external

: open ( -- ok? ) ... ;
```

external-token
            (--)   **code#** ca
            version 2

A token-type, used to indicate that this word should always be compiled with the name header present. Activated by external, all subsequent words are created with external-token until deactivated with either headers or headerless. See named-token for more details. This word should never be used in source code.

false
            (-- 0)   **code#** a5
            generates: 0

Leave the value for the false flag (which is zero) on the stack.

fb1-blink-screen

(--)   **code#** 1 74

The built-in default routine to blink or flash the screen momentarily on a generic 1-bit-per-pixel framebuffer. This routine is loaded into the `defer` word `blink-screen` by calling `fb1-install` .

This routine is invalid unless the FCode program has called `fb1-install` and has initialized `frame-buffer-adr` to a valid virtual address.

This word is implemented simply by calling `fb1-invert-screen` twice. In practice, this can be quite slow (around one full second). It is quite common for a framebuffer FCode program to replace `fb1-blink-screen` with a custom routine that simply disables the video for 20 milliseconds or so, i.e.

Code Example 11-2 `fb1-blink-screen` *sample*

```
: my-blink-screen  ( -- )  video-off  20 ms  video-on  ;
...
fb1-install
...
['] my-blink-screen   is blink-screen
```

fb1-delete-characters

(n --)   **code#** 1 77

The built-in default routine to delete n characters at and to the right of the cursor, on a generic 1-bit-per-pixel framebuffer. This routine is loaded into the `defer` word `delete-characters` by calling `fb1-install` .

This routine is invalid unless the FCode program has called `fb1-install` and `set-font` and has initialized `frame-buffer-adr` to a valid virtual address.

The cursor position is unchanged, the cursor character and the next n-1 characters to the right of the cursor are deleted, and the remaining characters to the right are moved left by n places. The end of the line is filled with blanks.

fb1-delete-lines

(n --)   **code#** 1 79

The built-in default routine to delete n lines, starting with the cursor line, on a generic 1-bit-per-pixel framebuffer. This routine is loaded into the `defer` word `delete-lines` by calling `fb1-install` .

This routine is invalid unless the FCode program has called `fb1-install` and `set-font` and has initialized `frame-buffer-adr` to a valid virtual address.

The cursor line and n-1 lines below it are deleted. All lines above the cursor line are unchanged. The cursor position is unchanged. All lines below the deleted lines are scrolled upwards by n lines, and n blank lines are placed at the bottom of the active text area.

fb1-draw-character
(char --)

code# 1 70

The built-in default routine for drawing a character on a generic 1-bit-per-pixel framebuffer, at the current cursor location. This routine is loaded into the `defer` word `draw-character` by calling `fb1-install` .

This routine is invalid unless the FCode program has called `fb1-install` and `set-font` and has initialized `frame-buffer-adr` to a valid virtual address.

If `inverse?` is `true` , then characters are drawn inverted (white-on-black). Otherwise (the normal case) they are drawn black-on-white.

fb1-draw-logo
(line# logoadr lwidth lheight --) **code#** 1 7a

The built-in default routine to draw the logo on a generic 1-bit-per-pixel framebuffer. This routine is loaded into the `defer` word `draw-logo` by calling `fb1-install` .

This routine is invalid unless the FCode program has called `fb1-install` and `set-font` and has initialized `frame-buffer-adr` to a valid virtual address.

See `draw-logo` for more information on the parameters passed.

fb1-erase-screen
(--)

code# 1 73

The built-in default routine to clear (erase) every pixel in a generic 1-bit-per-pixel framebuffer. This routine is loaded into the `defer` word `erase-screen` by calling `fb1-install` .

This routine is invalid unless the FCode program has called `fb1-install` and has initialized `frame-buffer-adr` to a valid virtual address.

All pixels are erased (not just the ones in the active text area). If `inverse-screen?` is `true` , then all pixels are set to 1, resulting in a black screen. Otherwise (the normal case) all pixels are set to 0, resulting in a white screen.

fb1-insert-characters
(n --)

code# 1 76

The built-in default routine to insert n blank characters to the right of the cursor, on a generic 1-bit-per-pixel framebuffer. This routine is loaded into the `defer` word `insert-characters` by calling `fb1-install` .

This routine is invalid unless the FCode program has called `fb1-install` and `set-font` and has initialized `frame-buffer-adr` to a valid virtual address.

The cursor position is unchanged, but the cursor character and all characters to the right of the cursor are moved right by n places. An error condition exists if an attempt is made to create a line longer than the maximum line size (the value in `#columns`).

fb1-insert-lines

(n --)   **code#** 1 78

The built-in default routine to insert n blank lines below the cursor on a generic 1-bit-per-pixel framebuffer. This routine is loaded into the `defer` word `insert-lines` by calling `fb1-install` .

This routine is invalid unless the FCode program has called `fb1-install` and `set-font` and has initialized `frame-buffer-adr` to a valid virtual address.

The cursor position on the screen is unchanged. The cursor line is pushed down, but all lines above it are unchanged. Any lines pushed off of the bottom of the active text area are lost.

fb1-install

(screen-width screen-height   **code#** 1 7b
  #cols #lines --)

This built-in routine installs all of the built-in default routines for driving a generic 1-bit-per-pixel framebuffer. It also initializes most necessary `values` needed for using these default routines.

`set-font` must be called, and `frame-buffer-adr` initialized, before `fb1-install` is called, because the `char-width` and `char-height` values set by `set-font` are needed when `fb1-install` is executed.

`fb1-install` loads the following `defer` routines with their corresponding `fb1-`(whatever) equivalents: `reset-screen` , `toggle-cursor` , `erase-screen` , `blink-screen` , `invert-screen` , `insert-characters` , `delete-characters`, `insert-lines` , `delete-lines` , `draw-character`, `draw-logo` .

The following `values` are also initialized:

   `screen-width` - set to the value of the passed-in parameter `screen-width` (screen width in pixels)

   `screen-height` - set to the value of the passed-in parameter `screen-height` (screen height in pixels)

   `#columns` - set to the smaller of the following two: the passed-in parameter `#cols` , and the NVRAM parameter `screen-#columns`

#lines - set to the smaller of the following two: the passed-in parameter #lines , and the NVRAM parameter screen-#rows

window-top - set to half of the difference between the total screen height (screen-height) and the height of the active text area (#lines times char-height)

window-left - set to half of the difference between the total screen width (screen-width) and the width of the active text area (#columns times charwidth), then rounded down to the nearest multiple of 32 (for performance reasons)

Several internal values used by various fb1- routine are also set.

fb1-invert-screen

(--)   **code#** 1 75

The built-in default routine to invert every visible pixel on a generic 1-bit-per-pixel framebuffer. This routine is loaded into the defer word invert-screen by calling fb1-install .

This routine is invalid unless the FCode program has called fb1-install and has initialized frame-buffer-adr to a valid virtual address.

All pixels are inverted (not just the ones in the active text area).

fb1-reset-screen

(--)   **code#** 1 71

The built-in default routine to enable a generic 1-bit-per-pixel framebuffer to display data. This routine is loaded into the defer word reset-screen by calling fb1-install. (reset-screen is called just after erase-screen during the terminal emulator initialization sequence.)

This word is initially a NOP. Typically, an FCode program will define a hardware-dependent routine to enable video, and then replace this generic function with:

Code Example 11-3   my-video-enable sample

```
: my-video-enable ( -- ) ... :
fb1-install
...
['] my-video-enable  is  reset-screen
```

fb1-slide-up

(n --)   **code#** 1 7c

This is a utility routine. It behaves exactly like fb1-delete-lines , except that it doesn't clear the lines at the bottom of the active text area. Its only purpose is to scroll the enable plane for framebuffers that have 1-bit overlay and enable planes.

This routine is invalid unless the FCode program has called `fb1-install` and `set-font` and has initialized `frame-buffer-adr` to a valid virtual address.

fb1-toggle-cursor
(--)   **code#** 1 72

The built-in default routine to toggle the cursor location in a generic 1-bit-per-pixel framebuffer. This routine is loaded into the `defer` word `toggle-cursor` by calling `fb1-install` . The behavior is to invert every pixel in the one-character-size space for the current position of the text cursor.

This routine is invalid unless the FCode program has called `fb1-install` and `set-font` and has initialized `frame-buffer-adr` to a valid virtual address.

fb8-blink-screen
(--)   **code#** 1 84

The built-in default routine to blink or flash the screen momentarily on a generic 8-bit-per-pixel framebuffer. This routine is loaded into the `defer` word `blink-screen` by calling `fb8-install` .

This routine is invalid unless the FCode program has called `fb8-install` and has initialized `frame-buffer-adr` to a valid virtual address.

This word is implemented simply by calling `fb8-invert-screen` twice. In practice, this can be very slow (several seconds). It is quite common for a framebuffer FCode program to replace `fb8-blink-screen` with a custom routine that simply disables the video for 20 milliseconds or so, i.e.

Code Example 11-4   my-blink-screen sample

```
: my-blink-screen  ( -- )  video-off  20 ms  video-on  ;
...
fb8-install
...
['] my-blink-screen   is blink-screen
```

fb8-delete-characters
(n --)   **code#** 1 87

The built-in default routine to delete n characters to the right of the cursor, on a generic 8-bit-per-pixel framebuffer. This routine is loaded into the `defer` word `delete-characters` by calling `fb8-install` .

This routine is invalid unless the FCode program has called `fb8-install` and `set-font` and has initialized `frame-buffer-adr` to a valid virtual address.

The cursor position is unchanged. The cursor character and the next n-1 characters to the right of the cursor are deleted, and the remaining characters to the right are moved left by n places. The end of the line is filled with blanks.

fb8-delete-lines

(n --)   **code#** 1 89

The built-in default routine to delete n lines, starting with the cursor line, on a generic 8-bit-per-pixel framebuffer. This routine is loaded into the `defer` word `delete-lines` by calling `fb8-install`.

This routine is invalid unless the FCode program has called `fb8-install` and `set-font` and has initialized `frame-buffer-adr` to a valid virtual address.

The cursor line and n-1 lines below it are deleted. All lines above the cursor line are unchanged. The cursor position is unchanged. All lines below the deleted lines are scrolled upwards by n lines, and n blank lines are placed at the bottom of the active text area.

fb8-draw-character

(char --)   **code#** 1 80

The built-in default routine for drawing a character on a generic 8-bit-per-pixel framebuffer, at the current cursor location. This routine is loaded into the `defer` word `draw-character` by calling `fb8-install`.

This routine is invalid unless the FCode program has called `fb8-install` and `set-font` and has initialized `frame-buffer-adr` to a valid virtual address.

If `inverse?` is `true`, then characters are drawn inverted (white-on-black). Otherwise (the normal case) they are drawn black-on-white.

fb8-draw-logo

(line# logoadr lwidth lheight --)**code#** 1 8a

The built-in default routine to draw the logo on a generic 8-bit-per-pixel framebuffer. This routine is loaded into the `defer` word `draw-logo` by calling `fb8-install`.

This routine is invalid unless the FCode program has called `fb8-install` and `set-font` and has initialized `frame-buffer-adr` to a valid virtual address.

The logo is drawn by painting every desired pixel with the value 01 (normal characters are painted with the value FF). Typically, color# 0xff is set to black (for normal black characters), whereas color#01 is set to Sun-blue so that the Sun logo is painted the proper color.

See `draw-logo` for more information on the parameters passed.

fb8-erase-screen

(--)   **code#** 1 83

The built-in default routine to clear (erase) every pixel in a generic 8-bit-per-pixel framebuffer. This routine is loaded into the `defer` word `erase-screen` by calling `fb8-install`.

This routine is invalid unless the FCode program has called `fb8-install` and has initialized `frame-buffer-adr` to a valid virtual address.

All pixels are erased (not just the ones in the active text area). If `inverse-screen?` is `true`, then all pixels are set to 0xff, resulting in a black screen. Otherwise (the normal case) all pixels are set to 0, resulting in a white screen.

fb8-insert-characters

(n --)   **code#** 1 86

The built-in default routine to insert n blank characters to the right of the cursor, on a generic 8-bit-per-pixel framebuffer. This routine is loaded into the `defer` word `insert-characters` by calling `fb8-install`.

This routine is invalid unless the FCode program has called `fb8-install` and `set-font` and has initialized `frame-buffer-adr` to a valid virtual address.

The cursor position is unchanged, but the cursor character and all characters to the right of the cursor are moved right by n places. An error condition exists if an attempt is made to create a line longer than the maximum line size (the value in `#columns`).

fb8-insert-lines

(n --)   **code#** 1 88

The built-in default routine to insert n blank lines below the cursor on a generic 8-bit-per-pixel framebuffer. This routine is loaded into the `defer` word `insert-lines` by calling `fb8-install`.

This routine is invalid unless the FCode program has called `fb8-install` and `set-font` and has initialized `frame-buffer-adr` to a valid virtual address.

The cursor position is unchanged. The cursor line is pushed down, but all lines above it are unchanged. Any lines pushed off of the bottom of the active text area are lost.

fb8-install

(screen-width screen-height #cols**code#** 1 8b
  #lines --)

This built-in routine installs all of the built-in default routines for driving a generic 8-bit-per-pixel framebuffer. It also initializes most necessary `values` needed for using these default routines.

`set-font` must be called, and `frame-buffer-addr` initialized, before `fb8-install` is called, because the `char-width` and `char-height` values set by `set-font` are needed when `fb8-install` is executed.

`fb8-install` loads the following `defer` routines with their corresponding `fb8-`(whatever) equivalents: `reset-screen`, `toggle-cursor`, `erase-screen`, `blink-screen`, `invert-screen`, `insert-characters`, `delete-characters`, `insert-lines`, `delete-lines`, `draw-character`, `draw-logo`

The following values are also initialized:

> `screen-width` - set to the value of the passed-in parameter `screen-width` (screen width in pixels)

> `screen-height` - set to the value of the passed-in parameter `screen-height` (screen height in pixels)

#columns - set to the smaller of the following two: the passed-in parameter #cols, and the NVRAM parameter screen-#columns

#lines - set to the smaller of the following two: the passed-in parameter #lines, and the NVRAM parameter screen-#rows

window-top - set to half of the difference between the total screen height (screen-height) and the height of the active text area (#lines times char-height)

window-left - set to half of the difference between the total screen width (screen-width) and the width of the active text area (#columns times char-width), then rounded down to the nearest multiple of 32 (for performance reasons)

Several internal values are also set that are used by various fb8- routines.

fb8-invert-screen

(--) **code#** 1 85

The built-in default routine to XOR (with hex 0xff) every visible pixel on a generic 8-bit-per-pixel framebuffer. This routine is loaded into the defer word invert-screen by calling fb8-install .

This routine is invalid unless the FCode program has called fb8-install and has initialized frame-buffer-adr to a valid virtual address.

All pixels are inverted (not just the ones in the active text area).

fb8-reset-screen

(--) **code#** 1 81

The built-in default routine to enable a generic 8-bit-per-pixel framebuffer to display data. This routine is loaded into the defer word reset-screen by calling fb8-install . (reset-screen is called just after erase-screen during the terminal emulator initialization sequence.)

This word is initially a NOP. Typically, an FCode program will define a hardware-dependent routine to enable video, and then replace this generic function with:

Code Example 11-5   my-video-enable sample

```
: my-video-enable ( -- ) ... :
fb8-install
...
['] my-video-enable  is  reset-screen
...
```

fb8-toggle-cursor

(--)   **code#** 1 82

The built-in default routine to toggle the cursor location in a generic 8-bit-per-pixel framebuffer. This routine is loaded into the `defer` word `toggle-cursor` by calling `fb8-install` . The behavior is to XOR every pixel with 0xff in the one-character-size space for the current position of the text cursor.

This routine is invalid unless the FCode program has called `fb8-install` and `set-font` and has initialized `frame-buffer-adr` to a valid virtual address.

fcode-version

(-- n)   **code#** 2 12
version 2

This FCode is obsolete, use `version` instead.

fcode-version1

(--) **code#**   fd 00   xx yy   aa bb cc dd
generates: version1 (null) (reserved) (length)

This word, or `fcode-version2`, *must* be the first command in your FCode program (except for tokenizer directives such as `hex` or `\` that do not generate any FCode bytes). The command `fcode-version1` creates an 8-byte header, as:

```
(fd) version1      ( 1 byte )
```

```
(00) null byte      ( 1 byte )

(xxyy) reserved     ( 2 bytes )

(aabbccdd) length   ( 4 bytes )
```

The `length` field specifies the total usable length of FCode data, from `version1` to `end0` inclusive. Additional `end0` bytes are appended to the end of the data, if needed, to leave a total length which is evenly divisible by 4. The "null byte" position may be used in the future to carry a version number or other information, but it is currently not used.

See Appendix D, "Changes in Version 1 FCode Usage".

fcode-version2

```
( -- )        code# f1 00 xx yy aa bb cc dd
generates: start1 (null) (reserved) (length)
version 2
```

Starts a version2 FCode program, generating an 8-byte header similar to `fcode-version1`, except that the starting byte is `start1` (f1) instead of `version1` (fd).

For example:

```
fcode-version2

" SUNW,nvsimm" xdrstring " name" attribute

...

end0
```

Caution – FCode programs created with `fcode-version2` will *only* run on OpenBoot 2 or later systems. They will *not* work on OpenBoot 1.0 systems.

> **Caution –** In most cases, use `fcode-version1`, along with an escape routine to prevent any version 1.0 systems from trying to execute, as shown in the following example:

```
: ?quit  ( -- ) version h# 2.0000 < if ['] end0 execute then ;

?quit
```

See Appendix D, "Changes in Version 1 FCode Usage".

ferror

```
( -- )                                        code#  fc
version 2.3
```

Displays an "Unimplemented FCode" error message and stops FCode interpretation. All unimplemented FCode numbers resolve to `ferror` in all existing OpenBoot implementations.

The intended use of `ferror` is to determine whether or not a particular FCode is implemented, without checking the FCode version number.

For example:

```
: implemented? ( acf -- flag) ['] ferror <> ;

: my-peer ( prev -- next )

  ['] peer implemented? if

    peer

  else

    ." peer is not implemented" cr

  then

:
```

field

```
                           ( offset size -- offset+size ) at creation
                           code# (header) be
                           ( base -- base+offset )        at execution
                           generates:  new header, b(type) = b(field)
```

struct and field are used to create named offset pointers into some array structure. For each field in the array structure, a name is assigned to the location of that field (as an offset from the beginning of the array). Here's a code example. (The numbers in parentheses show the stack *after* each word is created.) The structure being described is:

```
byte#

0 1  2 3 4 5  6    7    8 9    10 11 12 13 14 15 16 17   18 19

size flags.. bits key fullname....................   age

                         initials lastname..........

struct            ( 0 )

2 field size      ( 2 )   \ equivalent to:  : size     0 + ;

4 field flags     ( 6 )   \ equivalent to:  : flags    2 + ;

1 field bits      ( 7 )   \ equivalent to:  : bits     6 + ;

1 field key       ( 8 )   \ equivalent to:  : key      7 + ;

0 field fullname  ( 8 )   \ equivalent to:  : fullname 8 + ;

2 field initials  ( 10 )  \ equivalent to:  : initials 8 + ;

8 field lastname  ( 18 )  \ equivalent to:  : lastname 10 + ;

2 field age       ( 20 )  \ equivalent to:  : age      18 + ;

  constant /record ( )    \ equivalent to:  20 constant /record
```

Typical usage of these defined words would be:

```
/record buffer: myrecord    \ Create the "myrecord" buffer

myrecord flags 1@           \ get flags data

myrecord key   c@           \ get key data

myrecord size  w@           \ get size data

/record                     \ get total size of the array
```

Note that `struct` is merely a cross-compiler equivalent that puts the number 0 on the stack.

fill

(adr u byte --)   **code#** 79

Set u bytes of memory beginning at `adr` to `byte` . No action taken if u = 0.

$find

(adr len -- adr len false | acf +/-1)**code#**
cb

Takes a string from the stack, and tries to find that word in the OpenBoot PROM. This is an escape hatch, allowing an FCode program to perform any function that is available in the OpenBoot Forth Monitor but that is not defined as part of the standard FCode interface.

If the word is not found, the original string is left on the stack, with a `false` on top of the stack. If the word is found, the code field address of that word is left on the stack, and either a +1 or -1 is left on top. +1 is left if the found word is an `immediate` word, -1 is left otherwise.

Use `$find` with caution! Different CPUs or even different versions of the boot PROM may change or delete certain words in the Toolkit. If your FCode program depends on one of these words, you may suddenly find that your SBus card doesn't work properly with future releases.

 Caution – If you find yourself tempted to use `$find` , please contact the Sun SBus Support Group and tell them what function you need to use this way. This will help Sun to plan for future FCode features, and will let you know the likelihood of the needed Toolkit word being changed in the future.

Example of use:

```
" root-info" $find    ( adr len false | acf +/-1 )

if execute            \ if found, then do the function

                      \ in this example, we don't care about

                      \ immediate vs. non-immediate

else ( adr len ) type ." was not found!" cr

then
```

find-method

```
( adr len phandle -- false | acf true )code#
2 07
version 2
```

Locates the method named by `adr  len` within the package `phandle`. Returns `false` if the package has no such method, or `acf` and `true` if the operation succeeds. Subsequently, `acf` may be used with `call-package`.

For example:

```
: tftp-load-avail? ( -- exist? )

   " obp-tftp" find-package  if  ( phandle )

     " load"  rot find-method if ( acf )

        drop true exit

     then

   then

   false

;
```

find-package

(adr len -- false | phandle true)**code#** 2 04
version 2

Locates a package whose name is given by the string `adr len`. If the package can be located, returns its `phandle` and `true`. Otherwise returns `false`. The name is interpreted relative to the `/packages` device node. For example, if `adr len` represents the string "`disk-label`", the package in the device tree at "`/packages/disk-label`" will be located. If there are multiple packages with the same name (within the `/packages` node), the `phandle` for the most recently created one is returned.

For example:

```
: tftp-load-avail? ( -- exist? )

   " obp-tftp" find-package  if  ( phandle )

      " load"  rot find-method if ( acf )

         drop true exit

      then

   then

   false

;
```

finish-device

(--)   **code#** 1 27

The two words `finish-device` and `new-device` let a single FCode program declare more than one entry into the device tree. This capability is useful when a single SBus card contains two or more essentially independent devices, to be controlled by two or more separate SunOS device drivers. Typical usage:

```
fcode-version1

...driver#1...

finish-device    \ terminate device tree entry#1
```

```
new-device        \ begin a new device tree entry

...driver#2

finish-device     \ terminate device tree entry#2

new-device        \ begin a new device tree entry

...driver#3...

end0
```

There is an implicit new-device call at the beginning of an FCode program (at fcode-version1 or fcode-version2), and an implicit finish-device call at the end of an FCode program (at end0). Thus, FCode programs that only define a single device and driver will never need to call finish-device or new-device.

firmware-version

(-- n)   **code#**   2 11

version 2

Returns a 32-bit number identifying the version of the CPU firmware. The high 16 bits is the major version number and the low 16 bits is the minor version number.

This is the major/minor release number that is accessed by the ROMvec entry op_mon_id . For example, in version 2.1, firmware-version returns 0x00020001 . This is also the same number displayed by banner or .version.

For example:

```
: show-version ( -- )

  ." CPU bootprom version is " base @  d# 16 base !  ( old-base )

  firmware-version   ( old-base version )

  lwsplit (.) type ascii . emit .h cr base !          ( )

;
```

flip

(n1 -- n2)   **code#** 80

n2 is the result of exchanging the two low-order bytes of the number n1 . The two upper bytes of n1 must be zero, or erroneous results will occur.

fload

filename   (--)   **code#** none

Tokenizer command that begins tokenizing text in the named file. When the named file is done, tokenizing continues on the file that called filename with fload.

For example:

```
fload my-disk-package.fth
```

fload commands may be nested; an floaded file may include fload commands.

fload is useful for creating large FCode programs, making it easier to break them up into function blocks for better clarity and portability.

Note – fload commands won't work when downloading text in source-code form. You can either manually merge your text into one big file, download and execute the various file separately, or tokenize it first and then download and execute the FCode in binary form.

>font

(char -- adr)   **code#** 1 6e

This routine converts a character value (ASCII 0-0xff) into the address of the font table entry for that character. For the normal, built-in font, only ASCII values 0x21-0x7e result in a printable character, other values will be mapped to a font entry for "blank".

This word is only of interest if you are implementing your own character-drawing routines. Note that >font will generate invalid results unless set-font has been called to initialize the font table to be used.

fontbytes

(-- n)   **code#** 1 6f

A value, containing the interval between successive entries in the font table. Each entry contains the next scan line bits for the desired character. Each scan line is normally 12 pixels wide, and is stored as one bit per pixel, thus taking 1 1/2 bytes per scan line. The standard value for fontbytes is 2, meaning that the next scan line entry is 2 bytes after the previous one (the last 1/2 byte is wasted space).

This word *must* be set to the appropriate value if you wish to use *any* fb1- or fb8- utility routines or >font . This may be done with is, but is normally done by calling set-font.

The standard value for fontbytes is one of the parameters returned by default-font .

frame-buffer-adr

(-- virt) **code#** 1 62

This is a value that returns the address of the beginning of framebuffer memory. It *must* be set to an appropriate virtual address (using is) in order to use *any* of the fb1- or fb8- utility routines. It is suggested that this same value variable be used in any of your custom routines that require a frame

buffer address, although of course you are free to create and use your own variable if you wish.

Generally, you should only map in the framebuffer memory just before you are ready to use it, and unmap it if it is no longer needed. Typically, this means you should do your mapping in your "install" routine, and unmap it in your "remove" routine (see is-install and is-remove). Here's some sample code:

Code Example 11-6   Sample video-map install and remove routines

```
h# 2.0000  constant  /frame     \ # of bytes in frame buffer
h# 40.0000 constant  foffset    \ Location of frame buffer

: video-map  ( -- )
   my-address  foffset +  /frame  map-sbus  is  frame-buffer-adr
;
: video-unmap  ( -- )
   frame-buffer-adr  /frame  free-virtual
   -1  is  frame-buffer-adr     \ Flag accidental accesses to a
                                \ now-illegal address
;

: power-on-selftest  ( -- )
   video-map
   ( test video memory )
   video-unmap
```

Code Example 11-6   Sample video-map install and remove routines

```
;
power-on-selftest

: my-install   ( -- )
   video-map
   ...
;
: my-remove    ( -- )
   video-unmap
   ...
;
...
['] my-install   is-install
['] my-remove    is-remove
```

free-mem

(virtual #bytes --)   **code#** 8c

Frees up memory allocated by `alloc-mem`.

For example:

```
0 value my-string          \ Holds address of temporary

: .upc-string ( adr len -- ) \ convert to uppercase and print.

   dup alloc-mem is my-string               ( adr len )

   tuck my-string swap cmove                ( len )

   my-string over bounds ?do i c@ upc i c! loop   ( len )

   my-string over type                      ( len )

   my-string swap free-mem

;
```

free-virtual

(virtual size --)   **code#** 1 05

Undoes the MMU page map entries generated by obsolete FCodes `memmap`, `dma-alloc`, or `map-sbus`.

This FCode is obsolete for OpenBoot 2. (For use under OpenBoot 1, see Appendix D, "Changes in Version 1 FCode Usage".) To undo maps created with " `map-in`" `$call-parent` use:

```
" map-out" $call-parent
```

and to undo maps created with " `dma-map-in`" `$call-parent` use:

```
" dma-map-out" $call-parent
```

to undo maps created with " `dma-alloc`" `$call-parent`" use::

```
" dma-free" $call-parent
```

get-inherited-attribute

(name-adr name-len -- true | xdr-adr xdr-len false)
version 2   **code#** 2 1d

Locates, within the package associated with the current instance or any of its parents, the property whose name is name-adr name-len. If the property exists, returns the property value array xdr-adr xdr-len and false. Otherwise returns true.

The order in which packages is searched is the current instance first, followed by its immediate parent, followed by its parent's parent, and so on. This is useful for properties with default values established by a parent node, with the possibility of a particular child node "overriding" the default value.

For example:

```
: clock-frequency ( -- val.adr len false | true  )

   " clock-frequency" get-inherited-attribute

;
```

get-msecs

(-- ms)   **code#** 1 25

Returns the current value in a free-running system counter. The number returned is a running total, expressed in milliseconds. You can use this for measuring time intervals (by comparing the starting value with the ending value). No assumptions should be made regarding the absolute number returned; only relative interval comparisons are valid.

No assumptions should be made regarding the *precision* of the number returned. In many systems (including the SPARCstation 1), the value is derived from the system clock, which typically ticks once per second. Thus, the value returned by `get-msecs` on the SPARCstation 1 and 1+ will be seen to increase in jumps of 1000 (decimal), once per second. For a delay timer of millisecond accuracy, see `ms` .

get-my-attribute

```
( name-adr name-len -- true | val-adr val-len
false )                                code# 2 1a
version 2
```

Locates, within the package associated with the current instance, the property named by `name-adr name-len`. If the property exists, returns the property value array `val-adr val-len` and `false`. Otherwise returns `true`.

For example:

```
: show-model-name ( -- )

   " model" get-my-attribute 0= if  ( val.adr len )

      ." model name is " type cr

   else  ( )

      ." model  attribute is missing " cr

   then ( )

;
```

get-package-attribute

```
( name-adr name-len phandle -- true | xdr-adr
xdr-len false )
version 2                                code# 2 1f
```

Locates, within the package `phandle`, the property named by `name-adr name-len`. If the property exists, returns the property value array `xdr-adr xdr-len` and `false`. Otherwise returns `true`.

For example:

```
: show-model-name ( -- )

  my-self ihandle>phandle ( phandle )

  " model" rot get-package-attribute 0= if  ( val.adr len )

    ." model name is " type cr

  else  ( )

    ." model  attribute is missing " cr

  then ( )

;
```

group-code

(-- adr)   **code#** 1 23

This FCode is obsolete and should not be used.

.h

(n --)**code#** a0 6d 49 10 00 00 00 10 a0 72 9d
a0 72
generates: base @ swap d# 16 base ! . base !

Displays n in hex (using .) The value of `base` is not permanently affected.

h#

number (--)   **code#** 10 xx xx xx xx
generates: b(lit) value

Interpret the next number in hex (base 16), regardless of any previous settings of hex, decimal, binary, or octal. Only the immediately following number is affected, the default numeric base setting is unchanged. For example:

```
decimal

h# 100 ( equals decimal 256 )

100    ( equals decimal 100 )
```

See also b#, d#, and o#.

headerless

(--)   **code#** none

Causes all subsequent definitions to be created in FCode without the name field (the "head"). (See named-token and new-token .) This is sometimes done to save space in the final FCode PROM, or possibly to make it more difficult to reverse-engineer an FCode program.

All such headerless words may be used normally within the FCode program, but cannot be called interactively from the Toolkit for testing and development purposes.

Unless PROM space and/or dictionary space is a major consideration, Sun recommends not using headerless words, because they make debugging more difficult.

headerless remains in effect until headers or external is encountered.

For example:

```
headerless

h# 3 constant reset-scsi
```

headers

(--)   **code#** none

Causes all subsequent definitions to be saved with the name field (the "head") intact. This is the initial default behavior.

Note that even normal FCode words (with heads) cannot be called interactively from the Toolkit unless the NVRAM parameter fcode-debug? has been set to true before a system reset.

`headers` remains in effect until `headerless` or `external` is encountered.

For example:

```
headers

: cnt@  ( -- w )

    transfer-count-lo rb@

    transfer-count-hi rb@

    bwjoin

;
```

here

                `( -- adr )`   **code#** `ad`

`adr` is the address of the next available dictionary location.

hex

                `( -- )`   **code#** `none`
                `-or-`
                `generates: b(lit) 16 base !`**code#** `10 00 00 00 10 a0 72`

If outside of a definition, commands the tokenizer program to interpret subsequent numbers in hex (base 16). If within a definition, change the value in `base` affecting later numeric output when the FCode program is executed. See `base` .

hold

                `( char -- )`   **code#** `95`

Inserts `char` into a pictured numeric output string. Typically used between `<#` and `#>` .

For example:

```
: .32 ( n -- )

    base @ >r hex

    <# # # # #  ascii . hold # # # # #> type
```

```
    r> base !

    space

;
```

i

              (-- n)   **code#** 19

n is a copy of the loop index. May only be used inside of a do or ?do loop.

For example:

```
: simple-loop  ( start len -- )

    bounds ?do i .h cr loop

;
```

if

              (flag --)   **code#** 14 +offset
              generates: b?branch +offset

Execute the following code if flag is true. Used in the form:

```
flag if ... else ... then
```

or

```
flag if ... then
```

If flag is true, the words following if are executed and the words following else are skipped. The else part is optional. If flag is false, words from if through else , or from if through then (when no else is used), are skipped.

ihandle>phandle

              (ihandle -- phandle)   **code#** 2 0b
              version 2

Returns the `phandle` of the package from which the instance `ihandle` was created. This is often used with `get-package-attribute` to read the properties of the package corresponding to a given `ihandle`.

For example:

```
: show-parent ( -- )

   my-parent ihandle>phandle " name" rot

   get-package-attribute 0= if

     ." my-parent is " type cr

   then

;
```

insert-characters

(n --)   **code#** 1 5d

A `defer` word, called by the terminal emulator when needed to insert n blank characters to the right of the cursor. The cursor position is unchanged, but the cursor character and all characters to the right of the cursor are moved right by n places. (This command is used during command-line editing.) An error condition exists if an attempt is made to create a line longer that the maximum line size (the value in `#columns`).

This word is initially empty, but *must* be loaded with an appropriate routine in order for the terminal emulator to function correctly. This may be done with `is`, or it may be loaded automatically with `fb1-install` or `fb8-install` (which loads `fb1-insert-characters` or `fb8-insert-characters` , respectively).

insert-lines

(n --)   **code#** 1 5f

A `defer` word, called by the terminal emulator when needed to insert n blank lines just above the cursor. This could be used by a screen editor, for example.

The cursor's position on the screen is unchanged. The cursor line is pushed down, but all lines above it are unchanged. Any lines "pushed" off of the bottom of the active text area are lost.

This word is initially empty, but *must* be loaded with an appropriate routine in order for the terminal emulator to function correctly. This may be done with is, or it may be loaded automatically with fb1-install or fb8-install (which loads fb1-insert-lines or fb8-insert-lines, respectively).

instance

(--)   **code#** c0
version 2.1

Used to declare that new versions of data should be created for each new instance of a package (as opposed to global data). Valid for FCode version 2.1 or later.

instance should be called just before the data-creation defining word. Valid uses are with value, variable, defer and buffer:. For example:

```
: instance ( -- )  \ verify if "instance" is implemented.

   ['] instance ['] ferror  <>  if

      instance

   then

;

-1 instance value my-chip-reg
```

intr

(sbus-intr-level vector --)**code#** 1 17

This is a shorthand word for declaring the "intr" and "interrupts" properties.

See "intr" and "interrupts" in Chapter 5, "Properties".

See also attribute.

inverse-screen?

(-- flag)   **code#** 1 55

A `value`, set and controlled by the terminal emulator, that tells you how to paint the unused portions of each line, i.e. white or black? A value of `true` means paint the unused portion black.

This word can (and should) be looked at as needed if your FCode program is implementing its own set of framebuffer primitives.

inverse?

(-- flag)   **code#** 1 54

A `value`, set and controlled by the terminal emulator, that tells you whether to paint characters as white-on-black or black-on-white. A value of `true` means white-on-black. Unused characters on each line are not affected (see `inverse-screen?`).

This word can (and should) be looked at as needed if your FCode program is implementing its own set of framebuffer primitives.

invert-screen

(--)   **code#** 1 5c

A `defer` word, called by the terminal emulator when needed to invert the entire screen. This routine should XOR every visible pixel.

This word is initially empty, but *must* be loaded with an appropriate routine in order for the terminal emulator to function correctly. This may be done with `is`, or it may be loaded automatically with `fb1-install` or `fb8-install` (which loads `fb1-invert-screen` or `fb8-invert-screen`, respectively).

is

name   (n --)   **code#** c3 FCode
generates: b(is) FCode

Changes the contents of a `value` or a `defer` word:

```
number is name  ( for a value )

acf    is name  ( for a defer word )
```

is-install

(acf --)   **code#** 1 1c

Creates open, write, and draw-logo methods for display devices.

For any SBus framebuffer that is to be used by the boot PROM before or during booting, is-install declares the FCode procedure that should be used to install (i.e. initialize) that framebuffer. Note that this is distinct from any once-only power-on initialization, that should be performed during the probing process itself.

The is-install routine and is-remove routine should comprise a matched pair, that may be performed alternately as many times as needed. Typically, the is-install routine performs mapping functions and some initialization, and the is-remove performs any cleanup functions and then does a complementary unmapping.

A partial, typical code example follows:

```
fcode-version1

...

: power-on ( -- )          \ Once-only, power-on initialization

    map-register

    init-register

    unmap-register

;

...

: map-devices ( -- )       \ Map register and buffer

    map-register

    map-buffer

;

...
```

```
: install-me ( -- )          \ Do this to start using this device

    map-devices

    initialize-devices

;

: remove-me ( -- )           \ Do this to stop using this device

    reset-buffers

    unmap-devices

;

...

\ This routine executed during the probe of this FCode

: my-probe ( -- )                  \ First, define the routine

    power-on                       \ Power-on initialization

    ['] install-me is-install   \ Declare "install" routine

    ['] remove-me  is-remove    \ Declare "remove" routine

    ['] test-me    is-selftest  \ Declare "selftest" routine

;  \ End of the defintion

my-probe                           \ Now execute the routine

end0
```

is-remove

(acf --)   **code#** 1 1d

Creates a `close` method for display devices.

Declares the routine that will deallocate a framebuffer that is no longer going to be used. Typical deallocation would include unmapping memory and clearing buffers. For example:

```
fcode-version1

...

: remove-me   ( -- )      \ Do this to stop using this device

    reset-buffers

    unmap-devices

;

...

\ This routine executed during the "probe" of this FCode

: my-probe   ( -- )                \ First, define the routine

    power-on                       \ Power-on initialization

    ['] install-me  is-install  \ Declare "install" routine

    ['] remove-me   is-remove   \ Declare "remove" routine

    ['] test-me     is-selftest \ Declare "selftest" routine

;                                  \ End of the definition

my-probe                           \ Now, execute this routine

end0
```

The routine loaded with `is-remove` should form a matched pair with the routine loaded with `is-install` . See `is-install` for more details.

is-selftest

          (acf --)   **code#** 1 1e

Creates a `selftest` method for display devices.

Declares the routine that will perform a self test of the framebuffer. For example:

```
FCode-version1

...

: test-me   ( -- fail? )    \ self test method

   ...

;

...

\ This routine executed during the "probe" of this FCode

: my-probe  ( -- )               \ First, define the routine

   power-on                      \ Power-on initialization

    ['] install-me  is-install   \ Declare "install" routine

    ['] remove-me   is-remove    \ Declare "remove" routine

    ['] test-me     is-selftest  \ Declare "selftest" routine

;                                \ End of the definition

my-probe                         \ Now, execute this routine

end0
```

This declaration is typically performed in the same place in the code as `is-install` and `is-remove`.

The self test routine should return a status parameter on the stack indicating the results of the test. A zero value indicates that the test passed. Any nonzero value indicates that the self test failed, but the actual meaning for any nonzero value is not specified. (`memory-test-suite` returns a flag meeting these specifications.)

selftest is not automatically executed.

For automatic testing, devices should perform a quick sanity check as part of the install routine. See "selftest" on page 40.

(is-user-word)

(adr len acf --)   **code#** 2 14

version 2

Creates a Forth word (not a package method) whose name is given by adr len, and whose behavior is given by the compilation address acf (as returned by ['], for example). This allows an FCode program to define new user interface commands.

For example:

```
" xyz-abort" ' my-abort (is-user-word)
```

j

(-- n)   **code#** 1a

n is a copy of the index of the next outer loop. May only be used within a nested do or ?do loop. For example:

```
do

   ...

      do ... j ... loop

   ...

loop
```

Usually, do loops should not be nested this deeply inside a single definition. Forth programs are generally more readable if inner loops are defined inside a separate word.

key

(-- char)   **code#** 8e

A defer word that reads the next ASCII character from the keyboard. If no character has been typed since key was last executed, key waits until a new character is typed. All valid ASCII characters can be received. Control characters are not processed by the system for any editing purpose. Characters received by key are not displayed.

For example:

```
: continue? ( -- continue? )

   ." Want to Continue? Enter Y/N" key dup emit

   dup ascii Y = ascii y rot = or

;
```

key?

(-- flag)   **code#** 8d

A `defer` word returning `true` if a character has been typed on the keyboard since the last time that `key` or `expect` was executed. The keyboard character is not consumed.

Use `key?` to make simple, interruptable infinite loops:

```
begin  ...  key? until
```

The contents of the loop will repeat indefinitely until any key is pressed.

l!

(n adr --)   **code#** 73

The 32-bit value n is stored at location adr (through adr+3). The highest byte is stored at adr ; the lowest byte is stored at adr+3 . adr must be on a 32-bit boundary; it must be evenly divisible by 4.

l,

(n --)   **code#** d2

Compile 4-bytes into the dictionary, starting with the highest byte. See c, for limitations. The dictionary pointer must be 2-byte-aligned.

For example:

```
\ to create an array containing integers 40004000 23 45 6734

create my-array 40004000 l, 23 l, 45 l, 6734 l,
```

l@

(adr -- n)   **code#** 6e

Fetch the 32-bit number stored at `adr` (through `adr+3`). The highest byte is stored at `adr` ; the lowest byte is stored at `adr+3` . `adr` must be on a 32-bit boundary; it must be evenly divisible by 4.

/l

(-- n)

code# 5c

n is the size in bytes of a 32-bit word: 4.

/l*

(n1 -- n2)

code# 68

n2 is the result of multiplying n1 by the length in bytes of a (32-bit) long word. This is useful for converting an index into a byte offset. `/l*` is equivalent to 4 * , but should be used in preference to the less portable 4 * .

la+

(adr1 index -- adr2)

code# 60

adr2 is the address of the `index`'th 32-bit longword after `adr1` . For byte-addressed machines (such as this one), this is equivalent to 4 * + .

Use `la+` in preference to the less portable and less clear 4 * + .

la1+

(adr1 -- adr2)

code# 64

adr2 is the address of the next 32-bit word after `adr1` . For byte-addressed machines (such as this one), this is equivalent to 4 + . `la1+` should be used in preference to the less portable and clear 4 + .

lbsplit

(n -- byte.lo byte byte byte.hi) **code#** 7e

Splits a 32-bit value into four bytes. The upper bits of each byte are all zeroes.

lcc

(char1 -- char2)

code# 82

char2 is the lower case version of `char1` . If `char1` is not an upper case letter, it is unchanged. See `upc` .

For example:

```
ascii M lcc emit
```

shows m .

leave

```
( -- )
generates:  b(leave)
```

Transfers execution to just past the next `loop` or `+loop` . The loop is terminated and loop control parameters are discarded. May only be used within a `do` or `?do` loop.

`leave` may appear within other control structures that are nested within the `do` loop structure. More than one `leave` may appear within a `do` loop.

For example:

```
: search-pat ( pat adr len -- found? )

   rot false swap 2swap  ( false pat adr len )

   bounds ?do  ( flag pat )

      i @ over  =  if  drop true swap leave  then

   loop

   drop

;
```

?leave

```
( flag -- )                     code# 14 +offset 1b  b2
generates: if leave then
generates: b?branch +offset leave b(>resume)
```

If `flag` is `true` (nonzero), `?leave` transfers control to just beyond the next `loop` or `+loop` . The loop is terminated and loop control parameters are discarded. If flag is zero, no action is taken. May only be used within a `do` or `?do` loop.

`?leave` may appear within other control structures that are nested within the `do` loop structure. More than one `?leave` may appear within a `do` loop.

For example:

```
: show-mem ( vadr -- )  \ display h# 10 bytes

   dup h# 9 u.r 5 spaces h# 10 bounds  do  i c@ 3 u.r  loop

;

: .mem ( vaddr size -- )

   bounds  ?do  i show-mem key? ?leave  h# 10  +loop

;
```

left-parse-string

```
( adr len char -- adrR lenR adrL lenL )code#
2 40
version 2
```

A tool for separating fields within a string. For example:

```
" test;in;g" ascii ; left-parse-string
```

would leave the address and length of two strings on the stack:

"`in;g`" and "`test`".

The delimiter character may be any ASCII character. Note that if the delimiter is not found within the string, the effect is as if the delimiter was found at the very end. For example:

```
" testing" ascii q left-parse-string
```

would leave on the stack " " and " `testing`".

lflips

```
( adr len -- )                          code# 2 37
version 2
```

Swaps the order of the 16-bit words within each 32-bit longword in the memory buffer adr len. adr must be four-byte-aligned. len must be a multiple of four.

For example:

```
h# 12345678 8000 l!

8000 4 lflips

8000 l@ .h
```

shows 56781234 .

#line

       (-- adr)   **code#** 94

A `variable` that increments whenever `cr` executes. `#line` @ returns the current value of this `variable` . The value in this `variable` is used to determine when to pause during long display output, such as `dump`. Its value is reset each time the `ok` prompt displays.

line#

       (-- n)   **code#** 1 52

A `value`, set and controlled by the terminal emulator, that contains the current vertical position of the text cursor. A value of 0 represents the topmost line of available text space (this is *not* the topmost pixel of the framebuffer - see `window-top`).

This word can (and should) be looked at as needed if your FCode program is implementing its own set of framebuffer primitives.

For example:

```
: set-line  ( line -- ) 0 max  #lines   1- min  is line#   ;
```

linefeed

     (-- n)   **code#** 10 00 00 00 0a
     generates: b(lit)   10

n is the ASCII code for the linefeed character; decimal 10, hex 0a .

#lines

      (-- n)   **code#** 1 50

This is a `value` that returns the number of lines of text to be displayed using the boot PROM's terminal emulator. It *must* be set to a proper value in order for the terminal emulator to function correctly.

`#lines` is defined in the boot PROM with an initial value of 34 (decimal), but it should always be actively set by the FCode program. This may be done with `is`, or it may be handled automatically as one of the functions performed by `fb1-install` or `fb8-install`. The value set by `fbx-install` is the smaller of the passed *#lines* parameter and the *screen-#rows* NVRAM parameter.

For example:

```
: set-line  ( line -- ) 0 max  #lines   1- min  is line#   ;
```

loop

(--)   **code#** 15 -offset
generates: b(loop) -offset

Terminates a `do` or `?do` loop. Increments the loop index by one. If the index was incremented across the boundary between `limit-1` and `limit` , the loop is terminated and loop control parameters are discarded. When the loop is not terminated, execution continues to just after the corresponding `do` or `?do` .

For example, the following `do` loop:

```
8 0 do ... loop
```

terminates when the loop index changes from 7 to 8. Thus, the loop will iterate with loop index values from 0 to 7, inclusive.

+loop

(n --)   **code#** 16 -offset
generates: b(+loop) -offset

Terminates a `do` or `?do` loop. Increments the loop index by n (or decrements the index if n is negative). If the index was incremented (or decremented) across the boundary between `limit-1` and limit the loop is terminated and loop control parameters are discarded. When the loop is not terminated, execution continues to just after the corresponding `do` or `?do` .

The following do loop:

```
8 0 do ... 2 +loop
```

terminates when the loop index crosses the boundary between 7 and 8. Thus, the loop will iterate with loop index values of 0, 2, 4, 6.

By contrast, a do loop created as follows:

```
0 8 do ... -2 +loop
```

terminates when the loop index crosses the boundary between -1 and 0. Thus, the loop will iterate with loop index values of 8, 6, 4, 2, 0.

lpeek

```
( adr -- false | data true )    code# 2 22
version 2
```

Tries to read the 32-bit longword at address adr. Returns the data and true if the access was successful. A false return indicates that a read access error occurred. adr must be 32-bit aligned.

lpoke

```
( data adr -- ok? )             code# 2 25
version 2
```

Tries to write the 32-bit longword at address adr. Returns the data and true if the access was successful. A false return indicates a read access error. adr must be 32-bit aligned.

Note – lpoke may be unreliable on bus adapters that "buffer" write accesses.

---

lu>x

```
( ul -- ux )                    code# a5
generates: 0
```

Tokenizer instruction that zero-extends a 32-bit number to 64-bit.

lwsplit

```
( n -- word.lo word.hi )        code# 7c
```

Splits the 32-bit value n into two 16-bit words. The upper bits of the two generated words are zeroes.

mac-address

(-- adr len)   **code#** 1 a4
version 2

Usually used only by the network device-type, this FCode returns the value for the *Media Access Control*, or MAC address, that this SBus card should use for its own address. The data is encoded as a byte array, generally 6 bytes long.

The value returned by mac-address can either be supplied by the system, or by the card itself. If the card's FCode creates a property named local-mac-address, and the NVRAM parameter local-mac-address? (for typical systems) is set to true, then the value contained in the property local-mac-address will be returned by mac-address. Otherwise, the system will assign a value.

See also "mac-address", "local-mac-address", and "network" in Chapter 5, "Properties" and Chapter 9, "Network Devices".

map-sbus

(physoffset size -- virt)   **code#** 1 30

This FCode is obsolete in version 2. For version 1 usage, see Appendix D, "Changes in Version 1 FCode Usage".

For version 2, use:

```
" map-in" $call-parent
```

Creates a memory mapping for some SBus locations, usually within the address space of this SBus card. The MMU page maps are updated, and the generated virtual address is returned.

The memory mapping can (and should) be later undone with free-virtual. Used as:

```
( -1 value vregs )

...

my-address 10.0000 + 100

map-sbus ( virt )

is vregs
```

mask

(-- adr)   **code#** 1 24

This `variable` controls which bits out of every 32-bit longword which will be tested with `memory-test-suite` . To test all 32-bits, set `mask` to all ones with::

```
ffff.ffff mask !
```

To test only the low-order byte out of each longword, set just the lower bits of `mask` with:

```
0000.00ff mask !
```

Any arbitrary combination of bits may be tested or masked.

max

(n1 n2 -- n3)   **code#** 2f

n3 is the greater of n1 and n2.

memmap

(physoffset space size -- virtual)**code#** 1 04

Creates a memory mapping for some locations. It updates MMU page maps and returns the generated virtual address. The actual physical address is specified by (`physoffset space`), that indicates the device space and the physical offset within that space.

This fcode is obsolete in OpenBoot 2. For OpenBoot 1 usage, refer to Appendix D, "Changes in Version 1 FCode Usage". For version 2, use:

```
" map-in" $call-parent
```

The memory mapping can (and should) be later undone with `free-virtual`.

memory-test-suite

(adr len -- failed?)   **code#** 1 22

Performs a series of tests on some memory, to verify its proper functioning. A `true` flag is returned if any of the tests failed.

If `diagnostic-mode?` is `true` (`diag-switch?` NVRAM parameter is `true`), then a message is sent out to the current output device (to `ttya` if during probe time) giving the name of each test. If any test fails, a "Failed" message will also then be displayed.

For every one of the following tests, the value stored in the variable `mask` controls whether only some or all data lines are tested.

For example, to only test data bits 0-23 (skipping bits 24-31), `mask` would be set with: `00ffffff mask !`

The actual tests performed may vary from system to system. On current systems, the tests performed are:

- *Data lines test*. This test performs a walking ones and zeroes on each data line to test for stuck at zero or stuck at one.
- *Address quick test*. This tests each address line for being stuck at one, stuck at zero, shorted to another address line, or shorted to a data line.

- *Data size test*. Writes a constant 32-bit value to the starting location of the memory, both byte-at-a-time and shortword-at-a-time, then reads the data back with a 32-bit access and verifies the value. This test verifies proper 8-bit, 16-bit and 32-bit access.

The above tests are very fast. If the `diag-switch?` NVRAM parameter is set to `true`, then the following (slower) additional tests are also performed:

- Data bits test. Tests every bit in memory, by testing a write/read of 0 and a write/read of `ffffffff` at every location.

- Address=data test. Writes each longword location with its own address, then verifies. This checks for the uniqueness of individual locations with RAM chips.

For example:

```
: test-result ( -- )

    frame-buffer-adr my-frame-size memory-test-suite  ( failed? )

    xdrint " test-result" attribute

;
```

min
           (n1 n2 -- n3)   **code#** 2e

n3 is the lesser of n1 and n2 .

mod
           (n1 n2 -- rem)   **code#** 22

rem is the remainder after dividing n1 by the divisor n2 . rem has the same sign as n2 or is zero. An error condition results if the divisor is zero.

*/mod

(n1 n2 n3 -- rem quot) **code#** 30 20 31 2a
generates: >r * r> /mod

Calculates n1 * n2 / n3 , returns the remainder and quotient. The inputs, outputs, and intermediate products are all 32-bit. rem has the same sign as n3 or is zero. An error condition results if the divisor is zero.

/mod

(n1 n2 -- rem quot) **code#** 2a

rem is the remainder and quot is the quotient of n1 divided by the divisor n2. rem has the same sign as n2 or is zero. An error condition results if the divisor is zero.

model

(adr len --) **code#** 1 19

This is a shorthand word for creating a model property. By convention, model identifies the model name/number for an SBus card, for manufacturing and field-service purposes. A sample usage would be:

```
" SUNW,501-1415"  model
```

This is equivalent to:

```
" SUNW,501-1415" xdrstring  " model"  attribute
```

The model property is useful to identify the specific piece of hardware (the SBus card), as opposed to the name property (since several different but functionally-equivalent cards would have the same name property, thus calling the same SunOS device driver).

See also attribute , "model" in Chapter 5, "Properties".

move

(adr1 adr2 len --) **code#** 78

len bytes starting at adr1 (through adr1+len-1 inclusive) are moved to address adr2 (through adr2+len-1 inclusive). If len is zero then nothing is moved.

The data are moved such that the `len` bytes left starting at address `adr2` are the same data as was originally starting at address `adr1` . If `adr1` > `adr2` then the first byte of `adr1` is moved first, otherwise the last byte (`len`'th) of `adr1` is moved first. Thus, moves between overlapping fields are properly handled.

`move` will perform 16-bit, 32-bit or possibly even 64-bit operations (for better performance) if the alignment of the operands permits.

ms

(ms --)   **code#** 1 26

Delays all execution for the specified number of milliseconds, by executing an empty delay loop for an appropriate number of iterations. The maximum allowable delay will vary from system to system, but is guaranteed to be valid for all values up to at least 1,000,000 (decimal). No other CPU activity takes place during delays invoked with `ms` , although generally this is not a problem for FCode drivers since there is nothing else to do in the meantime anyway. If this word is used excessively, noticeable delays could result.

For example:

```
: probe-loop-wait ( adr -- )

   \ wait h# 10 ms before doing another probe at the location

   begin  dup 1@ drop h# 10 ms key?  until  drop

;
```

my-address

(-- physoffset)   **code#** 1 02

Returns a magic number, suitable for use with the `map-in` method, and with `reg`, `xdrphys`, `map-sbus` and `memmap`. The returned number, along with `my-space`, encodes the address of location 0 of this SBus device. The OpenBoot PROM automatically sets `my-address` to the correct value before each SBus slot is probed.

For example:

```
fcode-version1

  " audio" xdrstring " name" attribute

  my-address h# 130.0000 + my-space h# 8 reg


  ...

end0
```

my-args

        (-- adr len)   **code#** 2 02
        version 2

Returns the argument string `adr  len` that was passed to the current instance when it was created, if the argument string exists. Otherwise returns with a length of 0.

For example:

```
" /obio:TEST-ARGS" select-dev

my-args type
```

The above will display arguments passed to `/obio` at open time as TEST-ARGS

my-params

        (-- adr len)   **code#** 1 0f

This fcode is obsolescent and should not be used.

`my-params` returns a string that contains arbitrary customization information for this device. The string comments are the contents of the `params` property if present, otherwise returns a null string (adr,len equals 0,0).

`my-args` may be used in some situations to perform the same function.

my-parent

        (-- ihandle)   **code#** 2 0a
        version 2

Returns the `ihandle` of the instance that opened the current instance. For device driver packages, the relationships of parent/child instances mimic the parent/child relationships in the device tree.

For example:

```
: show-parent ( -- )

  my-parent ihandle>phandle " name" rot

  get-package-attribute 0= if

    ." my-parent is " type cr

  then

;
```

my-self

$$(\text{ -- ihandle })$$
version 2

code# 2 03

Returns the current instance `ihandle`.

For example:

```
: show-model-name ( -- )

  my-self ihandle>phandle ( phandle )

  " model" rot get-package-attribute 0= if  ( val.adr,len )

    ." model name is " type cr

  else  ( )

    ." model  attribute is missing " cr

  then  ( )

;
```

my-space

(-- space)   **code#** 1 03

Returns a "magic" number, representing the device space that this SBus card is plugged into.

For example:

```
fcode-version1

  " audio" xdrstring " name" attribute

  my-address h# 130.0000 + my-space h# 8 reg

  ...

end0
```

See my-address for more details.

my-unit

(-- low high)   **code#** 2 0d
version 2

Returns the unit address low high of the current instance. The unit address is set when the instance is created, as follows:

• If the *node-name* used to locate the instance's package contained an explicit *unit-address*, that is the instance's unit address. This would be used for a "wildcard" node with no associated "reg" property.

• Otherwise, if the device node associated with the package from which the instance was created contains a "reg" property, the first component of its property value is the instance's unit address.

• Otherwise, the instance's unit address is 0 0.

For example. on SPARCclassic systems:

```
" /iommu/sbus/ledma@4,840010" select-dev my-unit .s
```

displays

```
840010 4
```

/n

(-- n)   **code#** 5d

The number of bytes in a normal stack item; 4 in this implementation.

/n*

(n1 -- n2)   **code#** 69

n2 is the result of multiplying n1 by the length in bytes of a normal stack item. This is useful for converting an index into a byte offset. This word is equivalent to 4 * .

na+

(adr1 index -- adr2)   **code#** 61

adr2 is the address of the index'th "normal" sized word after adr1 . For this implementation, this is equivalent to 4 * + .

na+ should be used in preference to wa+ or la+ when the intent is to address items that are the same size as items on the stack.

na1+

(adr1 -- adr2)   **code#** 65

adr2 is the address of the next "normal" sized word after adr1 . For this implementation, this is equivalent to 4 + or la1+ .

na1+ should be used in preference to wa1+ or la1+ when the intent is to address items that are the same size as items on the stack.

name

(adr len --)**code#** 1 14 12 04 6e 61 6d 65 1 10
generates: xdrstring " name" attribute

A shorthand word for creating a "name" property, used to match a device node with the appropriate SunOS driver. The "name" declaration is required for booting with SunOS, and should be present in every FCode program. For example:

```
" SUNW,bison" name
```

is equivalent to:

```
" SUNW,bison" xdrstring " name" attribute
```

See also `attribute` , `device-name`.

See *"name"* in Chapter 5, *"Properties"*.

named-token

(--)**code#** b6 len xx xx xx ... 08 xx b(type)
generates: named-token string fcode# b(type)

`named-token`, `external-token` or `new-token` are called to create a new dictionary entry. If `headers` are active, use `named-token`.

The new header for a word created with `named-token` has the following format:

```
named-token, string, new FCode#, type
```

The first byte is b6, indicating a `named-token` format.

- Next is a string containing the name of the new created entry. The string is a length byte and then *length* bytes of text.
- Next is a new FCode# assigned by the tokenizer, starting at 08,00 then 08,01 and working upwards. If 08,ff is exceeded then 09,00 and so on is used, up to a maximum of 0b,ff.
- Finally, the b(*type*) byte indicates the type of word being created, such as b(:) for colon definition, b(value) for `values`, etc.

`named-token` should never be used directly in source code.

negate

(n1 -- n2)   **code#** 2c

n2 is the opposite sign of n1 . This is equivalent to -1 * .

new-device

(--)   **code#** 1 1f

Start a new entry in the device tree. This word is used for creating multiple devices in a single FCode program. See `finish-device`.

new-token

(--)   **code#** b5 xx xx b(type)
generates: new-token FCode# b(type)

named-token, external-token or new-token are called whenever a new dictionary entry is to be created. If headerless is active, then use new-token.

The format for new-token is identical to that for named-token , except that the string field is missing (and the first byte is b5 instead of b6). See named-token for more details.

new-token should never be used directly in source code.

newline

```
( -- n )                         code# 10 00 00 00 0a
generates: b(lit) 10
```

n is the ASCII code for the character that terminates a line; decimal 10, hex 0a. In this system this is the linefeed character.

newline is system-dependent, so its use is discouraged. Usually, it doesn't increment the line count, that results in problems with correct screen scrolling. Use of cr instead of newline is usually appropriate.

nip

```
( n1 n2 -- n2 )                                  code# 4d
```

Remove the second item on the stack.

noop

```
( -- )                                           code# 7b
```

Do nothing. This can be used to waste time or as a placeholder for something that will be patched in later.

not

```
( n1 -- n2 )                                     code# 26
```

n2 is the one's complement of n1 , i.e. all the one bits in n1 are changed to zero, and all the zero bits are changed to one.

For example:

```
: clear-lastbit ( -- )

   my-reg rl@ 1 not and my-reg rl!

;
```

See also 0=.

$number

```
( adr len -- true | n false )    code# a2
version 2
```

A numeric conversion primitive that converts a string to a number, according to the current `base` value (usually hexadecimal). An error flag is returned if an inconvertible character is encountered. For example, " `123f`" `$number` returns `123f 0` on the stack, while "123x" returns `-1`, indicating that the conversion failed.

For example:

```
: number-or-0   ( adr len -- true | number false )

   dup if  $number  else  2drop 0 false  then

;
```

o#

```
number ( -- n )    code# 10 xx xx xx xx
generates:  b(lit) value
```

Interpret the next number in octal (base 8), regardless of any previous settings of `hex`, `decimal`, `binary`, or `octal`. Only the immediately following number is affected, the default numeric base setting is unchanged. For example:

```
hex

o# 100 ( equals decimal 64 )

100 ( equals decimal 256 )
```

See also `b#`, `d#`, and `h#` .

octal

```
( -- )                              code# none
-or-                code# 10  00  00  00  08  a0  72
generates: b(lit)         8    base !
```

If outside a definition, commands the tokenizer program to interpret subsequent numbers in octal (base 8). If within a definition, changes the value in `base`, affecting later numeric output when the FCode program is executed.   See `base`.

of

```
( selector testval -- selector | null ) code#
1c +offset
generates:   b(of) +offset
```

Begin the next test clause in a `case` statement. See `case` for more details.

off

```
( adr -- )                                    code#  6b
```

Set the 32-bit contents at `adr` to zero (`false`).

offset16

```
( -- )                                        code#  cc
```

Instructs the tokenizer program, and the boot PROM, to expect all further branch offsets to be 16-bit values. This word is automatically generated by some current tokenizers.

on

```
( adr -- )                                    code#  6a
```

Set the 32-bit contents at `adr` to -1 or `ffff.ffff` (`true`).

open-package

```
( arg-adr arg-len phandle -- ihandle | 0 )
code#  2 05
version 2
```

Creates an instance of the package identified by `phandle`, saves in that instance an argument string specified by `arg-adr arg-len`, and invokes the package's `open` method. The parent instance of the new instance is the instance that invoked `open-package`.

Returns the instance handle `ihandle` of the new instance if it can be opened. It returns 0 if the package could not be opened, either because that package has no `open` method or because its `open` method returned false indicating an error. In this case, the current instance is not changed.

For example:

```
: test-tftp-open ( -- ok? )

   " obp-tftp" find-package  if  ( phandle )

      0 0 rot open-package  if  true  else  false  then

   else
```

Writing FCode Programs

```
        false

    then

  ;
```

$open-package

(arg-adr arg-len name-adr name-len -- ihandle
| 0)   **code#** 2 0f
version 2

Similar to using find-package open-package, except that if find-package fails, 0
is returned immediately, without calling open-package .

For example:

```
0 0  " obp-tftp" $open-package  ( ihandle )
```

or

(n1 n2 -- n3)   **code#** 24

n3 is the bit-by-bit inclusive-or of n1 with n2 .

#out

(adr --)   **code#** 93

A variable containing the current column number on the output device. This is
updated by emit and some other words that modify the cursor position. It is used for
display formatting.

For example:

```
: to-column  ( column -- )   #out @  -  1 max spaces  ;
```

over

(n1 n2 -- n1 n2 n1)   **code#** 48

The second stack item is copied to the top of the stack.

2over

(n1 n2 n3 n4 -- n1 n2 n3 n4 n1 n2)**code#** 54

Copies the third and fourth stack items to the stack top.

pack

(adr len pstr -- pstr)   **code#** 83

Convert a byte array (indicated by " adr len ") into a packed string, and store it at the location pstr . The byte at address pstr is the length of the string and the string itself starts at address pstr+1 .

Packed strings are generally not used in FCode. Virtually all string operations are in the " adr len " format.

For example:

```
h# 20 buffer: my-packed-string

" This is test string " my-packed-string pack
```

peer

(phandle -- next-phandle)   **code#** 2 3c
version 2.3

peer returns the phandle next-phandle of the package that is the next child of the parent of the package phandle.

If phandle is the last child of its parent, peer returns zero.

If phandle is zero, peer returns phandle of the root node.

Together with child, peer lets you enumerate (possibly recursively) the children of a particular device. A common application would be for a device driver to use child to determine the phandle of a node's first child, and use peer multiple times to determine the phandles of the node's other children. For example:

```
: my-children ( -- )
  my-self ihandle>phandle child  (first-child )
  begin ?dup while dup . peer repeat
;
```

>physical

(virtual -- physoffset space)**code#** 1 06

Given a virtual address, return the mapped physical address as a (physoffset space) pair, specifying the device space (as a "magic number") and the physical offset within that space.

This word has inconsistent behavior in current boot PROMs, and you should avoid using it in FCode programs.

For example:

```
: in-ram?      ( vadr  -- phys flag )

   >physical  ( padr space )

   \ code-to-verify if space and address refer to on-board memory

;
```

pick
(+n -- n2) **code#** 4e

n2 is a copy of the +n'th stack value, not counting +n itself. +n must be between 0 and the number of elements on the stack-1 inclusive.

```
0 pick is equivalent to dup    ( n1 -- n1 n1 )

1 pick is equivalent to over   ( n1 n2 -- n1 n2 n1 )

2 pick is equivalent to  ( n1 n2 n3 -- n1 n2 n3 n1 )
```

For readability's sake, the use of `pick` should be minimized.

probe
(arg-adr arg-len reg-adr reg-len fcode-adr
fcode-len --)
version 2.2   code# 2 38

This FCode is obsolete, and should not be used. Use `probe-self` method of a hierarchical device node.

probe-virtual
(arg-adr arg-len reg-adr reg-len fcode-adr --
)   code# 2 39
version 2.2

This FCode is obsolete, and should not be used. Use " `set-args`" and "`byte-load`" as shown below. In case you have downloaded the FCode PROM image of a SBus device at virtual address 4000, and the device is in SBus slot #1 use:

```
"  /sbus" select-dev

new-device

  0 0 "  1,0" "  set-args" $find if          ( arg-str reg-str acf )

      execute 4000 1 "  byte-load" $find if    ( adr offset acf )

         execute

      else

         ." byte-load missing "  cr 2drop 2drop

      then

   else

      ." set-args missing "  cr 2drop 2drop 2drop

   then

finish-device

unselect-dev
```

processor-type

                             (-- processor-type)   **code#** 2 10
                             version 2

Returns the type of processor (instruction set architecture). Obsolete.

.r

                             (n1 +n --)   **code#** 9e

$n1$ is converted using the value of `base` and then displayed right aligned in a field $+n$ characters wide. A leading minus sign is displayed if n is negative. A trailing space is *not* displayed.

If the number of characters required to display n1 is greater than +n, an error condition exists. In this implementation, all the characters required will be displayed, making the resulting field larger than +n.

For example:

```
: formatted-output ( -- )

   my-length h# 8 .r   ." length" cr

   my-width  h# 8 .r   ." width" cr

   my-depth  h# 8 .r   ." depth" cr

;
```

r>

(-- n)   **code#** 31

Removes n from the return stack and places it on the (regular) stack. See >r for restrictions on the use of this word.

For example:

```
: copyout  ( buf adr len -- len )   >r swap r@ move r>  ;
```

r@

(-- n)   **code#** 32

n is a copy of the top of the return stack.

For example:

```
: copyout  ( buf adr len -- len )   >r swap r@ move r>  ;
```

See >r for more details.

>r

(n --)   **code#** 30

Removes n from the stack and places it on the top of the return stack.

The return stack is a second stack, occasionally useful as a place to temporarily place numeric parameters, i.e. to "get them out of the way" for a little while. However, since the return stack is also used by the system for transferring control from word to word (and by do loops), improper use of >r or r> is guaranteed to crash your program.

For example:

```
: xdrintr   ( int-level vector -- )

    >r sbus-intr>cpu xdrint   r> xdrint   xdr+

;
```

Some restrictions that *must* be observed are:

- All values placed on the return stack within a colon definition must be removed before the colon definition is exited by normal termination, exit or throw, or else the program will crash.
- No values from the return stack should be removed from within a colon definition unless they were placed there within that definition.

- Entering a do loop automatically places values onto the return stack. Therefore,
  - Values placed on the return stack before the loop was started will not be accessible from within the loop.
  - Values placed on the return stack within the loop must be removed before loop , +loop , or leave is encountered.
  - The loop indices i or j will no longer be valid when additional values have been placed on the return stack within the loop.

rb!
(n adr --)
version 2

code# 2 31

Stores an 8-bit byte, preserving bit order.

For example:

```
: my-stat! ( byte -- ) my-stat rb! ;
```

rb@
(adr -- n)
version 2

code# 2 30

Fetches an 8-bit byte, preserving the bit order.

For example:

```
: my-stat@ ( -- byte ) my-stat rb@ ;
```

reg

(physoffset space size --) **code#** 1 16

This is a shorthand word for declaring a property named "reg" (by convention, reg is used for declaring the location and size of device registers). Typical usage:

```
my-address   40.0000 +   my-space   20   reg
```

This declares that the device registers are located at offset 40.0000 through 40.001f in this slot. The following code would accomplish the same thing::

```
my-address   40.0000 +   my-space   xdrphys

20 xdrint     xdr+

" reg" attribute
```

Note that if you need to declare more than one block of register addresses, you *must* use the longer, more explicit method in order to build the structure to be passed into the reg property.

For example, to declare two register fields at 10.0000-10.00ff and 20.0000-20.037f, use the following:

```
my-address   10.0000 +   my-space   xdrphys            \ Offset#1

100 xdrint                                      xdr+   \ Merge size#1

my-address   20.0000 +   my-space   xdrphys xdr+   \ Merge offset#2

380 xdrint                                      xdr+   \ Merge size#2

" reg" attribute
```

See also attribute. See also "reg" in Chapter 5, "Properties".

repeat

```
( -- )                              code# 13 -offset b2
generates:   bbranch, -offset, b(>resolve)
```

Terminates a `begin ... while ... repeat` conditional loop.
See `while` for more details.

reset-screen

```
( -- )                                        code# 1 58
```

A `defer` word, called by the boot PROM's terminal emulator (just after `erase-screen`). This word is called only once, during the terminal emulator initialization sequence, in order to enable the framebuffer to display information. A typical use for this function is to "enable video".

This word is initially empty, but *must* be loaded with an appropriate routine in order for the terminal emulator to function correctly. This may be done with `is`, or it may be loaded automatically with `fb1-install` or `fb8-install` (which loads `fb1-reset-screen` or `fb8-reset-screen` , respectively). These words are NOPs, so it is very common to first call `fbx-install` and then to override the default setting for `reset-screen` with:

Code Example 11-7   my-video-on code

```
['] my-video-on   is reset-screen
```

rl!

```
( n adr -- )                              code# 2 35
version 2
```

Stores a 32-bit longword, preserving bit order. `adr` must be 32-bit aligned.

For example:

```
: my-reg! ( n -- ) my-reg rl! ;
```

rl@

```
( adr -- n )                              code# 2 34
version 2
```

Fetches a 32-bit longword, preserving bit order. `adr` must be 32-bit aligned.

For example:

```
: my-reg@ ( -- n ) my-reg rl@ ;
```

roll

(+n --)   **code#** 4f

The +n'th stack value, not counting +n itself, is first removed and then transferred to the top of the stack, moving the remaining values into the vacated position. +n must be between 0 and the number of elements on the stack-1, inclusive.

```
0 roll is a null operation

1 roll is equivalent to swap      ( n1 n2 -- n2 n1 )

2 roll is equivalent to rot       ( n1 n2 n3 -- n2 n3 n1 )

3 roll is equivalent to           ( n1 n2 n3 n4 -- n2 n3 n4 n1 )
```

For readability's sake, minimize your use of roll. It is also relatively slow.

rot

(n1 n2 n3 -- n2 n3 n1)   **code#** 4a

Rotates the top three stack entries, bringing the deepest to the top.

-rot

(n1 n2 n3 -- n3 n1 n2)   **code#** 4b

Rotates the top three stack entries in the direction opposite from rot , putting the top number underneath the other two.

2rot

(n1 n2 n3 n4 n5 n6 -- n3 n4 n5 n6 n1 n2)
code# 56

Rotates the top three pairs of numbers, bringing the third pair to the top of the stack.

rw!

(n adr --)   **code#** 2 33
version 2

Stores a 16-bit word, preserving bit order. adr must be 16-bit aligned.

For example:

```
: my-count! ( w -- ) my-count rw! ;
```

rw@

              (adr -- n)   **code#** 2 32
              version 2

Fetches a 16-bit word, preserving bit order. adr must be 16-bit aligned.

For example:

```
: my-count@ ( -- w ) my-count rw@ ;
```

s.

              (n --) **code#** 47 2d 96 9a 49 98 97 90 a9 8f
              generates: (.)   type bl emit
              generates: dup abs <# #s swap sign #> type bl
              emit

Displays the absolute value of n in a free-field format with a leading minus sign if n is negative. A trailing space is also displayed. Even if the base is hexadecimal, the number will be printed in signed format (see .).

#s

              (+1 -- 0)   **code#** 9a

+1 is converted, appending each resultant character into the pictured numeric output string until the quotient is zero (see: #). A single zero is added to the output string if the number was initially zero. Typically used between <# and #> . See (.) and (u.) for typical usages.

This word is equivalent to calling # repeatedly until the number remaining is zero.

(s

              text) (--)   **code#** none

Ignore subsequent text after the (s up to a delimiting) . The same behavior occurs for (.

Although either (or \ works equally well for documentation, by common convention we use (...) or (s ...) for stack comments and \ ... for all other text comments and documentation.

Use (s to distinguish a definition's "interface" stack comment from stack comments *within* a definition (which clarify the current stack state). (This distinction could be of use for implementing automatic stack-checkers.) For example:

```
\ map in registers

: map-regs   (s size -- virt )

  reg-addr  swap    ( addr size )

  map-sbus          ( virt )

;
```

.s

                     (--)   **code#** 9f

Displays the contents of the data stack (using .) in the current base. The top of the stack appears on the right. The contents of the stack are unchanged.

For example:

```
: debug-abtest ( ??? -- ??? )

  debug-on? if ." input params: " .s cr then

  abtest

  debug-on? if ." output params: " .s cr then

;
```

sbus-intr>cpu

               (sbus-intr# -- cpu-intr#)   **code#** 1 31

Convert the SBus interrupt level (1-7) to the CPU interrupt level. The mapping performed will be system-dependent.

This word is called by the intr command.

For example:

```
3 sbus-intr>cpu xdrint 0 xdrint xdr+  " intr" attribute
```

See "`intr`" in Chapter 5, "Properties".

screen-height

(-- n)   **code#** 1 63

A `value`, containing the height of the display (in pixels). It may also be interpreted as the number of "lines" of memory.

This word is initially set to 900 (decimal), but should always be set explicitly to the appropriate value if you wish to use the `fb1-` or `fb8-` utility routines. This may be done with `is`, or it may be loaded as one of the parameters to `fb1-install` or `fb8-install`.

In particular, this value is used in `fbx-invert`, `fbx-erase-screen`, `fbx-blink-screen` and in calculating `window-top`.

Typical code might create a constant called `vres`. This would be used as the `height` parameter for `fbx-install`, and might also be passed as an attribute to SunOS if needed.

screen-width

(-- n)   **code#** 1 64

A `value`, containing the width of the display (in pixels). It may also be interpreted as the number of pixels (in memory) between one screen location and the next location immediately below it. The latter definition takes precedence if there is a conflict (e.g. there are unused/invisible memory locations at the end of each line).

Typical code might create a constant called `hres`. This would be used as the `width` parameter for `fbx-install`, and might also be passed as an attribute to SunOS if needed.

set-font

(fontbase charwidth charheight fontbytes
#firstchar #chars --)

code# 1 6b

This routine declares the font table to be used for printing characters on the screen. This routine *must* be called if you wish to use *any* of the fb1- or fb8- utility routines or >font .

Normally, set-font is called just after default-font . default-font leaves on the stack the exact set of parameters needed by set-font . This approach allows your FCode program to inspect and/or alter the default parameters if desired. See default-font for more information on these parameters.

sign

(n --)   **code#** 98

If n is negative, appends an ASCII "-" (minus sign) to the pictured numeric output string. Typically used between <# and #> . See (.) for a typical usage.

space

(--)   **code#** a9 8f
generates: bl emit

Display a single space character.

spaces

(+n --)**code#** a5 2f a5 18 +offset a9 8f 15 -
offset
generates: 0 max 0 ?do space loop
generates: 0 max 0 b(?do) +offset bl emit
b(loop) -offset

Display +n space characters. Nothing is displayed if +n is zero.

span

(-- adr)   **code#** 88

A variable containing the count of characters actually received and stored by the last execution of expect .

For example:

```
h# 10 buffer: my-name-buff

: hello ( -- )
```

```
        ." Enter Your First name " my-name-buff h# 10 expect

        ." Sun Microsystems Welcomes " my-name-buff span @ type cr

    ;
```

start*n*

        (--)**code#** f0 (start0) f1 (start1) f2 (start2) f3
        (start4)
        version 2

Four version 2.0 FCodes whose function is similar to `version1`, but for use with version 2.0 FCode programs. Their use is as follows:

- `start0`. Like `version1`, but for version 2 FCodes. Uses 16-bit branches. Fetches successive tokens from same address.
- `start1`. Like `version1`, but for version 2 FCodes. Uses 16-bit branches. Fetches successive tokens from consecutive addresses. Compiled by `fcode-version2`.
- `start2`. Like `version1`, but for version 2 FCodes. Uses 16-bit branches. Fetches successive tokens from consecutive 16-bit addresses.
- `start4`. Like `version1`, but for version 2 FCodes. Uses 16-bit branches. Fetches successive tokens from consecutive 32-bit addresses.

struct

        (-- 0)   **code#** a5
        generates: 0

Initializes a `struct ... field` structure. See `field` for details.

suspend-fcode

        (--)   **code#** 2 15
        version 2

Tells the FCode interpreter that the device identification properties for the active package have been declared, and that the interpreter may postpone interpreting the remainder of the package if it so chooses.

If the FCode interpreter postpones (suspends) interpretation, it saves the state of the interpretation process so that interpretation may continue later. Attempts to open a suspended package cause the FCode interpreter to resume and complete the interpretation of that package before executing the package's `open` method.

For example:

```
fcode-version1

    " SUNW,my-name" name

    " SUNW,my-model" xdrstring " model" attribute

    suspend-fcode

    . . .

end0
```

This feature is intended to save memory space and reduce the system startup time by preventing the compilation of FCode drivers that are not actually used.

swap

      (n1 n2 -- n2 n1)   **code#** 49

Exchanges the top two stack items.

2swap

      (n1 n2 n3 n4 -- n3 n4 n1 n2) **code#** 55

Exchanges the top two pairs of stack items.

then

      (--)   **code#** b2
      generates: b(>resolve)

Terminate an `if` ... `then` or an `if` ... `else` ... `then` conditional structure. See `if` for more details.

throw

      (error-code --)   **code#** 2 18
      version 2

Transfers control to the most recent dynamically enclosing error handling context, passing the indicated error code to that handler. Error code must be nonzero. If the value of `error-code` is zero, the zero is removed from the stack, but no other action is taken.

See `catch` for an example of use.

toggle-cursor

      (--)   **code#** 1 59

A `defer` word, called by the boot PROM's terminal emulator before and after any character or string is printed. (It is also called once during the terminal emulator initialization sequence.) The normal behavior of this word is to XOR the pixels at the current cursor position to leave a colored rectangle marking the next character to be output.

`toggle-cursor` is initially empty, but must be loaded with an appropriate routine in order for the terminal emulator to function correctly. This may be done with `is`, or it may be loaded automatically with `fb1-install` or `fb8-install` (which load `fb1-toggle-cursor` or `fb8-toggle-cursor`, respectively).

This is a good place to perform any necessary "cleanup" of display hardware state, such as resetting color maps or selecting the proper modes. For example, a window system may have set a color lookup table so that the color used for displaying text does not contrast with the background. If the PROM terminal emulator is then asked to display some system messages on the screen, the messages would be unreadable. Consequently, it would be a good idea to restore the text entries in the color lookup table in the `toggle-cursor` routine.

tokenizer[

(--)   **code#** none

This is a tokenizer command, used to end FCode byte generation and interpret following text as tokenizer commands (up to the closing `]tokenizer`). A `tokenizer[ ...` `]tokenizer` sequence may be used anywhere in an FCode program, either within any definition or outside of definitions.

One plausible use for `tokenizer[` would be to generate debugging text during the tokenizing process. (A `cr` flushes the text from the output buffer immediately, which is useful if the tokenizer crashes.) For example:

```
...

tokenizer[  .( step a)  cr  ]tokenizer
```

```
. . .

tokenizer[   .( step b)   cr   ]tokenizer

. . .
```

Another use for `tokenizer[` is together with `emit-byte`, to manually output a desired byte of FCode. This would be useful, for example, if you wished to generate a new FCode command that the tokenizer did not understand. For example:

```
. . .

tokenizer[   1 emit-byte   27 emit-byte   ]tokenizer

\ manually output finish-device fcode

. . .
```

]tokenizer

              (--)   **code#** none

Ends a tokenizer-only command sequence. See `tokenizer[` .

true

           (-- flag)   **code#** a4
           generates: -1

Leave the value for the `true` flag (which is -1) on the stack.

tuck

           (n1 n2 -- n2 n1 n2)   **code#** 4c

Copy the top stack item underneath the second item.

type

           (adr len --)   **code#** 90

A `defer` word that transfers `len` characters to the output, beginning with the character at address `adr`, continuing through `len` consecutive addresses. No action is taken if `len` is zero.

For example:

```
h# 10 buffer: my-name-buff

: hello ( -- )

    ." Enter Your First name " my-name-buff h# 10 expect

    ." Sun Microsystems Welcomes " my-name-buff span @ type cr

;
```

The output may go either to a framebuffer or to a serial port, depending on which is enabled.

u.

(n --)   **code#** 9b

Display n as an unsigned number in a free-field format, using the current value for base . A trailing space is also displayed.

For example:

```
hex -1 u.
```

shows

```
ffff.ffff
```

(u.)

(n -- adr len)   **code#** 96 9a 97
generates: <# #s #>

This is a numeric conversion primitive, used to implement display words such as u. . It converts an unsigned number into a string.

For example:

```
hex

d# -12 (u.)  type
```

shows:

```
fffffff4
```

u.r   (n1 +n --)   **code#** 9c

n1 is converted using the value of base and then displayed as an unsigned number right-aligned in a field +n characters wide. A trailing space is *not* displayed.

If the number of characters required to display n1 is greater than +n, an error condition exists. In this implementation, all the characters required will be displayed, making the resulting field larger than +n.

For example:

```
: formatted-output ( -- )

  my-base   h# 8 u.r  ." base" cr

  my-offset h# 8 u.r  ." offset" cr

;
```

u/mod   (n1 n2 -- rem quot)   **code#** 2b

rem is the remainder and quot is the quotient after dividing n1 by n2 . All values and arithmetic are unsigned. All values are 32-bit.

For example:

```
-1 5 u/mod .s
```

shows

```
0 3333.3333
```

u2/

           (n1 -- n2)   **code#** 58

n2 is the result of n1 logically shifted right one bit. A zero is shifted into the vacated sign bit.

For example:

```
-2 u2/ .s
```

shows

```
7fff.ffff
```

u<

           (n1 n2 -- flag)   **code#** 40

flag is true if n1 is less than n2 where n1 and n2 are treated as unsigned integers.

u<=

           (n1 n2 -- flag)   **code#** 3f

flag is true if n1 is less than or equal to n2 where n1 and n2 are treated as unsigned integers.

u>

           (n1 n2 -- flag)   **code#** 3e

flag is true if n1 is greater than n2 where n1 and n2 are treated as unsigned integers.

u>=

           (n1 n2 -- flag)   **code#** 41

flag is true if n1 is greater than or equal to n2 where n1 and n2 are treated as unsigned integers.

until

           (flag --)   **code#** 14 -offset
           generates: b?branch -offset

Marks the end of a begin ... (flag) until conditional loop. When until is encountered, a flag is removed and tested. If the flag is true, the loop is terminated and execution continues just after the until. If the flag is false, execution jumps back to just after the corresponding begin .

For example:

```
: probe-loop ( adr -- )

   \ generate tight probe-loop until a key is pressed.

   begin dup 1@ drop key? until drop

;
```

upc

(char1 -- char2)   **code#** 81

char2 is the upper case version of char1 . If char1 is not a lower case letter, it is left unchanged. See lcc .

For example:

```
: continue? ( -- continue? )

   ." Want to Continue? Enter Y/N" key dup emit

   upc ascii Y =

;
```

user-abort

(--)   **code#** 2 19
version 2.1

Used within an alarm routine to signify that the user has typed an abort sequence. When alarm finishes, instead of returning to the program that was interrupted by the execution of alarm, it enters the OpenBoot command interpreter. Valid for FCode version 2.1 or later.

For example:

```
: test-dev-status  ( -- error? )  ... ;

: my-checker  ( -- )  test-dev-status  if  user-abort  then  ;

: install-abort  ( -- )  ['] my-checker d# 10 alarm  ;
```

u*x

(u1[32] u2[32] -- product[64]) **code#** d4
version 2

Multiplies two unsigned 32-bit numbers, yielding an unsigned 64-bit product.

For example:

```
hex

3 3 u*x .s
```

gives

```
9 0
```

while

```
4 ffff.ffff u*x .s
```

gives

```
ffff.fffc 3
```

value

name(n1 --)at creation**code#** (header) b8
(-- n1)at execution
generates: new header, b(type) = b(value)

Creates a named, `value`-type variable. The name is initially created with:

```
456 value black
```

where the number before `value` is the initial value for `black`. Later occurrences of `black` will leave the correct value on the stack.

You can change the numeric contents of a `value` variable with `is` , as follows:

```
123 is black
```

`value`-type variables are widely used in this system.We encourage the use of `values` instead of `variables`. `values` act similarly to `constants` or colon definitions, in that execution of the word leaves the desired number on the stack. (With a `variable`, you always have to do a `@` .)

variable

```
name    ( -- )at creationcode# (header) b9
                      ( -- adr )at execution
generates:    new header, b(type) = b(value)
```

Create a named, `variable`-type variable. The name is initially created with:

```
variable red
```

Later occurrences of `red` leave an address on the stack.

The alignment of the returned address is system-dependent.The address holds a 32-bit value. To retrieve the value in a `variable` and leave it on the stack for subsequent use, enter:

```
red @
```

To change the value in a `variable` , enter:

```
123 red !
```

Sun encourages the use of `values` instead of `variables`. `values` act like `constants` or colon definitions, in that execution of the word leaves the desired number on the stack. (With a `variable` , you always have to do a @ .) This similarity between `values` and other words makes the FCode easier to read, write and maintain.

version

(-- n)

code# 87

Returns a 32-bit number identifying the version of the FCode interface supported by the CPU firmware. The high 16 bits is the major version number and the low 16 bits is the minor version number.

For example:

```
: exit-if-version1 ( -- )

    version  h# 20000  <   if   ['] end0  execute   then

;
```

This is not the same as the OpenBoot PROM version (see `firmware-version`). For example, the CPU PROM might be version 3.7, but the FCode version might still be 2.0 (= 0x00020000).

The value returned is less consistent on version 1 systems, but it is guaranteed to less than 0x0002.0000.

version1

(--)

code# fd

This byte is automatically generated by the `fcode-version1` command.

Never use the word `version1` in FCode source code.

version*x*?

(-- flag)

code# ??

A group of tokenizer macros to determine the FCode version of the system running the FCode interpreter. They include:

Table 11-2 Tokenizer macros

Word	Generates
version1?	version b(lit) 2000.0000 <
version2?	version b(lit) 2000.0000 >=
	version b(lit) 3000.0000 <
version2.0?	version b(lit) 2000.0000 =
version2.1?	version b(lit) 2000.0001 =
version2.2?	version b(lit) 2000.0002 =
version2.3?	version b(lit) 2000.0003 =

Each returns `true` if the named version matches the system running the FCode interpreter.

w!

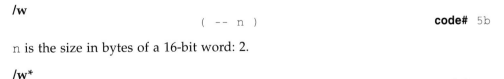

      (n adr --)   **code#** 74

The low-order 16-bits of n are stored at location `adr` (through `adr+1`). The higher byte is stored at `adr` ; the lower byte is stored at `adr+1` . `adr` must be on a 16-bit boundary; it must be evenly divisible by 2.

w,

      (n --)   **code#** d1

Compile two bytes into the dictionary. The dictionary pointer must be two-byte-aligned.

See `c,` for limitations.

w@

      (adr -- n)   **code#** 6f

Fetch the 16-bit number stored at `adr` (through `adr+1`). The higher byte is at `adr` ; the lower byte is at `adr+1` . The remaining high bytes of n are set to zero. `adr` must be on a 16-bit boundary; it must be evenly divisible by 2.

/w

      (-- n)   **code#** 5b

n is the size in bytes of a 16-bit word: 2.

/w*

      (n1 -- n2)   **code#** 67

n2 is the result of multiplying n1 by the length in bytes of a (16-bit) word. This is useful for converting an index into a byte offset. /w* is equivalent to 2* , but should be used in preference to 2* as it is more portable.

<w@

(adr -- n)   **code#** 70

Fetches the 16-bit number stored at adr (through adr+1). The higher byte is stored at adr; the lower byte is stored at adr+1 . The remaining high bytes of n are set by sign-extending the upper bit in the higher byte. adr must be two-byte-aligned.

For example:

```
9123 8000 w!

8000 <w@ .h
```

shows: ffff9123, while

```
8000 w@ .h
```

shows: 9123 .

wa+

(adr1 index -- adr2)   **code#** 5f

adr2 is the address of the index'th 16-bit word after adr1. For byte-addressed machines (such as this one), this is equivalent to 2* + .

Use wa+ in preference to 2* + because it more clearly expresses the intent of the operation and is more portable.

wa1+

(adr1 -- adr2)   **code#** 63

adr2 is the address of the next 16-bit word after adr1 . For byte-addressed machines (such as this one), this is equivalent to 2+ . wa1+ should be used in preference to 2+ because it more clearly expresses the intent of the operation and is more portable.

wbsplit

(w -- byte.lo byte.next)   **code#** af

Split the two lower bytes of w into two separate bytes (stored as the lower byte of each resulting item on the stack). The upper bytes of w must be zero.

wflip

```
( n1 -- n2 )                        code# 7c 49 7d
generates:  lwsplit swap wljoin
```

Swap the two 16-bit halves of a 32-bit number.

wflips

```
( adr len -- )                      code# 2 36
version 2
```

Swaps the order of the bytes within each 16-bit word in the memory buffer `adr len`.

`adr` must be two-byte-aligned. `len` must be a multiple of two.

while

```
( flag -- )                         code# 14 +offset
generates:  b?branch +offset
```

Test the exit condition for a `begin` ... `(flag)` `while` ... `repeat` conditional loop. When the `while` is encountered, a flag is removed from the stack and tested. If the flag is `true` , execution continues from just after the `while` through to the `repeat` which then jumps back to just after the `begin`. If the flag is `false` , the loop is exited by causing execution to jump ahead to just after the `repeat` .

For example:

```
: probe-loop ( adr -- )

  \ generate tight probe-loop until a key is pressed.

  begin key? 0=  while  dup 1@ drop  repeat  drop

;
```

window-left

```
( -- n )                            code# 1 66
```

A `value`, containing the offset (in pixels) of the left edge of the active text area from the left edge of the visible display. The "active text area" is where characters are actually printed. (There is generally a border of unused blank area surrounding it on all sides.) `window-left` contains the size of the left portion of the unused border.

The size of the right portion of the unused border is determined by the difference between `screen-width` and the sum of `window-left` plus the width of the active text area (`#columns` times `char-width`).

This word is initially set to 0, but should always be set explicitly to the appropriate value if you wish to use *any* `fb1-` or `fb8-` utility routines. This may be done with `is`, or it may be set automatically by calling `fb1-install` or `fb8-install`.

When set with `fbx-install`, a calculation is done to set `window-left` so that the available unused border area is evenly split between the left border and the right border. (The calculated value for `window-left` is rounded down to the nearest multiple of 32, though. This allows all pixel-drawing to proceed more efficiently.) If you wish to use `fbx-install` but desire a different value for `window-top`, simply change it with `is` *after* calling `fbx-install`.

window-top

(-- n)   **code#** 1 65

A `value`, containing the offset (in pixels) of the top of the active text area from the top of the visible display. The "active text area" is where characters are actually printed. (There is generally a border of unused blank area surrounding it on all sides.) `window-top` contains the size of the top portion of the unused border.

The size of the bottom portion of the unused border is determined by the difference between `screen-height` and the sum of `window-top` plus the height of the active text area (`#lines` times `char-height`).

This word is initially set to 0, but should always be set explicitly to the appropriate value if you wish to use *any* `fb1-` or `fb8-` utility routines. This may be done with `is`, or it may be set automatically by calling `fb1-install` or `fb8-install`. When set with `fbx-install`, a calculation is done to set `window-top` so that the available unused border area is evenly split between the top border and the bottom border. If you wish to use `fbx-install` but desire a different value for `window-top`, simply change it with `is` *after* calling `fbx-install`.

within

(n min max -- flag)   **code#** 45

flag is true if n is between min and max , inclusive of min and exclusive of max . (min <= n < max.) See between for another version.

wljoin

(word.lo word.hi -- n)   **code#** 7d

Merge two 16-bit numbers into a 32-bit number. The high bits of each 16-bit number must be zero.

wpeek

(adr -- false | data true)   **code#** 2 21
version 2

Tries to read the 16-bit half-word at address adr. Returns the data and true if the access was successful. A false return indicates that a read access error occurred. adr must be 16-bit aligned.

wpoke

(data adr -- ok?)   **code#** 2 24
version 2

Tries to write the 16-bit half-word at address adr. Returns true if the access was successful. A false return indicates that a write access error occurred. adr must be 16-bit aligned.

Note: wpoke may be unreliable on bus adapters that buffer write accesses.

x+

(x1 x2 -- x3)   **code#** d8
version 2

Adds two 64-bit numbers, leaving 64-bit sum.

For example:

```
1234.0000 0056.7800 9abc 3400.009a  x+  .s
```

shows

```
1234.9abc 3456.789a
```

x-

(x1 x2 -- x3)   **code#** d9
version 2

Subtracts two 64-bit numbers, leaving 64-bit result.

For example:

```
0 6  1 0  x- .s
```

shows

```
ffff.ffff 5
```

and

```
4444.8888 aaaa.bbbb 2222.1111 5555.2222  x-  .s
```

shows

```
2222.7777 5555.9999
```

xdr+

(xdr-adr1 xdr-len1 xdr-adr2 xdr-len2 -- xdr-
adr1 len1+2)

code# 1 12

Merge two xdr-format strings into a single xdr-format string. The two input strings must have been created sequentially with no intervening dictionary allocation or other xdr-format strings having been created. This can be called repeatedly, to create complex, multi-valued xdr-format strings for passing to attribute.

For example, suppose you wished to create a property named myprop with the following information packed sequentially:

```
"size" 2000 "vals" 3 128 40 22
```

This could be written in FCode as follows:

```
: xdrstring,num ( adr len number -- )

  >r xdrstring

  r> xdrint xdr+

;

" size" 2000 xdrstring,num

" vals"    3 xdrstring,num xdr+

128      xdrint      xdr+

40       xdrint      xdr+

22       xdrint      xdr+

" myprop"  attribute
```

xdrbytes

(adr len -- xdr-adr xdr-len)**code#** 1 15
version 2.1

Encodes a byte array into a property value array. The external representation of a byte array is the sequence of bytes itself, with no appended null byte.

For example:

```
my-idprom h# 20 xdrbytes " idprom" attribute
```

xdrint

(n1 -- xdr-adr xdr-len)   **code#** 1 11

Convert an integer into an xdr-format string, suitable for passing as a "value" to attribute . For example:

```
1152  xdrint  " hres"  attribute
```

xdrphys

```
( physoffset space -- xdr-adr xdr-len )code# 1
13
```

Convert a physical address (as a device space and a physical offset) into an `xdr`-format string suitable for `attribute` . For example:

```
my-address  20.0000 +   my-space  xdrphys

" resetloc" attribute
```

xdrstring

```
( adr len -- xdr-adr xdr-len )code# 1 14
```

Converts an ordinary string, such as created by `"` , into an `xdr`-format string suitable for `attribute` . For example:

```
" MJS,SEH" xdrstring " authors" attribute
```

xdrtoint

```
( xdr1-adr xdr1-len -- xdr2-adr xdr2-len n )
code# 2 1b
version 2
```

Decodes a number from the beginning of the property value array `xdr1-adr xdr1-len` , and returns the remainder of the property value array `xdr2-adr xdr2-len` and the number n.

For example:

```
: show-clock-frequency ( -- )

   " clock-frequency" get-inherited-attribute  0=  if

      ." Clock frequency: " xdrtoint .h cr 2drop

   then

;
```

xdrtostring

```
( xdr1-adr xdr1-len -- xdr2-adr xdr2-len adr
len )                              code# 2 1c
version 2
```

Decodes a string from the beginning of the property value array `xdr1-adr xdr1-len`, and returns the remainder of the property value array `xdr2-adr xdr2-len` and the string `adr3 len3`.

For example:

```
: show-model ( -- )

  " model" get-my-attribute 0= if xdrtostring type 2drop then

;
```

xor

```
( n1 n2 -- n3 )                         code# 25
```

n3 is the bit-by-bit exclusive-or of `n1` with `n2`.

xu>l

```
( ux -- ul )                            code# 46
generates: drop
```

Tokenizer instruction that truncates a 64-bit number to 32-bit.

xu/mod

```
( u1[64] u2[32] -- remainder[32] quot[32] )
code# d5
version 2
```

Divides an unsigned 64-bit number by an unsigned 32-bit number, yields a 32-bit remainder and quotient

FCode Reference

FCode Primitives

This appendix contains four lists:

- FCodes sorted according to functional group
- FCodes sorted by byte value
- FCodes sorted alphabetically by name
- Version 2 FCodes listed alphabetically

FCodes by Function

The following tables describe FCodes currently supported by the OpenBoot PROM. New 2.0 FCodes are indicated by V2. Both the FCode token values and Forth names are included. A token value entry of CR indicates a cross-compiler-generated sequence, while – indicates that no FCode is generated.

Table A-1 Stack Manipulation

Value	Function	Stack	Description
51	depth	(-- +n)	How many items on stack?
46	drop	(n --)	Removes n from the stack
52	2drop	(n1 n2 --)	Removes 2 items from stack
47	dup	(n -- n n)	Duplicates n
53	2dup	(n1 n2 -- n1 n2 n1 n2)	Duplicates 2 stack items
50	?dup	(n -- n n | 0)	Duplicates n if it is non-zero
CR	3dup	(n1 n2 n3 -- n1 n2 n3 n1 n2 n3)	Copies top 3 stack items
4d	nip	(n1 n2 -- n2)	Discards the second stack item
48	over	(n1 n2 -- n1 n2 n1)	Copies second stack item to top of stack
54	2over	(n1 n2 n3 n4 -- n1 n2 n3 n4 n1 n2)	Copies 2 stack items
4e	pick	(+n -- n2)	Copies +n-th stack item

Table A-1 Stack Manipulation

Value	Function	Stack	Description
30	>r	(n --) (rs: -- n)	Moves a stack item to the return stack*
31	r>	(-- n) (rs: n --)	Moves item from return stack to data stack*
32	r@	(-- n) (rs: --)	Copies the top of the return stack to the data stack
4f	roll	(+n --)	Rotates +n stack items
4a	rot	(n1 n2 n3 -- n2 n3 n1)	Rotates 3 stack items
4b	-rot	(n1 n2 n3 -- n3 n1 n2)	Shuffles top 3 stack items
56	2rot	(n1 n2 n3 n4 n5 n6 -- n3 n4 n5 n6 n1 n2)	Rotates 3 pairs of stack items
49	swap	(n1 n2 -- n2 n1)	Exchanges the top 2 stack items
55	2swap	(n1 n2 n3 n4 -- n3 n4 n1 n2)	Exchanges 2 pairs of stack items
4c	tuck	(n1 n2 -- n2 n1 n2)	Copies the top stack item below the second item

* Use these FCodes cautiously.

Table A-2 Arithmetic Operations

Value	Function	Stack	Description
20	*	(n1 n2 -- n3)	Multiplies n1 times n2
1e	+	(n1 n2 -- n3)	Adds n1+n2
1f	-	(n1 n2 -- n3)	Subtracts n1-n2
21	/	(n1 n2 -- quot)	Divides n1/n2
CR	1+	(n1 -- n2)	Adds one
CR	1-	(n1 -- n2)	Subtracts one
59	2*	(n1 -- n2)	Multiplies by 2
57	2/	(n1 -- n2)	Divides by 2
27	<<	(n1 +n -- n2)	Left shifts n1 by +n places
28	>>	(n1 +n -- n2)	Right shifts n1 by +n places
CR	<<a	(n1 +n -- n2)	Arithmetic left shifts (same as <<)
29	>>a	(n1 +n -- n2)	Arithmetic right shifts n1 by +n places
2d	abs	(n -- u)	Absolute value

Table A-2   Arithmetic Operations

Value	Function	Stack	Description
ae	aligned	(adr1 -- adr2)	Adjusts an address to a machine word boundary
23	and	(n1 n2 -- n3)	Logical and
ac	bounds	(startadr len -- endadr startadr)	Converts start,len to end,start for do loop
2f	max	(n1 n2 -- n3)	n3 is maximum of n1 and n2
2e	min	(n1 n2 -- n3)	n3 is minimum of n1 and n2
22	mod	(n1 n2 -- rem)	Remainder of n1/n2
CR	*/mod	(n1 n2 n3 -- rem quot)	Remainder, quotient of n1*n2/n3
2a	/mod	(n1 n2 -- rem quot)	Remainder, quotient of n1/n2
2c	negate	(n1 -- n2)	Changes the sign of n1
26	not	(n1 -- n2)	One's complement
24	or	(n1 n2 -- n3)	Logical or
2b	u/mod	(ul un -- un.rem un.quot)	Unsigned 32-bit divide of ul/un
58	u2/	(u1 -- u2)	Logical right shifts 1 bit
25	xor	(n1 n2 -- n3)	Exclusive or
d4	u*x	(u1[32] u2[32] -- product[64])	Multiplies two unsigned 32-bit numbers, yields an unsigned 64-bit product. V2
d5	xu/mod	(u1[64] u2[32] -- remainder[32] quot[32])	Divides an unsigned 64-bit number by an unsigned 32-bit number, yields a 32-bit remainder and quotient V2
d8	x+	(x1 x2 -- x3)	Adds two 64-bit numbers V2
d9	x-	(x1 x2 -- x3)	Subtracts two 64-bit numbers V2

Table A-3   Memory Operations

Value	Function	Stack	Description
72	!	(n adr --)	Stores a 32-bit number into the variable at adr
6c	+!	(n adr --)	Adds n to the 32-bit number stored in the variable at adr
77	2!	(n1 n2 adr --)	Stores 2 numbers at adr; n2 at lower address

Table A-3   Memory Operations

Value	Function	Stack	Description
76	2@	(adr -- n1 n2)	Fetches 2 numbers from adr; n2 from lower address
6d	@	(adr -- n)	Fetches a number from the variable at adr
CR	?	(adr --)	Displays the 32-bit number at adr
75	c!	(n adr --)	Stores low byte of n at adr
71	c@	(adr -- byte)	Fetches a byte from adr
CR	blank	(adr len --)	Sets len bytes of memory to ASCII space, starting at adr
CR	cmove	(adr1 adr2 u --)	Same as move
CR	cmove>	(adr1 adr2 u --)	Same as move
7a	comp	(adr1 adr2 len -- n)	Compares two byte arrays including case. n=0 if same
CR	erase	(adr len --)	Sets len bytes of memory to zero, starting at adr
79	fill	(adr u byte --)	Sets u bytes of memory to byte
0237	lflips	(adr len --)	Exchanges 16-bit words within 32-bit longwords in adr len V2
73	l!	(l adr --)	Stores the 32-bit number at adr, must be 32-bit aligned
6e	l@	(adr -- l)	Fetches the 32-bit longword at adr, must be 32-bit aligned
78	move	(adr1 adr2 u --)	Copies u bytes from adr1 to adr2, handles overlap correctly.
6b	off	(adr --)	Stores false (32-bit 0) at adr
6a	on	(adr --)	Stores true (32-bit -1) at adr
0236	wflips	(adr len --)	Exchanges bytes within 16-bit words in the specified region V2
74	w!	(w adr --)	Stores a 16-bit word at adr, must be 16-bit aligned
6f	w@	(adr -- w)	Fetches the unsigned 16-bit word at adr, must be 16-bit aligned
70	<w@	(adr -- n)	Fetches the signed 16-bit word at adr, must be 16-bit aligned

Table A-4   Atomic Access

Value	Function	Stack	Description
0230	rb@	(adr -- byte)	Reads the 8-bit value at the given address, atomically V2
0231	rb!	(byte adr --)	Writes the 8-bit value at the given address, atomically V2
0232	rw@	(adr -- word)	Reads the 16-bit value at the given address, atomically V2
0233	rw!	(word adr --)	Writes the 16-bit value at the given address, atomically V2
0234	rl@	(adr -- long)	Reads the 32-bit value at the given address, atomically V2
0235	rl!	(long adr --)	Writes the 32-bit value at the given address, atomically V2

Table A-5   Data Exception Test

Value	Function	Stack	Description
0220	cpeek	(adr -- false | byte true)	Reads the 8-bit value at the given address, returns false if unsuccessful V2
0221	wpeek	(adr -- false | word true)	Reads the 16-bit value at the given address, returns false if unsuccessful V2
0222	lpeek	(adr -- false | long true)	Reads the 32-bit value at the given address, returns false if unsuccessful V2
0223	cpoke	(byte adr -- ok?)	Writes the 8-bit value at the given address, returns false if unsuccessful V2
0224	wpoke	(word adr -- ok?)	Writes the 16-bit value at the given address, returns false if unsuccessful V2
0225	lpoke	(long adr -- ok?)	Writes the 32-bit value at the given address, returns false if unsuccessful V2

Table A-6   Comparison Operations

Value	Function	Stack	Description
36	0<	(n -- flag)	True if n < 0
37	0<=	(n -- flag)	True if n <= 0
35	0<>	(n -- flag)	True if n <> 0
34	0=	(n -- flag)	True if n = 0, also inverts any flag

Table A-6   Comparison Operations

Value	Function	Stack	Description
38	0>	(n -- flag)	True if n > 0
39	0>=	(n -- flag)	True if n >= 0
3a	<	(n1 n2 -- flag)	True if n1 < n2
43	<=	(n1 n2 -- flag)	True if n1 <= n2
3d	<>	(n1 n2 -- flag)	True if n1 <> n2
3c	=	(n1 n2 -- flag)	True if n1 = n2
3b	>	(n1 n2 -- flag)	True if n1 > n2
42	>=	(n1 n2 -- flag)	True if n1 >= n2
44	between	(n min max -- flag)	True if min <= n <= max
CR	false	(-- 0)	The value false
CR	true	(-- -1)	The value true
40	u<	(u1 u2 -- flag)	True if u1 < u2, unsigned
3f	u<=	(u1 n2 -- flag)	True if u1 <= u2, unsigned
3e	u>	(u1 n2 -- flag)	True if u1 > u2, unsigned
41	u>=	(u1 n2 -- flag)	True if u1 >= u2, unsigned
45	within	(n min max -- flag)	True if min <= n < max

Table A-7   Text Input

Value	Function	Stack	Description
-	(*text*)	(--)	Begins a comment (ignored)
-	\	(--)	Ignore rest of line (comment)
CR	ascii *x*	(-- char)	ASCII value of next character
CR	control *x*	(-- char)	Interprets next character as ASCII control character
8e	key	(-- char)	Reads a character from the keyboard
8d	key?	(-- flag)	True if a key has been typed on the keyboard
8a	expect	(adr +n --)	Gets a line of edited input from the keyboard; store at adr
88	span	(-- adr)	Variable containing the number of characters read by expect
-	(s *text*)	(--)	Begins a comment (ignored)

Table A-8 ASCII Constants

Value	Function	Stack	Description
ab	bell	(-- n)	The ASCII code for the bell character; decimal 7
a9	bl	(-- n)	The ASCII code for the space character; decimal 32
aa	bs	(-- n)	The ASCII code for the backspace character; decimal 8
CR	carret	(-- n)	The ASCII code for the carriage return character; decimal 13
CR	linefeed	(-- n)	The ASCII code for the linefeed character; decimal 10
CR	newline	(-- n)	The ASCII code for the newline character; decimal 10

Table A-9 Numeric Input

Value	Function	Stack	Description
a4	-1	(-- -1)	Constant -1
a5	0	(-- 0)	Constant 0
a6	1	(-- 1)	Constant 1
a7	2	(-- 2)	Constant 2
a8	3	(-- 3)	Constant 3
CR	b# *number*	(-- n)	Interprets next number in binary
-	binary	(--)	If outside definition, input text in binary
CR	d# *number*	(-- n)	Interprets next number in decimal
-	decimal	(--)	If outside definition, input text in decimal
CR	h# *number*	(-- n)	Interprets next number in hexadecimal
-	hex	(--)	If outside definition, input text in hexadecimal
CR	o# *number*	(-- n)	Interprets next number in octal
-	octal	(--)	If outside definition, input text in octal

Table A-10 Numeric Primitives

Value	Function	Stack	Description
99	#	(+l1 -- +l2)	Converts a digit in pictured numeric output
97	#>	(l -- adr +n)	Ends pictured numeric output
96	<#	(--)	Initializes pictured numeric output
a0	base	(-- adr)	Variable containing number base
a3	digit	(char base -- digit true | char false)	Converts a character to a digit
95	hold	(char --)	Inserts the char in the pictured numeric output string
9a	#s	(+l -- 0)	Converts the rest of the digits in pictured numeric output
98	sign	(n --)	Sets sign of pictured output
a2	$number	(adr len -- true | n false)	Converts a string to a number V2

Table A-11 Numeric Output

Value	Function	Stack	Description
9d	.	(n --)	Displays a number
CR	.d	(n --)	Displays number in decimal
CR	binary	(--)	If inside definition, output in binary
CR	decimal	(--)	If inside definition, output in decimal
CR	.h	(n --)	Displays number in hexadecimal
CR	hex	(--)	If inside definition, output in hexadecimal
CR	octal	(--)	If inside definition, output in octal
9e	.r	(n +n --)	Displays a number in a fixed width field
9f	.s	(--)	Displays the contents of the data stack
CR	s.	(n --)	Displays n as a signed number
9b	u.	(u --)	Displays an unsigned number
9c	u.r	(u +n --)	Prints an unsigned number in a fixed width field

Table A-12 General-purpose Output

Value	Function	Stack	Description
CR	." *text*"	(--)	Compiles string for later output
CR	.(*text*)	(--)	Displays a string now
91	(cr	(--)	Outputs ASCII CR character; decimal 13
92	cr	(--)	Starts a new line of display output
8f	emi	(char --)	Displays the character
CR	space	(--)	Outputs a single space character
CR	spaces	(+n --)	Outputs +n spaces
90	type	(adr +n --)	Displays n characters

Table A-13 Formatted Output

Value	Function	Stack	Description
94	#line	(-- adr)	Variable holding the line number on the output device
93	#out	(-- adr)	Variable holding the column number on the output device

Table A-14 `begin` Loops

Value	Function	Stack	Description
CR	again	(--)	Ends begin..again (infinite) loop
CR	begin	(--)	Starts conditional loop
CR	repeat	(--)	Returns to loop start
CR	until	(flag --)	If true, exits begin..until loop
CR	while	(flag --)	If true, continues begin..while..repeat loop, else exits loop

Table A-15 Conditionals

Value	Function	Stack	Description
CR	if	(flag --)	If true, executes next FCode(s)
CR	else	(--)	(optional) Executes next FCode(s) if if failed
CR	then	(--)	Terminates if..else..then

Table A-16 *do Loops*

Value	Function	Stack	Description
CR	do	(end start --)	Loops, index *start* to *end-1* inclusive
CR	?do	(end start --)	Like do, but skips loop if *end = start*
19	i	(-- n)	Returns current loop index value
1a	j	(-- n)	Returns value of next outer loop index
CR	leave	(--)	Exits do loop immediately
CR	?leave	(flag --)	If flag is true, exits do loop
CR	loop	(--)	Increments index, returns to do
CR	+loop	(n --)	Increments by n, returns to do. If n<0, index *start* to *end*

Table A-17 *Control Words*

Value	Function	Stack	Description
1d	execute	(acf --)	Executes the word whose compilation address is on the stack
33	exit	(--)	Returns from the current word
0238	probe	(arg-adr arg-len reg-adr reg-len fcode-adr fcode-len --)	V2.2
0239	probe-virtual	(arg-adr arg-len reg-adr reg-len fcode-adr --)	V2.2

Table A-18 *Strings*

Value	Function	Stack	Description
CR	" *text*"	(-- adr len)	Collects a string
84	count	(pstr -- adr +n)	Unpacks a packed string
82	lcc	(char -- lower-case-char)	Converts char to lower case
83	pack	(adr len pstr -- pstr)	Makes a packed string from adr len, placing it at pstr

Table A-18 Strings

Value	Function	Stack	Description
81	upc	(char -- upper-case-char)	Converts char to upper case
0240	left-parse-string	(adr len char -- adrR lenR adrL lenL)	Splits a string at the given delimiter (which is discarded) V2
011b	decode-2int	(adr len -- phys space)	Converts a string into a physical address and space V2

Table A-19 Defining Words

Value	Function	Stack	Description
CR	: (colon) *name*	(--)	Begins colon definition
CR	; (semicolon)	(--)	Ends colon definition
-	alias *newname oldname*	(--)	Creates newname with behavior of oldname
CR	buffer: *name*	(size --)	Creates data array of size bytes
CR	constant *name*	(n --)	Creates a constant
CR	create *name*	(--)	Generic defining word
CR	defer *name*	(--)	Execution vector (change with is)
CR	field *name*	(offset size -- offset+size)	Creates a named offset pointer
c0	instance	(--)	Declare a data type to be local V2.1
CR	struct	(-- 0)	Initializes for field creation
CR	variable *name*	(--)	Creates a data variable
CR	value *name*	(n --)	Creates named value-type variable (change with is)

Table A-20 Dictionary Compilation

Value	Function	Stack	Description
d3	,	(n --)	Places a number in the dictionary
d0	c,	(n --)	Places a byte in the dictionary
ad	here	(-- adr)	Address of top of dictionary

Table A-20 Dictionary Compilation

Value	Function	Stack	Description
d2	l,	(l --)	Places a 32-bit longword in the dictionary
d1	w,	(w --)	Places a 16-bit word in the dictionary
CR	is *name*	(n --)	Changes value in a defer word or a value

Table A-21 Dictionary Search

Value	Function	Stack	Description
CR	' *name*	(-- acf)	Finds the word (while executing)
CR	['] *name*	(-- acf)	Finds word (while compiling)
cb	$find	(adr len -- adr len false | acf +-1)	Finds a name in the OpenBoot PROM
cd	eval	(??? adr len -- ?)	Executes Forth commands within a string V2

Table A-22 Conversion Operators

Value	Function	Stack	Description
7f	bljoin	(b.low b2 b3 b.hi -- l)	Joins four bytes to form a longword
b0	bwjoin	(b.low b.hi -- w)	Joins two bytes to form a 16-bit word
5a	/c	(-- n)	Address increment for a byte; 1
66	/c*	(n1 -- n2)	Multiplies by /c
5e	ca+	(adr1 index -- adr2)	Increments adr1 by index times /c
62	ca1+	(adr1 -- adr2)	Increments adr1 by /c
80	flip	(w1 -- w2)	Swaps the bytes within a 16-bit word
5c	/l	(-- n)	Address increment for a 32-bit longword; 4
68	/l*	(n1 -- n2)	Multiplies by /l
60	la+	(adr1 index -- adr2)	Increments adr1 by index times /l
64	la1+	(adr1 -- adr2)	Increments adr1 by /l
7e	lbsplit	(l -- b.low b2 b3 b.high)	Splits a longword into four bytes
7c	lwsplit	(l -- w.low w.high)	Splits a longword into two words
5d	/n	(-- n)	Address increment for a normal; 4

Table A-22 Conversion Operators

Value	Function	Stack	Description
69	/n*	(n1 -- n2)	Multiplies by /n
61	na+	(adr1 index -- adr2)	Increments adr1 by index times /n
65	na1+	(adr1 -- adr2)	Increments adr1 by /n
5b	/w	(-- n)	Address increment for a 16-bit word; 2
67	/w*	(n1 -- n2)	Multiplies by /w
5f	wa+	(adr1 index -- adr2)	Increments adr1 by index times /w
63	wa1+	(adr1 -- adr2)	Increments adr1 by /w
af	wbsplit	(w -- b.low b.high)	Splits a 16-bit word into two bytes
CR	wflip	(l1 -- l2)	Swaps halves of 32-bit longword
7d	wljoin	(w.low w.high -- l)	Joins two words to form a longword

Table A-23 Memory Buffers Allocation

Value	Function	Stack	Description
8b	alloc-mem	(nbytes -- adr)	Allocates nbytes of memory and returns its address
8c	free-mem	(adr nbytes --)	Frees memory allocated by alloc-mem

Table A-24 Miscellaneous Operators

Value	Function	Stack	Description
86	>body	(acf -- apf)	Finds parameter field address from compilation address
85	body>	(apf -- acf)	Finds compilation address from parameter field address
CR	emit-byte	(n --)	Outputs FCode byte (use with tokenizer[)
00	end0	(--)	Marks the end of FCode
ff	end1	(--)	Alternates form for end0 (not recommended)
CR	fcode-version1	(--)	Begins FCode program
-	fload *filename*	(--)	Begins tokenizing *filename*
-	headerless	(--)	Creates new names with new-token (no name fields)

Table A-24 Miscellaneous Operators

Value	Function	Stack	Description
-	headers	(--)	Creates new names with named-token (default)
7b	noop	(--)	Does nothing
cc	offset16	(--)	All further branches use 16-bit offsets (instead of 8-bit)
-	tokenizer[	(--)	Begins tokenizer program commands
-	]tokenizer	(--)	Ends tokenizer program commands
CR	fcode-version2	(--)	Begins 2.0 FCode program, compiles start1 V2
-	external	(--)	Creates new names with external-token V2

Table A-25 Internal Operators, (invalid for program text)

Value	Function	Stack	Description
1-f	{ table#1-15 }		Reserved byte codes, used for 2-byte entries
10	b(lit)	(-- n)	Followed by 32-bit#. Compiled by numeric data
11	b(')	(-- acf)	Followed by a token (1 or 2-byte code) . Compiled by ['] or '
12	b(")	(-- adr len)	Followed by count byte, text. Compiled by " or ."
c3	b(is)	(n --)	Compiled by is
fd	version1	(--)	Followed by reserved byte, checksum (2 bytes) , length (4 bytes). Compiled by fcode-version1, as the first FCode bytes
fe	4-byte-id	(--)	Followed by 3 identifier bytes. First FCode byte. Not supported.
13	bbranch	(--)	Followed by offset. Compiled by else or again
14	b?branch	(--)	Followed by offset. Compiled by if or until
15	b(loop)	(--)	Followed by offset. Compiled by loop
16	b(+loop)	(n --)	Followed by offset. Compiled by +loop
17	b(do)	(end start --)	Followed by offset. Compiled by do
18	b(?do)	(end start --)	Followed by offset. Compiled by ?do
1b	b(leave)	(--)	Compiled by leave or ?leave
b1	b(<mark)	(--)	Compiled by begin

Table A-25 Internal Operators, (invalid for program text)

Value	Function	Stack	Description
b2	b(>resolve)	(--)	Compiled by else or then
c4	b(case)	(--)	Compiled by case
c5	b(endcase)	(--)	Compiled by endcase
c6	b(endof)	(--)	Compiled by endof
1c	b(of)	(sel testval -- sel | none)	Followed by offset. Compiled by of
b5	new-token	(--)	Followed by table#, code#, token-type. Compiled by any defining word. Headerless, not used normally.
b6	named-token	(--)	Followed by packed string (count,text), table#, code#, token-type. Compiled by any defining word (: value constant etc.)
b7	b(:)		Token-type compiled by :
b8	b(value)		Token-type compiled by value
b9	b(variable)		Token-type compiled by variable
ba	b(constant)		Token-type compiled by constant
bb	b(create)		Token-type compiled by create
bc	b(defer)		Token-type compiled by defer
bd	b(buffer:)		Token-type compiled by buffer:
be	b(field)		Token-type compiled by field
c2	b(;)	(--)	End a colon definition. Compiled by ;
ca	external-token	(--)	Like named-token, but name header is always created at probe time V2
f0	start0	(--)	Like version1, but for version 2.0 FCodes. Uses 16-bit branches. Fetches successive tokens from same address V2
f1	start1	(--)	Like version1, but for version 2.0 FCodes. Uses 16-bit branches. Fetches successive tokens from consecutive addresses. Compiled by fcode-version2 V2
f2	start2	(--)	Like version1, but for version 2.0 FCodes. Uses 16-bit branches. Fetches successive tokens from consecutive 16-bit addresses V2
f3	start4	(--)	Like version1, but for version 2.0 FCodes. Uses 16-bit branches. Fetches successive tokens from consecutive 32-bit addresses V2

Table A-26 Memory Allocation

Value	Function	Stack	Description
0101	dma-alloc	(nbytes -- virt)	Maps in nbytes of DMA space, return virtual adr
0104	memmap	(phys space nbytes -- virt)	Maps in a region, return virtual address
0105	free-virtual	(virt nbytes --)	Frees virtual memory from memmap, dma-alloc,or map-sbus
0106	>physical	(virt -- phys space)	Returns physical adr and space for virtual adr

Table A-27 Non-volatile Parameters

Value	Function	Stack	Description
010f	my-params	(-- adr len)	Returns a data array for this plug-in device. The data format is defined specifically for each plug-in device, in order to customize the device. Params for each device, as needed, will be stored in the system NVRAM

Table A-28 Properties

Value	Function	Stack	Description
0110	attribute	(xdr-adr xdr-len name-adr name-len --)	Declares a property with the given value structure, for the given name string.
0111	xdrint	(n -- xdr-adr xdr-len)	Converts a number into an xdr-format string
0112	xdr+	(xdr-adr1 xdr-len1 xdr-adr2 xdr-len2 -- xdr-adr xdr-len1+2)	Merges two xdr-format strings. They must have been created sequentially
0113	xdrphys	(phys space -- xdr-adr xdr-len)	Converts physical address and space into an xdr-format string
0114	xdrstring	(adr len -- xdr-adr xdr-len)	Converts a string into an xdr-format string

Table A-28 Properties

Value	Function	Stack	Description
0115	xdrbytes	(adr len -- xdr-adr xdr-len)	Converts a byte array into an xdr-format string V2.1
021a	get-my-attribute	(nam-adr nam-len -- true | xdr-adr xdr-len false)	Returns the xdr-format string for the given property name V2
021b	xdrtoint	(xdr-adr xdr-len -- xdr2-adr xdr2-len n)	Converts the beginning of an xdr-format string to an integer V2
021c	xdrtostring	(xdr-adr xdr-len -- xdr2-adr xdr2-len adr len)	Converts the beginning of an xdr-format string to a normal string V2
021d	get-inherited-attribute	(nam-adr nam-len -- true | xdr-adr xdr-len false)	Returns the value string for the given property, searches parents' properties if not found V2
021e	delete-attribute	(nam-adr nam-len --)	Deletes the property with the given name V2
021f	get-package-attribute	(adr len phandle -- true | xdr-adr xdr-len false)	Returns the xdr-format string for the given property name in the package "phandle" V2

Table A-29 Commonly-used Properties

Value	Function	Stack	Description
0116	reg	(phys space size --)	Declares location and size of device registers
0117	intr	(intr-level vector --)	Declares interrupt level and vector for this device
0118	driver	(adr len --)	Not supported
0119	model	(adr len --)	Declares model# for this device, such as " SUNW,501-1415-01"
011a	device-type	(adr len --)	Declares type of device, e.g. " display", " block", " network", or " byte"
CR	name	(adr len --)	Declares SunOS driver name, as in " SUNW,zebra"
0201	device-name	(adr len --)	Creates the "name" attribute with the given value V2

Table A-30 System Version Information

Value	Function	Stack	Description
0210	processor-type	(-- processor-type)	Obsolete V2
0211	firmware-version	(-- n)	Returns major/minor CPU firmware version V2
0212	fcode-version	(-- n)	Obsolete V2
87	version	(-- n)	Returns major/minor FCode interface version

Table A-31 Device Activation Vector Setup

Value	Function	Stack	Description
011c	is-install	(acf --)	Identifies "install" routine to allocate a framebuffer
011d	is-remove	(acf --)	Identifies "remove" routine, to deallocate a framebuffer
011e	is-selftest	(acf --)	Identifies "selftest" routine for this framebuffer
011f	new-device	(--)	Opens an additional device, using this driver package
0127	finish-device	(--)	Closes out current device, ready for new-device

Table A-32 Self-test utility Routines

Value	Function	Stack	Description
0120	diagnostic-mode?	(-- flag)	Returns "true" if extended diagnostics are desired
0121	display-status	(n --)	Obsolete
0122	memory-test-suite	(adr len -- status)	Calls memory tester for given region
0123	group-code	(-- adr)	Obsolete
0124	mask	(-- adr)	Variable, holds "mask" used by memory-test-suite

Table A-33 Time Utilities

Value	Function	Stack	Description
0125	get-msecs	(-- ms)	Returns the current time, in milliseconds, approx.
0126	ms	(n --)	Delays for n milliseconds. Resolution is 1 millisecond
0213	alarm	(acf n --)	Periodically execute acf. If n=0, stop. V2

Table A-34 Machine-specific Support

Value	Function	Stack	Description
0130	map-sbus	(phys size -- virt)	Maps a region of memory in 'sbus' address space
0131	sbus-intr>cpu	(sbus-intr# -- cpu-intr#)	Translates SBus interrupt# into CPU interrupt#

Note – Table A-35 through apply only to *display* device-types.

Table A-35 User-set terminal Emulation Values

Value	Function	Stack	Description
0150	#lines	(-- n)	Number of lines of text being used for display. This word must be initialized (using is). fbx-install does this automatically, and also properly incorporates the NVRAM parameter "screen-#rows"
0151	#columns	(-- n)	Number of columns (chars/line) used for display. This word must be initialized (using is). fbx-install does this automatically, and also properly incorporates the NVRAM parameter "screen-#columns"

Table A-36 Terminal Emulator-set Terminal Emulation Values

Value	Function	Stack	Description
0152	line#	(-- n)	Current cursor position (line#). 0 is top line
0153	column#	(-- n)	Current cursor position (column#). 0 is left char.
0154	inverse?	(-- flag)	True if output is inverted (white-on-black)
0155	inverse-screen?	(-- flag)	True if screen has been inverted (black background)

Table A-37 Terminal Emulation Routines*

Value	Function	Stack	Description
0157	draw-character	(char --)	Paints the given character and advance the cursor
0158	reset-screen	(--)	Initializes the display device
0159	toggle-cursor	(--)	Draws or erase the cursor
015a	erase-screen	(--)	Clears all pixels on the display
015b	blink-screen	(--)	Flashes the display momentarily
015c	invert-screen	(--)	Changes all pixels to the opposite color
015d	insert-characters	(n --)	Inserts n blanks just before the cursor
015e	delete-characters	(n --)	Deletes n characters starting at with cursor character, rightward. Remaining chars slide left
015f	insert-lines	(n --)	Inserts n blank lines just before the current line, lower lines are scrolled downward
0160	delete-lines	(n --)	Deletes n lines starting with the current line, lower lines are scrolled upward
0161	draw-logo	(line# logoaddr logowidth logoheight --)	Draws the logo

*defer-type loadable routines.

Table A-38 Frame Buffer Parameter Values*

Value	Function	Stack	Description
016c	char-height	(-- n)	Height (in pixels) of a character (usually 22)
016d	char-width	(-- n)	Width (in pixels) of a character (usually 12)
016f	fontbytes	(-- n)	Number of bytes/scan line for font entries (usually 2)
0162	frame-buffer-adr	(-- adr)	Address of frame buffer memory
0163	screen-height	(-- n)	Total height of the display (in pixels)
0164	screen-width	(-- n)	Total width of the display (in pixels)
0165	window-top	(-- n)	Distance (in pixels) between display top and text window
0166	window-left	(-- n)	Distance (in pixels) between display left edge and text window left edge

*These must all be initialized before using any fbx- routines.

Table A-39 Font Operators

Value	Function	Stack	Description
016a	default-font	(-- fontbase charwidth charheight fontbytes #firstchar #chars)	Returns default font values, plugs directly into set-font
016b	set-font	(fontbase charwidth charheight fontbytes #firstchar #chars --)	Sets the character font for text output
016e	>font	(char -- adr)	Returns font address for given ASCII character

Table A-40 One-bit Framebuffer Utilities

Value	Function	Stack	Description
0170	fb1-draw-character	(char --)	Paints the character and advance the cursor
0171	fb1-reset-screen	(--)	Initializes the display device (noop)
0172	fb1-toggle-cursor	(--)	Draws or erases the cursor
0173	fb1-erase-screen	(--)	Clears all pixels on the display

Table A-40 One-bit Framebuffer Utilities

Value	Function	Stack	Description
0174	fb1-blink-screen	(--)	Inverts the screen, twice (slow)
0175	fb1-invert-screen	(--)	Changes all pixels to the opposite color
0176	fb1-insert-characters	(n --)	Inserts n blanks just before the cursor
0177	fb1-delete-characters	(n --)	Deletes n characters, starting at with cursor character, rightward. Remaining chars slide left
0178	fb1-insert-lines	(n --)	Inserts n blank lines just before the current line, lower lines are scrolled downward
0179	fb1-delete-lines	(n --)	Deletes n lines starting with the current line, lower lines are scrolled upward
017a	fb1-draw-logo	(line# logoaddr logowidth logoheight --)	Draws the logo
017b	fb1-install	(width height #columns #lines --)	Installs the one-bit built-in routines
017c	fb1-slide-up	(n --)	Like fb1-delete-lines, but doesn't clear lines at bottom

Table A-41 Eight-bit Framebuffer Utilities

Value	Function	Stack	Description
0180	fb8-draw-character	(char --)	Paints the character and advance the cursor
0181	fb8-reset-screen	(--)	Initializes the display device (noop)
0182	fb8-toggle-cursor	(--)	Draws or erases the cursor
0183	fb8-erase-screen	(--)	Clears all pixels on the display
0184	fb8-blink-screen	(--)	Inverts the screen, twice (slow)
0185	fb8-invert-screen	(--)	Changes all pixels to the opposite color
0186	fb8-insert-characters	(n --)	Inserts n blanks just before the cursor
0187	fb8-delete-characters	(n --)	Deletes n characters starting at with cursor character, rightward. Remaining chars slide left
0188	fb8-insert-lines	(n --)	Inserts n blank lines just before the current line, lower lines are scrolled downward

Table A-41 Eight-bit Framebuffer Utilities

Value	Function	Stack	Description
0189	fb8-delete-lines	(n --)	Deletes n lines starting with the current line, lower lines are scrolled upward
018a	fb8-draw-logo	(line# logoaddr logowidth logoheight --)	Draws the logo
018b	fb8-install	(width height #columns #lines --)	Installs the eight-bit built-in routines

Table A-42 Package Support

Value	Function	Stack	Description
023c	peer	(phandle -- next-phandle)	Returns phandle of package that is the next child of the the parent of the package V2.3
023b	child	(parent-phandle -- child-phandle)	Returns phandle of the package that is the first child of the package parent-phandle V2.3
0204	find-package	(adr len -- false | phandle true)	Finds a package named "adr len" V2
0205	open-package	(adr len phandle -- ihandle | 0)	Opens an instance of the package "phandle," passes arguments "adr len" V2
020f	$open-package	(arg-adr arg-len adr len -- ihandle | 0)	Finds a package "adr len," then opens it with arguments "arg-adr arg-len" V2
020a	my-parent	(-- ihandle)	Returns the ihandle of the parent of the current package instance V2
0203	my-self	(-- ihandle)	Returns the instance handle of currently-executing package instance V2
020b	ihandle>phandle	(ihandle -- phandle)	Converts an ihandle to a phandle V2
0206	close-package	(ihandle --)	Closes an instance of a package V2

Table A-42 Package Support

Value	Function	Stack	Description
0207	find-method	(adr len phandle -- false | acf true)	Finds the method (command) named "adr len" within the package "phandle" V2
0208	call-package	([...] acf ihandle -- [...])	Executes the method "acf" within the instance "ihandle" V2
020e	$call-method	([...]adr len ihandle -- [...])	Executes the method named "adr len" within the instance "ihandle" V2
0209	$call-parent	([...] adr len -- [...])	Executes the method "adr len" within the parent's package V2
0202	my-args	(-- adr len)	Returns the argument string "adr len" passed when this package was opened V2
020d	my-unit	(-- low high)	Returns the physical unit number pair for this package V2
0102	my-address	(-- phys)	Returns the physical adr of this plug-in device. "phys" is a "magic" number, usable by other routines V2
0103	my-space	(-- space)	Returns address space of plug-in device. "space" is a "magic" number, usable by other routines V2

Table A-43 Asynchronous Support

Value	Function	Stack	Description
0213	alarm	(acf n --)	Executes the method (command) indicated by "acf" every "n" milliseconds V2
0219	user-abort	(--)	Abort after alarm routine finishes execution

Table A-44 Miscellaneous Operations

Value	Function	Stack	Description
0214	(is-user-word)	(adr len acf --)	Creates a new word called "adr len" which executes "acf" V2
01a4	mac-address	(-- adr len)	Returns the MAC address V2

Table A-45 Interpretation

Value	Function	Stack	Description
0215	suspend-fcode	(--)	Suspends execution of FCode, resumes later if an undefined command is required V2

Table A-46 Error Handling

Value	Function	Stack	Description
0216	abort	(--)	Aborts FCode execution, returns to the "ok" prompt V2
0217	catch	([...] acf -- [...] error-code)	Executes "acf," returns throw error code or 0 if throw not encountered V2
0218	throw	(error-code --)	Returns given error code to catch V2
fc	ferror	(--)	Displays "Unimplemented FCode" and stops FCode interpretation

FCodes by Byte Value

The following table lists, in hexadecimal order, currently-assigned FCode byte values.

Table A-47 FCodes by Byte Value

Value	Function	Stack	Version 2?
00	end0	(--)	
10	b(lit)	(-- n)	
11	b(')	(-- acf)	
12	b(")	(-- adr len)	
13	bbranch	(--)	
14	b?branch	(--)	
15	b(loop)	(--)	
16	b(+loop)	(n --)	
17	b(do)	(end start --)	
18	b(?do)	(end start --)	
19	i	(-- n)	

Table A-47 FCodes by Byte Value

Value	Function	Stack	Version 2?
1a	j	(-- n)	
1b	b(leave)	(--)	
1c	b(of)	(sel testval -- sel | none)	
1d	execute	(acf --)	
1e	+	(n1 n2 -- n3)	
1f	-	(n1 n2 -- n3)	
20	*	(n1 n2 -- n3)	
21	/	(n1 n2 -- quot)	
22	mod	(n1 n2 -- rem)	
23	and	(n1 n2 -- n3)	
24	or	(n1 n2 -- n3)	
25	xor	(n1 n2 -- n3)	
26	not	(n1 -- n2)	
27	<<	(n1 +n -- n2)	
28	>>	(n1 +n -- n2)	
29	>>a	(n1 +n -- n2)	
2a	/mod	(n1 n2 -- rem quot)	
2b	u/mod	(ul un -- un.rem un.quot)	
2c	negate	(n1 -- n2)	
2d	abs	(n -- u)	
2e	min	(n1 n2 -- n3)	
2f	max	(n1 n2 -- n3)	
30	>r	(n --) (rs: -- n)	
31	r>	(-- n) (rs: n --)	
32	r@	(-- n) (rs: --)	
33	exit	(--)	
34	0=	(n -- flag)	
35	0<>	(n -- flag)	
36	0<	(n -- flag)	
37	0<=	(n -- flag)	
38	0>	(n -- flag)	
39	0>=	(n -- flag)	

Writing FCode Programs

Table A-47 FCodes by Byte Value

Value	Function	Stack	Version 2?
3a	<	(n1 n2 -- flag)	
3b	>	(n1 n2 -- flag)	
3c	=	(n1 n2 -- flag)	
3d	<>	(n1 n2 -- flag)	
3e	u>	(u1 n2 -- flag)	
3f	u<=	(u1 n2 -- flag)	
40	u<	(u1 u2 -- flag)	
41	u>=	(u1 n2 -- flag)	
42	>=	(n1 n2 -- flag)	
43	<=	(n1 n2 -- flag)	
44	between	(n min max -- flag)	
45	within	(n min max -- flag)	
46	drop	(n --)	
47	dup	(n -- n n)	
48	over	(n1 n2 -- n1 n2 n1)	
49	swap	(n1 n2 -- n2 n1)	
4a	rot	(n1 n2 n3 -- n2 n3 n1)	
4b	-rot	(n1 n2 n3 -- n3 n1 n2)	
4c	tuck	(n1 n2 -- n2 n1 n2)	
4d	nip	(n1 n2 -- n2)	
4e	pick	(+n -- n2)	
4f	roll	(+n --)	
50	?dup	(n -- n n | 0)	
51	depth	(-- +n)	
52	2drop	(n1 n2 --)	
53	2dup	(n1 n2 -- n1 n2 n1 n2)	
54	2over	(n1 n2 n3 n4 -- n1 n2 n3 n4 n1 n2)	
55	2swap	(n1 n2 n3 n4 -- n3 n4 n1 n2)	
56	2rot	(n1 n2 n3 n4 n5 n6 -- n3 n4 n5 n6 n1 n2)	
57	2/	(n1 -- n2)	
58	u2/	(u1 -- u2)	
59	2*	(n1 -- n2)	

Table A-47 FCodes by Byte Value

Value	Function	Stack	Version 2?
5a	/c	(-- n)	
5b	/w	(-- n)	
5c	/l	(-- n)	
5d	/n	(-- n)	
5e	ca+	(adr1 index -- adr2)	
5f	wa+	(adr1 index -- adr2)	
60	la+	(adr1 index -- adr2)	
61	na+	(adr1 index -- adr2)	
62	ca1+	(adr1 -- adr2)	
63	wa1+	(adr1 -- adr2)	
64	la1+	(adr1 -- adr2)	
65	na1+	(adr1 -- adr2)	
66	/c*	(n1 -- n2)	
67	/w*	(n1 -- n2)	
68	/l*	(n1 -- n2)	
69	/n*	(n1 -- n2)	
6a	on	(adr --)	
6b	off	(adr --)	
6c	+!	(n adr --)	
6d	@	(adr -- n)	
6e	l@	(adr -- l)	
6f	w@	(adr -- w)	
70	<w@	(adr -- n)	
71	c@	(adr -- byte)	
72	!	(n adr --)	
73	l!	(l adr --)	
74	w!	(w adr --)	
75	c!	(n adr --)	
76	2@	(adr -- n1 n2)	
77	2!	(n1 n2 adr --)	
78	move	(adr1 adr2 u --)	
79	fill	(adr u byte --)	

Table A-47 FCodes by Byte Value

Value	Function	Stack	Version 2?
7a	comp	(adr1 adr2 len -- n)	
7b	noop	(--)	
7c	lwsplit	(l -- w.low w.high)	
7d	wljoin	(w.low w.high -- l)	
7e	lbsplit	(l -- b.low b2 b3 b.high)	
7f	bljoin	(b.low b2 b3 b.hi -- l)	
80	flip	(w1 -- w2)	
81	upc	(char -- upper-case-char)	
82	lcc	(char -- lower-case-char)	
83	pack	(adr len pstr -- pstr)	
84	count	(pstr -- adr +n)	
85	body>	(apf -- acf)	
86	>body	(acf -- apf)	
87	version	(-- n)	
88	span	(-- adr)	
8a	expect	(adr +n --)	
8b	alloc-mem	(nbytes -- adr)	
8c	free-mem	(adr nbytes --)	
8d	key?	(-- flag)	
8e	key	(-- char)	
8f	emit	(char --)	
90	type	(adr +n --)	
91	(cr	(--)	
92	cr	(--)	
93	#out	(-- adr)	
94	#line	(-- adr)	
95	hold	(char --)	
96	<#	(--)	
97	#>	(l -- adr +n)	
98	sign	(n --)	
99	#	(+l1 -- +l2)	
9a	#s	(+l -- 0)	

Table A-47 FCodes by Byte Value

Value	Function	Stack	Version 2?
9b	u.	(u --)	
9c	u.r	(u +n --)	
9d	.	(n --)	
9e	.r	(n +n --)	
9f	.s	(--)	
a0	base	(-- adr)	
a2	$number	(adr len -- true | n false)	V2
a3	digit	(char base -- digit true | char false)	
a4	-1	(-- -1)	
a5	0	(-- 0)	
a6	1	(-- 1)	
a7	2	(-- 2)	
a8	3	(-- 3)	
a9	bl	(-- n)	
aa	bs	(-- n)	
ab	bell	(-- n)	
ac	bounds	(startadr len -- endadr startadr)	
ad	here	(-- adr)	
ae	aligned	(adr1 -- adr2)	
af	wbsplit	(w -- b.low b.high)	
b0	bwjoin	(b.low b.hi -- w)	
b1	b(<mark)	(--)	
b2	b(>resolve)	(--)	
b5	new-token	(--)	
b6	named-token	(--)	
b7	b(:)		
b8	b(value)		
b9	b(variable)		
ba	b(constant)		
bb	b(create)		
bc	b(defer)		
bd	b(buffer:)		

Table A-47 FCodes by Byte Value

Value	Function	Stack	Version 2?
be	b(field)		
c0	instance	(--)	V2.1
c2	b(;)	(--)	
c3	b(is)	(n --)	
c4	b(case)	(--)	
c5	b(endcase)	(--)	
c6	b(endof)	(--)	
ca	external-token	(--)	V2
cb	$find	(adr len -- adr len false | acf +-1)	
cc	offset16	(--)	
cd	eval	(??? adr len -- ?)	V2
d0	c,	(n --)	
d1	w,	(w --)	
d2	l,	(l --)	
d3	,	(n --)	
d4	u*x	(u1[32] u2[32] -- product[64])	V2
d5	xu/mod	(u1[64] u2[32] -- remainder[32] quot[32])	V2
d8	x+	(x1 x2 -- x3)	V2
d9	x-	(x1 x2 -- x3)	V2
f0	start0	(--)	V2
f1	start1	(--)	V2
f2	start2	(--)	V2
f3	start4	(--)	V2
fc	ferror	(--)	V2.3
fd	version1	(--)	
fe	4-byte-id	(--)	
ff	end1	(--)	
0101	dma-alloc	(nbytes -- virt)	
0102	my-address	(-- phys)	V2
0103	my-space	(-- space)	V2
0104	memmap	(physoffset space size -- virtual)	
0105	free-virtual	(virt nbytes --)	

Table A-47 FCodes by Byte Value

Value	Function	Stack	Version 2?
0106	>physical	(virt -- phys space)	
010f	my-params	(-- adr len)	
0110	attribute	(xdr-adr xdr-len name-adr name-len --)	
0111	xdrint	(n -- xdr-adr xdr-len)	
0112	xdr+	(xdr-adr1 xdr-len1 xdr-adr2 xdr-len2 -- xdr-adr xdr-len1+2)	
0113	xdrphys	(phys space -- xdr-adr xdr-len)	
0114	xdrstring	(adr len -- xdr-adr xdr-len)	
0115	xdrbytes	(adr len -- xdr-adr xdr-len)	V2.1
0116	reg	(phys space size --)	
0117	intr	(intr-level vector --)	
0118	driver	(adr len --)	
0119	model	(adr len --)	
011a	device-type	(adr len --)	
011b	decode-2int	(xdr-adr xdr-len -- phys space)	V2
011c	is-install	(acf --)	
011d	is-remove	(acf --)	
011e	is-selftest	(acf --)	
011f	new-device	(--)	
0120	diagnostic-mode?	(-- flag)	
0121	display-status	(n --)	
0122	memory-test-suite	(adr len -- status)	
0123	group-code	(-- adr)	
0124	mask	(-- adr)	
0125	get-msecs	(-- ms)	
0126	ms	(n --)	
0127	finish-device	(--)	
0130	map-sbus	(phys size -- virt)	
0131	sbus-intr>cpu	(sbus-intr# -- cpu-intr#)	
0150	#lines	(-- n)	
0151	#columns	(-- n)	
0152	line#	(-- n)	

Table A-47 FCodes by Byte Value

Value	Function	Stack	Version 2?
0153	column#	(-- n)	
0154	inverse?	(-- flag)	
0155	inverse-screen?	(-- flag)	
0157	draw-character	(char --)	
0158	reset-screen	(--)	
0159	toggle-cursor	(--)	
015a	erase-screen	(--)	
015b	blink-screen	(--)	
015c	invert-screen	(--)	
015d	insert-characters	(n --)	
015e	delete-characters	(n --)	
015f	insert-lines	(n --)	
0160	delete-lines	(n --)	
0161	draw-logo	(line# logoaddr logowidth logoheight --)	
0162	frame-buffer-adr	(-- adr)	
0163	screen-height	(-- n)	
0164	screen-width	(-- n)	
0165	window-top	(-- n)	
0166	window-left	(-- n)	
016a	default-font	(-- fontbase charwidth charheight fontbytes #firstchar #chars)	
016b	set-font	(fontbase charwidth charheight fontbytes #firstchar #chars --)	
016c	char-height	(-- n)	
016d	char-width	(-- n)	
016e	>font	(char -- adr)	
016f	fontbytes	(-- n)	
0170	fb1-draw-character	(char --)	
0171	fb1-reset-screen	(--)	
0172	fb1-toggle-cursor	(--)	
0173	fb1-erase-screen	(--)	
0174	fb1-blink-screen	(--)	

Table A-47 FCodes by Byte Value

Value	Function	Stack	Version 2?
0175	fb1-invert-screen	(--)	
0176	fb1-insert-characters	(n --)	
0177	fb1-delete-characters	(n --)	
0178	fb1-insert-lines	(n --)	
0179	fb1-delete-lines	(n --)	
017a	fb1-draw-logo	(line# logoaddr logowidth logoheight --)	
017b	fb1-install	(width height #columns #lines --)	
017c	fb1-slide-up	(n --)	
0180	fb8-draw-character	(char --)	
0181	fb8-reset-screen	(--)	
0182	fb8-toggle-cursor	(--)	
0183	fb8-erase-screen	(--)	
0184	fb8-blink-screen	(--)	
0185	fb8-invert-screen	(--)	
0186	fb8-insert-characters	(n --)	
0187	fb8-delete-characters	(n --)	
0188	fb8-insert-lines	(n --)	
0189	fb8-delete-lines	(n --)	
018a	fb8-draw-logo	(line# logoaddr logowidth logoheight --)	
018b	fb8-install	(width height #columns #lines --)	
01a4	mac-address	(-- adr len)	V2
0201	device-name	(adr len --)	V2
0202	my-args	(-- adr len)	V2
0203	my-self	(-- ihandle)	V2
0204	find-package	(adr len -- false | phandle true)	V2
0205	open-package	(adr len phandle -- ihandle | 0)	V2
0206	close-package	(ihandle --)	V2
0207	find-method	(adr len phandle -- false | acf true)	V2
0208	call-package	([...] acf ihandle -- [...])	V2

Table A-47 FCodes by Byte Value

Value	Function	Stack	Version 2?
0209	$call-parent	([...] adr len -- [...])	V2
020a	my-parent	(-- ihandle)	V2
020b	ihandle>phandle	(ihandle -- phandle)	V2
020d	my-unit	(-- low high)	V2
020e	$call-method	([...]adr len ihandle -- [...])	V2
020f	$open-package	(arg-adr arg-len adr len -- ihandle | 0)	V2
0210	processor-type	(-- processor-type)	V2
0211	firmware-version	(-- n)	V2
0212	fcode-version	(-- n)	V2
0213	alarm	(acf n --)	V2
0214	(is-user-word)	(adr len acf --)	V2
0215	suspend-fcode	(--)	V2
0216	abort	(--)	V2
0217	catch	([...] acf -- [...] error-code)	V2
0218	throw	(error-code --)	V2
0219	user-abort	(--)	V2.1
021a	get-my-attribute	(nam-adr nam-len -- true | xdr-adr xdr-len false)	V2
021b	xdrtoint	(xdr-adr xdr-len -- xdr2-adr xdr2-len n)	V2
021c	xdrtostring	(xdr-adr xdr-len -- xdr2-adr xdr2-len adr len)	V2
021d	get-inherited-attribute	(nam-adr nam-len -- true | xdr-adr xdr-len false)	V2
021e	delete-attribute	(nam-adr nam-len --)	V2
021f	get-package-attribute	(adr len phandle -- true | xdr-adr xdr-len false)	V2
0220	cpeek	(adr -- false | byte true)	V2
0221	wpeek	(adr -- false | word true)	V2
0222	lpeek	(adr -- false | long true)	V2
0223	cpoke	(byte adr -- ok?)	V2
0224	wpoke	(word adr -- ok?)	V2
0225	lpoke	(long adr -- ok?)	V2
0230	rb@	(adr -- byte)	V2

Table A-47 FCodes by Byte Value

Value	Function	Stack	Version 2?
0231	rb!	(byte adr --)	V2
0232	rw@	(adr -- word)	V2
0233	rw!	(word adr --)	V2
0234	rl@	(adr -- long)	V2
0235	rl!	(long adr --)	V2
0236	wflips	(adr len --)	V2
0237	lflips	(adr len --)	V2
0238	probe	(arg-adr arg-len reg-adr reg-len fcode-adr fcode-len --)	V2.2
0239	probe-virtual	(arg-adr arg-len reg-adr reg-len fcode-adr --)	V2.2
023b	child	(phandle -- child-phandle)	V2.3
023c	peer	(phandle -- peer-phandle)	V2.3
0240	left-parse-string	(adr len char -- adrR lenR adrL lenL)	V2.2
-	(text)	(--)	
-	(s text)	(--)	
-	]tokenizer	(--)	
-	\	(--)	
-	alias	(--)	
-	binary	(--)	
-	decimal	(--)	
-	external	(--)	V2
-	fload filename	(--)	
-	headerless	(--)	
-	headers	(--)	
-	hex	(--)	
-	octal	(--)	
-	tokenizer[	(--)	
CR	" text"	(-- adr len)	
CR	' name	(-- acf)	
CR	*/mod	(n1 n2 n3 -- rem quot)	
CR	+loop	(n --)	

Table A-47 FCodes by Byte Value

Value	Function	Stack	Version 2?
CR	." text"	(--)	
CR	.(text)	(--)	
CR	.d	(n --)	
CR	.h	(n --)	
CR	1+	(n1 -- n2)	
CR	1-	(n1 -- n2)	
CR	3dup	(n1 n2 n3 -- n1 n2 n3 n1 n2 n3)	
CR	: (colon) name	(--)	
CR	; (semicolon)	(--)	
CR	<<a	(n1 +n -- n2)	
CR	?	(adr --)	
CR	?do	(end start --)	
CR	?leave	(flag --)	
CR	['] name	(-- acf)	
CR	again	(--)	
CR	ascii x	(-- char)	
CR	b# number	(-- n)	
CR	begin	(--)	
CR	blank	(adr len --)	
CR	buffer: name	(size --)	
CR	carret	(-- n)	
CR	cmove	(adr1 adr2 u --)	
CR	cmove>	(adr1 adr2 u --)	
CR	constant name	(n --)	
CR	control x	(-- char)	
CR	create name	(--)	
CR	d# number	(-- n)	
CR	decimal	(--)	
CR	defer name	(--)	
CR	do	(end start --)	
CR	else	(--)	
CR	emit-byte	(n --)	

Table A-47 FCodes by Byte Value

Value	Function	Stack	Version 2?
CR	erase	(adr len --)	
CR	false	(-- 0)	
CR	fcode-version1	(--)	
CR	fcode-version2	(--)	V2
CR	field name	(offset size -- offset+size)	
CR	h# number	(-- n)	
CR	hex	(--)	
CR	if	(flag --)	
CR	is name	(n --)	
CR	leave	(--)	
CR	linefeed	(-- n)	
CR	loop	(--)	
CR	name	(adr len --)	
CR	newline	(-- n)	
CR	o# number	(-- n)	
CR	repeat	(--)	
CR	s.	(n --)	
CR	space	(--)	
CR	spaces	(+n --)	
CR	struct	(-- 0)	
CR	then	(--)	
CR	true	(-- -1)	
CR	until	(flag --)	
CR	value name	(n --)	
CR	variable name	(--)	
CR	wflip	(l1 -- l2)	
CR	while	(flag --)	

FCodes by Name

The following table lists, in alphabetic order, currently-assigned FCodes.

Table A-48 FCodes by Name

Value	Function	Stack	Version 2?
a5	0	(-- 0)	
36	0<	(n -- flag)	
37	0<=	(n -- flag)	
35	0<>	(n -- flag)	
34	0=	(n -- flag)	
38	0>	(n -- flag)	
39	0>=	(n -- flag)	
a6	1	(-- 1)	
CR	1+	(n1 -- n2)	
CR	1-	(n1 -- n2)	
a7	2	(-- 2)	
77	2!	(n1 n2 adr --)	
59	2*	(n1 -- n2)	
57	2/	(n1 -- n2)	
76	2@	(adr -- n1 n2)	
52	2drop	(n1 n2 --)	
53	2dup	(n1 n2 -- n1 n2 n1 n2)	
54	2over	(n1 n2 n3 n4 -- n1 n2 n3 n4 n1 n2)	
56	2rot	(n1 n2 n3 n4 n5 n6 -- n3 n4 n5 n6 n1 n2)	
55	2swap	(n1 n2 n3 n4 -- n3 n4 n1 n2)	
a8	3	(-- 3)	
CR	3dup	(n1 n2 n3 -- n1 n2 n3 n1 n2 n3)	
fe	4-byte-id	(--)	
0216	abort	(--)	V2
2d	abs	(n -- u)	
CR	again	(--)	
0213	alarm	(acf n --)	V2
-	alias	(--)	
ae	aligned	(adr1 -- adr2)	

Table A-48 FCodes by Name

Value	Function	Stack	Version 2?
8b	alloc-mem	(nbytes -- adr)	
23	and	(n1 n2 -- n3)	
CR	ascii x	(-- char)	
0110	attribute	(xdr-adr xdr-len name-adr name-len --)	
CR	b# number	(-- n)	
12	b(")	(-- adr len)	
11	b(')	(-- acf)	
16	b(+loop)	(n --)	
b7	b(:)		
c2	b(;)	(--)	
b1	b(<mark)	(--)	
b2	b(>resolve)	(--)	
18	b(?do)	(end start --)	
bd	b(buffer:)		
c4	b(case)	(selector -- selector)	
ba	b(constant)		
bb	b(create)		
bc	b(defer)		
17	b(do)	(end start --)	
c5	b(endcase)	(--)	
c6	b(endof)	(--)	
be	b(field)		
c3	b(is)	(n --)	
1b	b(leave)	(--)	
10	b(lit)	(-- n)	
15	b(loop)	(--)	
1c	b(of)	(sel testval -- sel | none)	
b8	b(value)		
b9	b(variable)		
14	b?branch	(--)	
a0	base	(-- adr)	
13	bbranch	(--)	

Table A-48 FCodes by Name

Value	Function	Stack	Version 2?
CR	begin	(--)	
ab	bell	(-- n)	
44	between	(n min max -- flag)	
-	binary	(--)	
a9	bl	(-- n)	
CR	blank	(adr len --)	
015b	blink-screen	(--)	
7f	bljoin	(b.low b2 b3 b.hi -- l)	
85	body>	(apf -- acf)	
ac	bounds	(startadr len -- endadr startadr)	
aa	bs	(-- n)	
CR	buffer: name	(size --)	
b0	bwjoin	(b.low b.hi -- w)	
75	c!	(n adr --)	
d0	c,	(n --)	
71	c@	(adr -- byte)	
5e	ca+	(adr1 index -- adr2)	
62	ca1+	(adr1 -- adr2)	
0208	call-package	([...] acf ihandle -- [...])	V2
CR	carret	(-- n)	
0217	catch	([...] acf -- [...] error-code)	V2
016c	char-height	(-- n)	
016d	char-width	(-- n)	
0236	child	(phandle -- child-phandle)	V2.3
0206	close-package	(ihandle --)	V2
CR	cmove	(adr1 adr2 u --)	
CR	cmove>	(adr1 adr2 u --)	
0153	column#	(-- n)	
7a	comp	(adr1 adr2 len -- n)	
CR	constant name	(n --)	
CR	control x	(-- char)	
84	count	(pstr -- adr +n)	

Table A-48 FCodes by Name

Value	Function	Stack	Version 2?
0220	cpeek	(adr -- false | byte true)	V2
0223	cpoke	(byte adr -- ok?)	V2
92	cr	(--)	
CR	create name	(--)	
CR	d# number	(-- n)	
-	decimal	(--)	
CR	decimal	(--)	
011b	decode-2int	(xdr-adr xdr-len -- phys space)	V2
016a	default-font	(-- fontbase charwidth charheight fontbytes #firstchar #chars)	
CR	defer name	(--)	
021e	delete-attribute	(nam-adr nam-len --)	V2
015e	delete-characters	(n --)	
0160	delete-lines	(n --)	
51	depth	(-- +n)	
0201	device-name	(adr len --)	V2
011a	device-type	(adr len --)	
0120	diagnostic-mode?	(-- flag)	
a3	digit	(char base -- digit true | char false)	
0121	display-status	(n --)	
0101	dma-alloc	(nbytes -- virt)	
CR	do	(end start --)	
0157	draw-character	(char --)	
0161	draw-logo	(line# logoaddr logowidth logoheight --)	
0118	driver	(adr len --)	
46	drop	(n --)	
47	dup	(n -- n n)	
CR	else	(--)	
8f	emit	(char --)	
CR	emit-byte	(n --)	
00	end0	(--)	

Table A-48 FCodes by Name

Value	Function	Stack	Version 2?
ff	end1	(--)	
CR	erase	(adr len --)	
015a	erase-screen	(--)	
cd	eval	(??? adr len -- ?)	V2
1d	execute	(acf --)	
33	exit	(--)	
8a	expect	(adr +n --)	
-	external	(--)	V2
ca	external-token	(--)	V2
CR	false	(-- 0)	
0174	fb1-blink-screen	(--)	
0177	fb1-delete-characters	(n --)	
0179	fb1-delete-lines	(n --)	
0170	fb1-draw-character	(char --)	
017a	fb1-draw-logo	(line# logoaddr logowidth logoheight --)	
0173	fb1-erase-screen	(--)	
0176	fb1-insert-characters	(n --)	
0178	fb1-insert-lines	(n --)	
017b	fb1-install	(width height #columns #lines --)	
0175	fb1-invert-screen	(--)	
0171	fb1-reset-screen	(--)	
017c	fb1-slide-up	(n --)	
0172	fb1-toggle-cursor	(--)	
0184	fb8-blink-screen	(--)	
0187	fb8-delete-characters	(n --)	
0189	fb8-delete-lines	(n --)	
0180	fb8-draw-character	(char --)	

A

Table A-48 FCodes by Name

Value	Function	Stack	Version 2?
018a	fb8-draw-logo	(line# logoaddr logowidth logoheight --)	
0183	fb8-erase-screen	(--)	
0186	fb8-insert-characters	(n --)	
0188	fb8-insert-lines	(n --)	
018b	fb8-install	(width height #columns #lines --)	
0185	fb8-invert-screen	(--)	
0181	fb8-reset-screen	(--)	
0182	fb8-toggle-cursor	(--)	
0212	fcode-version	(-- n)	V2
CR	fcode-version1	(--)	
CR	fcode-version2	(--)	V2
fc	ferror	(--)	V2.3
CR	field name	(offset size -- offset+size)	
79	fill	(adr u byte --)	
0207	find-method	(adr len phandle -- false | acf true)	V2
0204	find-package	(adr len -- false | phandle true)	V2
0127	finish-device	(--)	
0211	firmware-version	(-- n)	V2
80	flip	(w1 -- w2)	
-	fload filename	(--)	
016f	fontbytes	(-- n)	
0162	frame-buffer-adr	(-- adr)	
8c	free-mem	(adr nbytes --)	
0105	free-virtual	(virt nbytes --)	
021d	get-inherited-attribute	(nam-adr nam-len -- true | xdr-adr xdr-len false)	V2
0125	get-msecs	(-- ms)	
021a	get-my-attribute	(nam-adr nam-len -- true | xdr-adr xdr-len false)	V2

Table A-48 FCodes by Name

Value	Function	Stack	Version 2?
021f	get-package-attribute	(adr len phandle -- true | xdr-adr xdr-len false)	V2
0123	group-code	(-- adr)	
CR	h# number	(-- n)	
-	headerless	(--)	
-	headers	(--)	
ad	here	(-- adr)	
-	hex	(--)	
CR	hex	(--)	
95	hold	(char --)	
19	i	(-- n)	
CR	if	(flag --)	
020b	ihandle>phandle	(ihandle -- phandle)	V2
015d	insert-characters	(n --)	
015f	insert-lines	(n --)	
c0	instance	(--)	V2.1
0117	intr	(intr-level vector --)	
0155	inverse-screen?	(-- flag)	
0154	inverse?	(-- flag)	
015c	invert-screen	(--)	
CR	is name	(n --)	
011c	is-install	(acf --)	
011d	is-remove	(acf --)	
011e	is-selftest	(acf --)	
1a	j	(-- n)	
8e	key	(-- char)	
8d	key?	(-- flag)	
73	l!	(l adr --)	
d2	l,	(l --)	
6e	l@	(adr -- l)	
60	la+	(adr1 index -- adr2)	

Table A-48 FCodes by Name

Value	Function	Stack	Version 2?
64	la1+	(adr1 -- adr2)	
7e	lbsplit	(l -- b.low b2 b3 b.high)	
82	lcc	(char -- lower-case-char)	
CR	leave	(--)	
0240	left-parse-string	(adr len char -- adrR lenR adrL lenL)	V2
0237	lflips	(adr len --)	V2
0152	line#	(-- n)	
CR	linefeed	(-- n)	
CR	loop	(--)	
0222	lpeek	(adr -- false | long true)	V2
0225	lpoke	(long adr -- ok?)	V2
7c	lwsplit	(l -- w.low w.high)	
01a4	mac-address	(-- adr len)	V2
0130	map-sbus	(phys size -- virt)	
0124	mask	(-- adr)	
2f	max	(n1 n2 -- n3)	
0122	memory-test-suite	(adr len -- status)	
0104	memmap	(physoffset space size -- virtual)	
2e	min	(n1 n2 -- n3)	
22	mod	(n1 n2 -- rem)	
0119	model	(adr len --)	
78	move	(adr1 adr2 u --)	
0126	ms	(n --)	
0102	my-address	(-- phys)	V2
0202	my-args	(-- adr len)	V2
010f	my-params	(-- adr len)	
020a	my-parent	(-- ihandle)	V2
0203	my-self	(-- ihandle)	V2
0103	my-space	(-- space)	V2
020d	my-unit	(-- low high)	V2
61	na+	(adr1 index -- adr2)	

Table A-48 FCodes by Name

Value	Function	Stack	Version 2?
65	na1+	(adr1 -- adr2)	
CR	name	(adr len --)	
b6	named-token	(--)	
2c	negate	(n1 -- n2)	
011f	new-device	(--)	
b5	new-token	(--)	
CR	newline	(-- n)	
4d	nip	(n1 n2 -- n2)	
7b	noop	(--)	
26	not	(n1 -- n2)	
CR	o# number	(-- n)	
-	octal	(--)	
6b	off	(adr --)	
cc	offset16	(--)	
6a	on	(adr --)	
0205	open-package	(adr len phandle -- ihandle | 0)	V2
24	or	(n1 n2 -- n3)	
48	over	(n1 n2 -- n1 n2 n1)	
83	pack	(adr len pstr -- pstr)	
023c	peer	(phandle -- peerhandle)	V2.3
4e	pick	(+n -- n2)	
0238	probe	(arg-adr arg-len reg-adr reg-len fcode-adr fcode-len --)	V2.2
0239	probe-virtual	(arg-adr arg-len reg-adr reg-len fcode-adr --)	V2.2
0210	processor-type	(-- processor-type)	V2
31	r>	(-- n) (rs: n --)	
32	r@	(-- n) (rs: --)	
0231	rb!	(byte adr --)	V2
0230	rb@	(adr -- byte)	V2
0116	reg	(phys space size --)	
CR	repeat	(--)	

Table A-48 FCodes by Name

Value	Function	Stack	Version 2?
0158	reset-screen	(--)	
0235	rl!	(long adr --)	V2
0234	rl@	(adr -- long)	V2
4f	roll	(+n --)	
4a	rot	(n1 n2 n3 -- n2 n3 n1)	
0233	rw!	(word adr --)	V2
0232	rw@	(adr -- word)	V2
CR	s.	(n --)	
0131	sbus-intr>cpu	(sbus-intr# -- cpu-intr#)	
0163	screen-height	(-- n)	
0164	screen-width	(-- n)	
016b	set-font	(fontbase charwidth charheight fontbytes #firstchar #chars --)	
98	sign	(n --)	
CR	space	(--)	
CR	spaces	(+n --)	
88	span	(-- adr)	
f0	start0	(--)	V2
f1	start1	(--)	V2
f2	start2	(--)	V2
f3	start4	(--)	V2
CR	struct	(-- 0)	
0215	suspend-fcode	(--)	V2
49	swap	(n1 n2 -- n2 n1)	
CR	then	(--)	
0218	throw	(error-code --)	V2
0159	toggle-cursor	(--)	
-	tokenizer[	(--)	
CR	true	(-- -1)	
4c	tuck	(n1 n2 -- n2 n1 n2)	
90	type	(adr +n --)	
d4	u*x	(u1[32] u2[32] -- product[64])	V2

Table A-48 FCodes by Name

Value	Function	Stack	Version 2?
9b	u.	(u --)	
9c	u.r	(u +n --)	
2b	u/mod	(ul un -- un.rem un.quot)	
58	u2/	(u1 -- u2)	
40	u<	(u1 u2 -- flag)	
3f	u<=	(u1 u2 -- flag)	
3e	u>	(u1 u2 -- flag)	
41	u>=	(u1 u2 -- flag)	
CR	(u.)	(n -- adr len)	
CR	until	(flag --)	
81	upc	(char -- upper-case-char)	
0219	user-abort	(--)	V2.1
CR	value name	(n --)	
CR	variable name	(--)	
87	version	(-- n)	
fd	version1	(--)	
74	w!	(w adr --)	
d1	w,	(w --)	
6f	w@	(adr -- w)	
5f	wa+	(adr1 index -- adr2)	
63	wa1+	(adr1 -- adr2)	
af	wbsplit	(w -- b.low b.high)	
CR	wflip	(l1 -- l2)	
0236	wflips	(adr len --)	V2
CR	while	(flag --)	
0166	window-left	(-- n)	
0165	window-top	(-- n)	
45	within	(n min max -- flag)	
7d	wljoin	(w.low w.high -- l)	
0221	wpeek	(adr -- false | word true)	V2
0224	wpoke	(word adr -- ok?)	V2
d8	x+	(x1 x2 -- x3)	V2

A

Table A-48 FCodes by Name

Value	Function	Stack	Version 2?
d9	x-	(x1 x2 -- x3)	V2
0112	xdr+	(xdr-adr1 xdr-len1 xdr-adr2 xdr-len2 -- xdr-adr xdr-len1+2)	
0115	xdrbytes	(adr len -- xdr-adr xdr-len)	V2.1
0111	xdrint	(n -- xdr-adr xdr-len)	
0113	xdrphys	(phys space -- xdr-adr xdr-len)	
0114	xdrstring	(adr len -- xdr-adr xdr-len)	
021b	xdrtoint	(xdr-adr xdr-len -- xdr2-adr xdr2-len n)	V2
021c	xdrtostring	(xdr-adr xdr-len -- xdr2-adr xdr2-len adr len)	V2
25	xor	(n1 n2 -- n3)	
d5	xu/mod	(u1[64] u2[32] -- remainder[32] quot[32])	V2
CR	: (colon) name	(--)	
CR	; (semicolon)	(--)	
3a	<	(n1 n2 -- flag)	
96	<#	(--)	
27	<<	(n1 +n -- n2)	
CR	<<a	(n1 +n -- n2)	
43	<=	(n1 n2 -- flag)	
3d	<>	(n1 n2 -- flag)	
70	<w@	(adr -- n)	
3c	=	(n1 n2 -- flag)	
3b	>	(n1 n2 -- flag)	
42	>=	(n1 n2 -- flag)	
28	>>	(n1 +n -- n2)	
29	>>a	(n1 +n -- n2)	
86	>body	(acf -- apf)	
016e	>font	(char -- adr)	
0106	>physical	(virt -- phys space)	
30	>r	(n --) (rs: -- n)	
CR	?	(adr --)	
CR	?do	(end start --)	

Table A-48 FCodes by Name

Value	Function	Stack	Version 2?
50	?dup	(n -- n n | 0)	
CR	?leave	(flag --)	
6d	@	(adr -- n)	
CR	['] name	(-- acf)	
-	\	(--)	
-	]tokenizer	(--)	
72	!	(n adr --)	
CR	" text"	(-- adr len)	
99	#	(+l1 -- +l2)	
97	#>	(l -- adr +n)	
0151	#columns	(-- n)	
94	#line	(-- adr)	
0150	#lines	(-- n)	
93	#out	(-- adr)	
9a	#s	(+l -- 0)	
020e	$call-method	([...]adr len ihandle -- [...])	V2
0209	$call-parent	([...] adr len -- [...])	V2
cb	$find	(adr len -- adr len false | acf +-1)	
a2	$number	(adr len -- true | n false)	V2
020f	$open-package	(arg-adr arg-len adr len -- ihandle | 0)	V2
CR	' name	(-- acf)	
-	(text)	(--)	
91	(cr	(--)	
CR	(.)	(n -- adr len)	
0214	(is-user-word)	(adr len acf --)	V2
-	(s text)	(--)	
20	*	(n1 n2 -- n3)	
CR	*/mod	(n1 n2 n3 -- rem quot)	
1e	+	(n1 n2 -- n3)	
6c	+!	(n adr --)	
CR	+loop	(n --)	
d3	,	(n --)	

Table A-48 FCodes by Name

Value	Function	Stack	Version 2?
1f	-	(n1 n2 -- n3)	
a4	-1	(-- -1)	
4b	-rot	(n1 n2 n3 -- n3 n1 n2)	
9d	.	(n --)	
CR	." text"	(--)	
CR	.(text)	(--)	
CR	.d	(n --)	
CR	.h	(n --)	
9e	.r	(n +n --)	
9f	.s	(--)	
21	/	(n1 n2 -- quot)	
5a	/c	(-- n)	
66	/c*	(n1 -- n2)	
5c	/l	(-- n)	
68	/l*	(n1 -- n2)	
2a	/mod	(n1 n2 -- rem quot)	
5d	/n	(-- n)	
69	/n*	(n1 -- n2)	
5b	/w	(-- n)	
67	/w*	(n1 -- n2)	

Version 2 FCodes

The following table lists, in alphabetic order, Version 2 FCodes.

Table A-49 Version 2 FCodes

Value	Function	Stack	Version
0216	abort	(--)	V2
0213	alarm	(acf n --)	V2
0208	call-package	([...] acf ihandle -- [...])	V2
0217	catch	([...] acf -- [...] error-code)	V2
0236	child	(phandle -- child-phandle)	V2.3

Table A-49 Version 2 FCodes

Value	Function	Stack	Version
0206	close-package	(ihandle --)	V2
0220	cpeek	(adr -- false | byte true)	V2
0223	cpoke	(byte adr -- ok?)	V2
011b	decode-2int	(xdr-adr xdr-len -- phys space)	V2
021e	delete-attribute	(nam-adr nam-len --)	V2
0201	device-name	(adr len --)	V2
cd	eval	(??? adr len -- ?)	V2
-	external	(--)	V2
ca	external-token	(--)	V2
0212	fcode-version	(-- n)	V2
CR	fcode-version2	(--)	V2
fc	ferror	(--)	V2.3
0207	find-method	(adr len phandle -- false | acf true)	V2
0204	find-package	(adr len -- false | phandle true)	V2
0211	firmware-version	(-- n)	V2
021d	get-inherited-attribute	(nam-adr nam-len -- true | xdr-adr xdr-len false)	V2
021a	get-my-attribute	(nam-adr nam-len -- true | xdr-adr xdr-len false)	V2
021f	get-package-attribute	(adr len phandle -- true | xdr-adr xdr-len false)	V2
020b	ihandle>phandle	(ihandle -- phandle)	V2
c0	instance	(--)	V2.1
0240	left-parse-string	(adr len char -- adrR lenR adrL lenL)	V2
0237	lflips	(adr len --)	V2
0222	lpeek	(adr -- false | long true)	V2
0225	lpoke	(long adr -- ok?)	V2
01a4	mac-address	(-- adr len)	V2
0102	my-address	(-- phys)	V2
0202	my-args	(-- adr len)	V2
020a	my-parent	(-- ihandle)	V2
0203	my-self	(-- ihandle)	V2

Table A-49 Version 2 FCodes

Value	Function	Stack	Version
0103	my-space	(-- space)	V2
020d	my-unit	(-- low high)	V2
0205	open-package	(adr len phandle -- ihandle | 0)	V2
023c	peer	(phandle -- peerhandle)	V2.3
0238	probe	(arg-adr arg-len reg-adr reg-len fcode-adr fcode-len --)	V2.2
0239	probe-virtual	(arg-adr arg-len reg-adr reg-len fcode-adr --)	V2.2
0210	processor-type	(-- processor-type)	V2
0231	rb!	(byte adr --)	V2
0230	rb@	(adr -- byte)	V2
0235	rl!	(long adr --)	V2
0234	rl@	(adr -- long)	V2
0233	rw!	(word adr --)	V2
0232	rw@	(adr -- word)	V2
f0	start0	(--)	V2
f1	start1	(--)	V2
f2	start2	(--)	V2
f3	start4	(--)	V2
0215	suspend-fcode	(--)	V2
0218	throw	(error-code --)	V2
d4	u*x	(u1[32] u2[32] -- product[64])	V2
0219	user-abort	(--)	V2.1
0236	wflips	(adr len --)	V2
0221	wpeek	(adr -- false | word true)	V2
0224	wpoke	(word adr -- ok?)	V2
d8	x+	(x1 x2 -- x3)	V2
d9	x-	(x1 x2 -- x3)	V2
0115	xdrbytes	(adr len -- xdr-adr xdr-len)	V2.1
021b	xdrtoint	(xdr-adr xdr-len -- xdr2-adr xdr2-len n)	V2
021c	xdrtostring	(xdr-adr xdr-len -- xdr2-adr xdr2-len adr len)	V2
d5	xu/mod	(u1[64] u2[32] -- remainder[32] quot[32])	V2

Table A-49 Version 2 FCodes

Value	Function	Stack	Version
020e	$call-method	([...]adr len ihandle -- [...])	V2
0209	$call-parent	([...] adr len -- [...])	V2
a2	$number	(adr len -- true | n false)	V2
020f	$open-package	(arg-adr arg-len adr len -- ihandle | 0)	V2
0214	(is-user-word)	(adr len acf --)	V2

OpenBoot Interrupt Testing

An important, and not always obvious, part of programming peripheral devices is dealing with interrupts. Table B-1 describes Open Boot 2.0 words for testing interrupts from the Forth Monitor. Note that these cannot be used in FCode programs because of their highly system-dependent nature.

Table B-1   Interrrupt-handling words

Word	Stack Diagram	Descriptions
catch-interrupt	(level --)	Establishes a handler for interrupt "level" (1-15). If an interrupt occurs on that level, the handler sets the value of the `interrupt-occurred?` variable to -1 and sets the value of the `vector-used` variable to the interrupt level.
interrupt-occurred?	(-- adr)	Returns the address of a variable whose value will be set to "-1" when an interrupt occurs.
vector-used	(-- adr)	Returns the address of a variable whose value will be set to the interrupt level when an interrupt occurs on a level guarded by `catch-interrupt`.
pil@ pil!	(-- level) (level --)	Gets (`pil@`) and sets (`pil!`) the current processor interrupt level. The system will only respond to interrupts *above* the current setting of the PIL. After the first interrupt is handled, the PIL is automatically raised to the level of the interrupt (thus disabling further interrupts at the same level). Re-lower the PIL if you wish to process additional interrupts.

Assume a device which interrupts on level 3. Here is a sample Forth program for testing the device's ability to interrupt.

```
: test-interrupt   ( -- )

   pil@ >r                          \ Remember old priority level

   interrupt-occurred? off
```

```
3 catch-interrupt

2 pil!                                 \ Allow level 3 interrupts

<do whatever is necessary to make the device interrupt>

1000 0  do  loop               \ Wait awhile; may not be necessary

interrupt-occurred? @  if

    <do whatever is necessary to turn off the device's interrupt
request>

    ." Interrupt on level " vector-used @ .  cr

else

    ." No interrupt." cr

then

r> pil!

;
```

Note – If you want to test interrupts on CPU levels 14, 10 or 8, you will also need to set the `interrupt-enable` register to the appropriate value as well. (SBus level 6 is equivalent to CPU level 8 on most current systems.) See comments at end for more details.

Caution – There is a bug in Open Boot PROMs 1.1 thru 2.1 in the `interrupt-occurred?` flag, causing it to return a 0 even after an interrupt has occurred.

For example:

```
interrupt-occurred? off  \ Clear flag

6 catch-interrupt          \ Establish handler

5 pil!                     \ Lower CPU priority to allow level 6 interrupts

89 interrupt-enable!     \ Cause a level 6 "software interrupt"

interrupt-occurred? ?    \ Examine flag; it should be ffffffff but it's
0 (bug)
```

Here is a workaround patch for this bug.

```
ok see catch-interrupt

: catch-interrupt

   10 + (ffeac10c) swap vector!


;
```

Note the number shown in parentheses (ffeac10c in this example). In the following step, substitute that number in place of the example number ffeac10c.

```
ok ramforth

ok 8000.0000 ffeac10c execute 4 + !

ok
```

A way to determine this magic value from a program would be (for any Open Boot 2.0-based system) as follows:

```
['] catch-interrupt       (addr of catch-interrupt)

h# 0a +    w@             (offset pointer for ffxxxxxx routine)

4 * origin +              (ffeac10c)
```

An interrupt can be generated just by writing the proper value to the interrupt register. Here is the format of this register:

Table B-2   Interrupt register format

Bit #	Bit Name	Function
7	A	Enable level 14 interrupts.
6	B	None (always 0).
5	C	Enable level 10 interrupts.
4	D	Enable level 8 interrupts.
3	E	Software interrupt level 6.
2	F	Software interrupt level 4.
1	G	Software interrupt level 1.
0	H	Enable all interrupts.

Writing a zero to bits A, C, or D only masks that interrupt, it does not clear the source.

Writing a one to a software interrupt bit requests an interrupt on that level; the bit must be cleared to clear the request.

Merely writing a one to register bit H will *not* enable interrupts on levels 14, 10 and 8, since these also have a separate mask.

To enable level 8, for example, You need to write a one to *both* bits D and H. After power-up or after any Forth traps, the Open Boot writes this interrupt register to "81".

Note – Writing a zero to bit H will clear the Asynchronous Memory (level 15) Interrupt, as well as masking *all* interrupts. Interrupts should be immediately re-enabled by writing a one to bit 0.

On reset, all bits are cleared and all interrupts are reset.

Finally, here is a complete test example. All known bugs are accounted for.

Code Example B-1   Interrupt-testing program

```
\ Interrupt-testing program
hex
: patch-bugs  ( -- )
   ramforth
   8000.0000
   ['] catch-interrupt  0a +  w@  2*  ( 8000.0000 token )

\ If "firmware-version" found and >=2.0 (2.0000), then 2* again
\ 2.0 boot PROMS use a 4* multiplier, to expand the available dictionary
   p" firmware-version" find   ( acf n | pstr 0 )
   if  execute  ( version )  2.0000 >=  if  2*  then
   else  drop   then                ( 8000.0000 token' )

   origin +                          ( 8000.0000 acf )
   execute  4 +  !
;

: catch-level  ( level -- )
   interrupt-occurred? off

   dup d#  8 =  if  91 interrupt-enable!  then
   dup d# 10 =  if  a1 interrupt-enable!  then
\ Or, just always do  "b1 interrupt-enable!" to enable all masks...

   dup catch-interrupt      ( level )
   1- pil!        \ Set priority level to allow this interrupt
;

: check-interrupt  ( -- )
   <do whatever is necessary to make the device interrupt>
   20 ms \ Wait awhile; may not be necessary
   interrupt-occurred? @    ( flag )
   if
     <do whatever is necessary to turn off the device's interrupt request>
     ." Interrupt on level " vector-used @ .  cr
   else   ." No interrupt." cr
   then
;

7 value my-level      \ My device's interrupt level

\ Alternatively...
\ 5 value my-sbus-level
```

Code Example B-1   Interrupt-testing program

```
\ Interrupt-testing program
\ : my-level  ( -- int-level )  my-sbus-level  sbus-intr>cpu  ;

0 value old-pil      \ Holder for system interrupt level
: test-interrupt  ( -- )
  patch-bugs        \ Overkill, only needs to be called once per session
  pil@  is old-pil         \ Save old interrupt level
  my-level catch-level     \ Setup handler
  check-interrupt          \ Do the test
  old-pil pil!             \ Restore old interrupt level
;
```

FCode Memory Allocation

For OpenBoot 2

To get general-purpose memory, use `buffer:` or `alloc-mem`. Use `free-mem` to deallocate memory obtained with `alloc-mem`.

To map in portions of your device for ordinary access, use `" map-in" $call-parent` (adr space size -- virt), as in:

```
my-address  offset +  my-space  size  " map-in" $call-parent  ( virt )
```

To later map out those portions of your device, use `" map-out" $call-parent` (virt size --), as in:

```
( virt )  size  " map-out" $call-parent
```

To use a region of system memory for DMA (for example, for both direct CPU access and DMA access from a device), first define the following mapping and allocation routines, then follow the steps below to ensure data coherency.

```
: dma-alloc  ( n -- virt )  " dma-alloc" $call-parent  ;

: dma-free  ( virt n -- )    " dma-free" $call-parent  ;

: dma-map-in  ( virt n cache? -- devaddr )  " dma-map-in" $call-parent ;

: dma-map-out  ( virt devaddr n -- )    " dma-map-out" $call-parent  ;

: dma-sync  ( virt devaddr size -- )  \ Correct even if "dma-sync"
missing

   " dma-sync" ['] $call-parent catch  if
```

```
    2drop 3drop

then

;
```

1. **Allocate the DMA region with:**
   - dma-alloc
   - dma-map-in

2. **CPU accesses the region using virt from dma-alloc, then perform:**
   - dma-sync

3. **Start DMA operation, using devaddr from dma-map-in.**
   - Wait for DMA complete status.
   - Repeat DMA as needed, then perform dma-sync

4. **Repeat steps 2 and 3 as needed**

5. **Deallocate the region when completed, with:**
   - dma-map-out
   - dma-free

For OpenBoot 1

To obtain general-purpose memory, use buffer: or alloc-mem for small amounts (less than several hundred bytes). Use dma-alloc for larger amounts.

Use free-mem to deallocate memory allocated with alloc-mem. Use free-virtual to deallocate memory allocated with dma-alloc.

To map in portions of your device for ordinary access, use map-sbus.

To map out portions of your device, use free-virtual.

To use a region of system memory for DMA (for example, both direct CPU access and DMA access from a device), map it in with dma-alloc. CPU accesses and DMA accesses may be performed interchangeably.

When the memory is no longer needed, unmap it with free-virtual.

When unmapping multiple regions using free-virtual, you must perform the unmapping in the reverse order that the memory was originally mapped in.

Changes in OpenBoot 1 FCode Usage

FCode For OpenBoot 1 Systems

There are two groups of FCode functions - OpenBoot 1 and OpenBoot 2. You will need to keep the differences in mind while writing your FCode program (depending on your intended system market).

The first SBus systems shipped by Sun used only OpenBoot 1 FCodes. Such systems, including SPARCstation1, 1+, 1E, original IPC, have a Open Boot PROM with a version number of 1.x. All later SPARC systems from Sun have an Open Boot PROM with a version number of 2.x. These systems recognize both Open Boot 1 and OpenBoot 2 FCodes. (2.x upgrade PROMs are available for SPARCstation 1, 1+ and IPC.)

Most basic FCode functions are OpenBoot 1. Framebuffer support FCodes are also OpenBoot 1. OpenBoot 2 FCodes support package access, bootable devices, and several other miscellaneous functions. The individual FCode descriptions state whether that FCode is version 2 or not. (See Appendix A, "FCode Reference" for a list of all OpenBoot 2 FCodes.)

Any OpenBoot 2 FCode encountered by a OpenBoot 1 system will not be recognized, causing the FCode program to fail. To deal with this possibility, write your FCode to conform to one of the several styles shown here. The correct choice of style will depend on your FCode requirements, and the intended system targets.

FCode Programming Style 1

```
fcode-version1

    ...

    (version 1 FCodes only)

    ...

end0
```

This style will operate correctly on either OpenBoot 1 or OpenBoot 2 systems.

FCode Programming Style 2

```
fcode-version2

    ...

    (version 1 plus version 2 FCodes)

    ...

end0
```

This style operates correctly only on OpenBoot 2 systems. Any such FCode will abort immediately if encountered on a OpenBoot 1 system, as the `fcode-version2` header will be rejected. This style is suitable for any device is not intended for operation on any OpenBoot 1 system.

FCode Programming Style 3

```
fcode-version1

  ...

  (version 1 FCodes only)

  ...

: v1-exit  ( -- )  version  h# 2.0000 <  if ['] end0 execute then  ;

v1-exit

  ...

  (version 1 plus version 2 FCodes)

  ...

end0
```

This style will operate correctly on either OpenBoot 1 or OpenBoot 2 systems. It is used when OpenBoot 2 functionality is needed, but where a limited OpenBoot 1 functionality is also acceptable on OpenBoot 1 systems. It works by initially restricting usage to OpenBoot 1 FCodes only, and then ending FCode execution on a OpenBoot 1 system. On a OpenBoot 2 system, execution continues with subsequent OpenBoot 1 plus OpenBoot 2 FCodes.

Style 1 is suitable for framebuffers, and for other devices with simple non-boot FCode requirements.

Style 2 or 3 is appropriate for bootable devices, depending on whether an abbreviated non-boot functionality on OpenBoot 1 systems is appropriate or desired.

Other OpenBoot 1 Restrictions

FCode that will operate on OpenBoot 1 systems must also take into account the following restrictions and limitations:

Total FCode Program Size

OpenBoot 1 systems only have about 13K of dictionary space to accomodate *all* plug-in SBus cards. Combinations of cards each containing FCode exceeding 5K or so in size may fail. (The actual size of the FCode binary can be used as a first estimate of the consumed dictionary space in many instances. For a more precise measure, look at the value in `here` at the start and end of FCode compilation.)

OpenBoot 2 systems have substantially more available dictionary space.

Old-style Memory Mapping And Unmapping

On OpenBoot 2 systems, the standard technique for device-dependent memory mapping/unmapping is with " *xxxx*" `$call-parent` (where " *xxxx*" could be " `map-in`", " `map-out`", " `dma-alloc`", " `dma-free`", " `dma-map-in`", " `dma-map-out`").

Since `$call-parent` is not defined on OpenBoot 1 systems, you must use the obsolescent FCode functions `dma-alloc`, `map-sbus`, `memmap` and `free-virtual` in FCode programs that will run on OpenBoot 1 systems.

Memory Mapping Size Limits

On OpenBoot 1 systems, the total available mapping (for all devices) is hex 12.4000, divided into two regions: 10.0000 and 2.4000. The 10.0000 region is typically used up by the active framebuffer.

To ensure correct behavior with multiple devices, Sun recommends:

- limit large mappings to only 1.0000 (64K)
- have only one such mapping active at any time
- return the mapping when done.

It is also best to perform a single larger mapping in preference to several smaller mappings, where possible.

Large General-purpose Mappings

On OpenBoot 1 systems, memory allocated with `alloc-mem` or `buffer:` uses up limited dictionary space. For general-purpose memory allocations larger than several hundred bytes or so, `dma-alloc` should be used instead to avoid this limitation. (OpenBoot 2 systems do not have this limitation, so `alloc-mem` and `buffer:` may be freely used.)

Memory De-allocation

Memory allocated with `alloc-mem`, `memmap`, `dma-alloc` or `map-sbus` must be deallocated in a specific sequence on OpenBoot 1 systems. When de-allocating memory on OpenBoot 1 systems, you should de-allocate in the reverse order that the memory was allocated. (OpenBoot 2 systems do not have this restriction.)

Total Properties

On OpenBoot 1 systems, each device is limited to 16 properties total. (OpenBoot 2 systems do not have this restriction.)

Interpretation of `my-address` and `my-space`

The interpretation of these numbers differs between OpenBoot 1 and OpenBoot 2.

In OpenBoot 1, `my-address` is a slot offset (200.0000, 400.0000, etc.) and `my-space` is a magic number representing the SBus address space. In OpenBoot 2, `my-address` is typically 0 and `my-space` is typically the SBus slot number. Properly-written FCode programs will operate correctly in both versions.

To do this, make sure that `my-address` and `my-space` are not interpreted directly, but are only used as input parameters to mapping functions (`map-sbus`, `memmap`, `" map-in" $call-parent`) or property declarations (`reg`, `xdrphys`).

`my-address` Volatility

On OpenBoot 1 systems, `my-address` will change when other slots are probed, so later execution of your routines which use `my-address` could generate illegal results. The best workaround is to save `my-address` into a `constant` or `value` during the initial probe, and then always use that saved value instead. (This precaution is not necessary on OpenBoot 2 systems.)

`free-virtual` and Properties

Execution of `free-virtual` on any OpenBoot 2 system will automatically delete an `address` property with the same virtual address contents.

Changes in `new-device` and `finish-device` Usage

Nested `new-device` FCodes will create "children-of-children" on FCode 2.0 systems. This feature is not supported on OpenBoot 1 systems: they will create only sibling children (children of the parent of the nested `new-device` operations).

`finish-device` is not implemented on SPARCstation 1 PROM versions 1.0 and 1.1. It is implemented as a NOP in other OpenBoot 1 systems.

OpenBoot 1 systems are limited to a maximum of eight plug-in device nodes per system. Each plug-in device occupies a node, and each `new-device` call uses up an additional node.

Index

Symbols

+n, 9
.attributes, 26
:, 6
;, 6
?, 9
???, 9
|, 9

Numerics

0xfd, 2
n, 9

A

accessing
    method, 46
    packages, 40
acf, 9
addressing
    package, 44
    SBus, 116
    VMEbus, 116
adr, 9
attribute, 70

B

binary executable programs, 21
binary format
    FCode, 5
block device, 75
byte, 9

C

catch-interrupt, 394, 395
cd, 26
char, 9
close, 37
cnt, 9
:, 6
colon definition, 6
    and stack comment, 7
commands
    forth monitor, 43
compile state, 6
configuration
    operating system, 53

D

data
    packages, 36
data definition
    package, 39
deblocker support, 50
debugging
    packages, 47
defining
    FCode, 5
    Forth words, 5
device
    drivers, plug-in, 36
    identification, 2
    interrupt vectors, 53
    interrupts, 53
    node, 2
    tree, 2, 264, 296
device addressing

SBus, 116
VMEbus, 116
device methods
    block-size, 76
    decode-unit, 111
    dma-alloc, 111
    dma-free, 112
    dma-map-in, 112
    dma-map-out, 113
    dma-sync, 114
    install-abort, 189
    load, 76, 146
    map-in, 115
    map-out, 115
    max-transfer, 76
    probe-self, 114
    read, 76, 146, 189
    read-blocks, 77
    remove-abort, 189
    seek, 77
    write, 77, 147, 189
    write-blocks, 77
device node
    and package, 36
device-end, 26
devices
    block, 75
    display, 99
    hierarchical, 111
    network, 145
    serial, 189
display device, 99
driver
    and boot PROM, 1
    function, 1
    SunOS, 1

E

end0, 2
end1, 2
execute
    method, 44

F

FCode
    #columns, 231
    #line, 287
    #lines, 287
    #out, 303
    #s, 312
    $call-method, 224
    $call-parent, 225
    $find, 262
    $number, 301, 302
    $open-package, 43, 303
    (cr, 234
    (is-user-word), 282
    */mod, 293
    +loop, 288
    .d, 234
    .h, 271
    /c, 223
    /c*, 224
    /l, 284
    /l*, 284
    /mod, 293
    /n, 298
    /n*, 298
    /w, 327
    /w*, 327
    <<a, 210
    <w@, 328
    >>a, 210
    >body, 222
    >font, 266
    >physical, 304
    >r, 307
    ?do, 241
    ?dup, 244
    ?leave, 285
    \, 209
    ]tokenizer, 319
    ‹s, 312
    ‹u›, 320
    ˙r, 306
    ˙s, 313
    2drop, 244
    2dup, 244
    2over, 303

2rot, 311
2swap, 317
3drop, 244
3dup, 244
4-byte-id, 223
abort, 210
abs, 211
again, 211
alarm, 211
alias, 212
aligned, 212
alloc-mem, 212
and, 213
and Forth-83, 5
ascii, 213
attribute, 70, 213
b#, 214
base, 218
begin, 220
begin-package, 22, 43
bell, 220
between, 221
binary, 221
binary format, 5
bl, 221
blank, 221
blink-screen, 221
bljoin, 222
body>, 222
bounds, 222
bs, 222
buffer:, 222
bwjoin, 223
byte-load, 23, 24
c!, 223
c,, 223
c@, 223
ca+, 224
ca1+, 224
call-package, 224
carret, 226
case, 226
catch, 227
char-height, 228
char-width, 229
child, 229

close-package, 229
cmove, 230
cmove>, 230
column#, 230
comp, 231
compile state, 6
constant, 232
control, 232
count, 232
cpeek, 233
cpoke, 233
cr, 233
create, 234
d#, 234
decimal, 235
decode-2int, 235
default-font, 235
defer, 236
defining words, 5
delete-attribute, 238
delete-characters, 238
delete-lines, 238
depth, 239
device identification, 2
device-name, 239
device-type, 239
diagnostic-mode?, 240
digit, 240
display-status, 241
dma-alloc, 242
do, 241
draw-character, 243
draw-logo, 243
drop, 244
dup, 244
else, 244
emit, 244
emit-byte, 245
end0, 245
end1, 245
endcase, 245
endof, 245
erase, 246
erase-screen, 246
eval, 23, 246
execute, 246

executing, 22
exit, 247
expect, 247
external, 248
external-token, 248
false, 248
fb1-blink-screen, 249
fb1-delete-characters, 249
fb1-delete-lines, 249
fb1-draw-character, 250
fb1-draw-logo, 250
fb1-erase-screen, 250
fb1-insert-characters, 250
fb1-install, 251
fb1-invert-lines, 251
fb1-invert-screen, 252
fb1-reset-screen, 252
fb1-slide-up, 252
fb1-toggle-cursor, 253
fb8-blink-screen, 253
fb8-delete-characters, 253
fb8-delete-lines, 254
fb8-draw-character, 254
fb8-draw-logo, 254
fb8-erase-screen, 255
fb8-insert-characters, 255
fb8-insert-lines, 256
fb8-install, 256
fb8-invert-screen, 257
fb8-reset-screen, 257
fb8-toggle-cursor, 258
fcode-version, 258
fcode-version1, 258
fcode-version2, 259
ferror, 260
field, 261
fill, 262
find-method, 44, 263
find-package, 264
finish-device, 264
firmware-version, 265
flip, 265
fload, 266
fontbytes, 266
frame-buffer-adr, 267
free-mem, 268
free-virtual, 268

get-inherited-attribute, 269
get-msecs, 269
get-my-attribute, 270
get-package-attribute, 270
group-code, 271
h#, 271
headerless, 272
headers, 272
here, 273
hex, 273
hold, 273
i, 274
if, 274
ihandle>phandle, 274
in PROM, 1
insert-characters, 275
insert-lines, 275
instance, 276
interpret state, 6
interpretation, 2
intr, 276
inverse?, 277
inverse-screen?, 276
invert-screen, 277
is, 277
is-install, 278
is-remove, 279
is-selftest, 280
j, 282
key, 282
key?, 283
l!, 283
l,, 283
l@, 283
la+, 284
la1+, 284
lbsplit, 284
lcc, 284
leave, 285
left-parse-string, 42, 286
lflips, 286
line#, 287
linefeed, 287
loop, 288
lpeek, 289
lpoke, 289
lu>x, 289

lwsplit, 289
mac-address, 290
map-sbus, 290
mask, 291
max, 291
memmap, 291
min, 292
mod, 292
model, 70, 293
move, 293
ms, 294
my-address, 294
my-args, 42, 43, 295
my-params, 295
my-parent, 295
my-self, 296
my-space, 297
my-unit, 297
na+, 298
na1+, 298
name, 70, 298
named-token, 299
negate, 299
new-device, 299
newline, 300
new-token, 299
nip, 300
noop, 300
not, 300
o#, 301
octal, 301
off, 302
offset16, 302
on, 302
open-package, 43, 302
or, 303
over, 303
pack, 304
peer, 304
pick, 305
primitives, 11
probe, 305
probe-virtual, 305
processor-type, 306
programming style, ?? to 8, ?? to 9
r>, 307

r@, 307
rb!, 308
rb@, 308
reg, 309
repeat, 310
reset-screen, 310
rl!, 310
rl@, 310
roll, 311
rot, 311
rot, 311
rw!, 311
rw@, 312
s´, 312
sbus-intr>cpu, 313
screen-height, 314
screen-width, 314
select-dev, 29
set-args, 43
set-font, 314
sign, 315
soace, 315
source format, 5
spaces, 315
span, 315
stack, 6
start$n$, 316
struct, 316
suspend-fcode, 316
swap, 317
testing, 29, 30
then, 317
throw, 317
toggle-cursor, 317
tokenizer[, 318
true, 319
tuck, 319
type, 319
u*x, 324
u.r, 321
u/mod, 321
u<, 322
u<=, 322
u>, 322
u>=, 322
u´, 320

u2/, 322
unselect-dev, 31
until, 322
upc, 323
user-abort, 323
valid program, 2
value, 324
variable, 325
version, 326
version1, 326
versionx?, 326
w!, 327
w,, 327
w@, 327
wa+, 328
wa1+, 328
wbsplit, 328
wflip, 329
wflips, 329
while, 329
window-left, 329
window-top, 330
within, 330
wljoin, 331
words, 5
wpeek, 331
wpoke, 331
x-, 331
x+, 331
xdr+, 332
xdrbytes, 333
xdrint, 333
xdrphys, 334
xdrstring, 334
xdrtoint, 334
xdrtostring, 335
xor, 335
xu/mod, 335
xu>l, 335
FCode programs, 21
FCode PROM
    body, 2
    end token, 2
    header, 2
    magic number, 2
    organization, 2

size, 1
FCodes
    and properties, 72
    interface, 11, 12
    local, 11, 13
    one-byte, 11
    system, 11
    two-byte, 11
flag, 9
Forth
    compile state, 6
    interpret state, 6
    stack, 6
    words, 5
forth monitor
    commands, 43
Forth-83
    and FCode, 5

H

hierarchical device, 111

I

ihandle, 40, 275
instance
    arguments, 42
    package, 35, 36
    parameters, 42
interpret, 35
interpret state, 6
interpreting FCode, 2
interrupt
    device, 53
    vectors, 53
interrupt-enable!, 395
interrupt-occurred?, 393, 395

L

len, 9
long L, 9
ls, 26

M

mapping
    packages, 47
method
    accessing, 46
    execute, 44
methods, 248
    package, 36
model, 70

N

n, 9
name, 70
network device, 145
node
    machine, 66
    SBus, 66
    scsi, 66
NVRAM parameters
    setting, 18
nvramrc, 47

O

open, 37
operating system
    configuring, 53

P

package, 35
    accessing, 40, 41
    addressing, 44
    and device node, 36
    and methods, 37
    data definition, 39
    deblocker, 50
    debugging, 47
    instances, 36
    mapping, 47
    standard, 48
    TFTP, 49
package method
    close, 37

    open, 37
    reset, 37
    selftest, 37
packages
    and linking, 35
    data, 36
    instance, 35
    interface, 35
    methods, 36
    plug-in, 35
    properties, 36
phandle, 40, 271, 275
phys, 9
pil!, 394
pil@, 393
plug-in device drivers, 36
plug-in package, 35
probe, 35
programming style
    FCode, ?? to 8, ?? to 9
PROM
    contents, 1
properties
    packages, 36
property
    create, 70
    creation, 53
    decoding of, 72
    encoding of, 71
    list, 2
    modify, 70
    name, 2, 53
    ranges, 66
    reg, 297
    reg, 66
    retrieval of, 71
    value, 2, 53
    value of, 70
pstr, 10
pwd, 27

R

ranges
    property, 66

rb!, 308
rb@, 308
reg
    property, 66, 297
reset, 37
restricting system use, 15
reverse polish notation, 5
rl!, 310
rl@, 310
ROMvec
    op_mon_id, 265
rw!, 311
rw@, 312

S

SBus
    node, 66
SBus addressing, 116
sbus-probe-list, 19
scsi
    node, 66
selftest, 37
;, 6
serial device, 189
show-devs, 27
size, 9
    FCode PROM, 1
source format
    Fcode, 5
stack, 6
    operation, 7
stack comment, 7
    and colon definition, 7
standard packages, 48

T

testing
    FCode, 30
TFTP
    support, 49
Tokenizer, 22
tokenizer, 5

tools
    tokenizer, 5

U

unit-address, 297

V

value
    property, 2
virt, 10

W

word, 10
words, 27
    Fcode, 5
    Forth, 5